salt & pepper

**also by
michele anna jordan**

California Home Cooking

Polenta

Pasta with Sauces

Ravioli & Lasagne

The Good Cook's Book of Days: A Food Lover's Journal

The Good Cook's Book of Tomatoes

The Good Cook's Book of Mustard

The Good Cook's Book of Oil & Vinegar

A Cook's Tour of Sonoma

michele anna jordan

salt & pepper

135 Perfectly Seasoned Recipes

broadway books · new york

BROADWAY

Broadway Books titles may be purchased for business or promotional use or for special sales. For information, please write to: Special Markets Department, Random House, Inc., 1540 Broadway, New York, NY 10036.

BROADWAY BOOKS and its logo, a letter B bisected on the diagonal, are trademarks of Broadway Books, a division of Random House, Inc.

Visit our website at www.broadwaybooks.com.

Library of Congress Cataloging-in-Publication Data

Jordan, Michele Anna.
    Salt and pepper : 135 perfectly seasoned recipes / Michele Anna Jordan. — 1st ed.
        p.   cm.
    Includes bibliographical references and index.
    ISBN 0-7679-0027-8
    1. Cookery (Pepper) 2. Salting of food. 3. Salt. 4. Pepper (Spice) I. Title.
    TX819.P3J67   1999
    641.6'384—dc21   98-45798
                                                            CIP

FIRST EDITION

Photographs by Quentin Bacon
Designed by Pei Loi Koay

99 00 01 02 03 10 9 8 7 6 5 4 3 2 1

for gina and nicolle

I love you more than salt.

Imagine a Carthage sown with salt, and all the sowers gone, and the seeds lain however long in the earth, till there rose finally in vegetable profusion leaves and trees of rime and brine. What flowering would there be in such a garden? Light would force each salt calyx to open in prisms, and to fruit heavily with bright globes of water—peaches and grapes are little more than that, and where the world was salt there would be greater need of slaking. For need can blossom into all the compensations it requires.

—Marilynne Robinson
Housekeeping

"A loaf of bread," the walrus said,
"Is what we chiefly need:
 Pepper and vinegar besides
 Are very good indeed —
 Now if you're ready, Oysters dear,
 We can begin to feed."

—Lewis Carroll
Through the Looking Glass

Acknowledgments   **xi**

Introduction   **xiii**

s a l t

Magical Salt   **1**

Common Salt, Common Sense   **4**

The Flowering Sea   **8**

Salt, Salt Everywhere   **12**

Red Rocks, Crimson Crystals   **14**

Salt's Mystery   **15**

Jewish Barbecue, the Best Bacon, and Other Salty Miracles   **16**

Koshering and Kashering   **21**

Snowflakes on the Windshield   **22**

Brining for Flavor   **26**

p e p p e r

The King of Spice   **29**

Citizenship of Pepper   **32**

The Question of Quality   **33**

Cat City   **35**

Rice Wine and a Crescent Moon   **40**

A Brief History of the World   **42**

a salt & pepper cookbook

Seasoning to Taste **47**

The Shaker Dilemma **49**

Shake It, Don't Break It **50**

Freshly Ground Pepper **50**

The Best Pepper Mills **51**

Repetitive Pepper Syndrome **52**

APPETIZERS **53**

SOUPS **70**

PASTA, RICE & OTHER GRAINS **83**

MAIN COURSES **96**

SIDE DISHES **136**

SALADS **147**

SPICE MIXTURES, CONDIMENTS & PRESERVES **159**

DESSERTS **186**

BEVERAGES **195**

CRAFTS **205**

appendix: tasting notes & recommendations

Common Culinary Salts **211**

Commonly Available Peppercorns **214**

Resources **216**

Glossary **221**

Bibliography **228**

Index **231**

acknowledgments

Although *Salt & Pepper* is what I like to call a love letter, a personal tribute, and a song of praise shaped by my delight in two things that many people take for granted (more than one eyebrow has been raised whenever I've mentioned this project), I could not have succeeded without the help of dozens of people, old friends who laugh at my exuberance, new friends who share it. I feel enormous gratitude to everyone who has helped, whether they have been aware of their assistance or not.

First, I must acknowledge writer Sallie Tisdale, whom I do not know. Her remarkable book *Lot's Wife: Salt and the Human Condition* is the finest treatise I have read on salt. Her writing, which seems so driven by passion and curiosity, is an inspiration.

As I worked on this book, Mollie Katzen, Deborah Madison, and Paula Wolfert became new friends; their enthusiasm helped spur me on in moments of doubt.

Tourism Malaysia provided crucial support and introduced me to a region of the world I might not have discovered on my own. A heartfelt *terima kasih* to Lily Musni and Sharifah Danial in the Los Angeles office, Raja H. J. Normala and her associates in the Kuala Lumpur office, and Talib H. J. Long in Kuching, Sarawak.

Had it not been for Bill Penzey of Penzeys, Ltd., I might not have gone to Malaysia at all, so Bill, *thank you,* again and again.

In Malaysia, so many people were kind and helpful that I am sure I will forget to name them all, and I offer my apologies in advance of my thanks. That said, thank you very much to Elizabeth Foo of the Legend Hotel in Kuala Lumpur, to Fiona Fong of the Holiday Inn in Kuching, and to Anandan Adnan Abdullah, general manager of the Pepper Marketing Board and a gracious and charming host. It was through Anandan's efforts, and those of his assistants Chong Vui Hok and Joseph Lau, that I was able to return to Sarawak for a second visit not long after my first. I have fallen completely in love with the city and the state of Sarawak, and the island of Borneo. And to Narain Nallathamby, who was my guide in Kuala Lumpur, thank you for indulging my whims and curiosity, and for being a wonderful companion.

Malaysia Airlines deserves its reputation as one of the best airlines in the world. The service is the best I've experienced on any carrier, and the food is remarkably good. Thanks to Vladimir Valasco, marketing manager for Malaysia Airlines in North

America, and to Jim Burke, of the same office, for helping me get to Malaysia ready and eager to explore rather than sleep.

Thanks to everyone who helped along the salt trail, especially Jill Singleton and Skip Niman of Cargill Corporation; Andy Briscoe of the Salt Institute; Brian Abendroth, and the folks at the Grain and Salt Society. And to Elizabeth Erman of ASTA, thanks for leads to pepper traders.

Thanks to Harriet Bell for being such a smart editor, understanding friend, and all-around cool person, and to Doe Coover and Skip Dye, for believing in *Salt & Pepper*. It is difficult to know exactly how to thank Frances Bowles, who must be the world's kindest, gentlest, and most dedicated copyeditor on the planet. In the wrong hands, copyediting can be brutal; with Frances, it is a pleasure, and I appreciate her guidance and enthusiasm more than I can say.

My assistant Lesa Tanner continues to leave me speechless with gratitude, too, for her unwavering support, constant good humor, and willingness to help me with anything, at any time. I wouldn't have been able to do the extensive traveling this book merited had it not been for Lesa's attention to the feline trio, Olive, Jamaica, and Mario, and I can tell by their plump tummies and feisty spirits that they're grateful, too. They hardly missed me at all.

Thanks to Betty Ellsworth for the kitchen assistance and to Joseph Wagner, my brother-in-law, for helping me understand the basic chemistry of salt. And to Peter Perrone, for the salt cross and for being a good friend for so long.

To my family, my close friends, and my colleagues at KRCB-FM, thank you for understanding my long absences, both emotionally and physically. I value tremendously the opportunity to work with Robin Pressman, program director at the public radio station where I do both of my shows, *Mouthful* and *Red Shoes Rodeo*. (And thanks to Bob Sala, for engineering *Mouthful,* and to Evelyn Anderson, for her continued assistance in producing the show.) And to Diane Holt, of the *Press Democrat,* thanks for being such a great editor.

To my daughters Gina and Nicolle; John Boland and James Carroll; John Kramer, Nancy Dobbs, and their children Andrew and Annie; David Browne; Amy Rennert; Patrick Bouquet; and Ginny Stanford, thank you again. *Whatever would I do without you?*

Finally, to Ramlee Eli, who began as my guide in Borneo but quickly became a dear friend, *terima kasih,* thank you, and see you soon.

Salt seasons the self so that the self's own
true flavor emerges.
Sallie Tisdale, *Lot's Wife*

You know me. I'm the shy girl from elementary school who gave you her ice cream, the one who scraped the chocolate frosting off the birthday cake and *ate the cake*. Take me out for a drink and you have to keep an eye on me or I'll lick the salt off your margarita glass.

My friend John loves desserts, looking forward with relish to the end of the meal and its last, sweet pleasure. I look across the table and appreciate John's delight, though such pleasure is mostly unavailable to me. I have little interest in sweets. I was born without a sweet tooth and I am an outsider, my nose pressed up against the window of another's joy. Certainly, I can appreciate a voluptuous cheesecake, admire a luscious chocolate mousse, and sincerely believe that *tarte tatin* is one of the great contributions France has made to world culture. But I am almost always satisfied by a single bite. I don't have a chocolate jones. Ahh, but that salty flourish. I crave it.

When I was a little kid, I'd sneak into the kitchen and find lemons to squeeze on my hands. Then I'd sprinkle salt over the juice, sit in front of the television, and slowly lick off the tangy film. If I was in the mood for a more elaborate snack, I might peel a lemon, cut it into the thinnest slices, and sprinkle the slices with salt, a pleasure I gave up only in my early twenties, when a friend warned that the acid would eat the enamel off my teeth. He knew; it had already happened to him.

This book began more than a decade ago as self-defense. The salt police were everywhere, ripping shakers out of hands and wagging fingers at the loosely indulgent, me among them. I took them to task in my column "The Jaded Palate," published then in the *Sonoma County Independent*. The response was encouraging, and I was buoyed by the realization that I was not alone in my salty sea.

The column soon grew into a book proposal, something I worked on late at night when I was done with my serious assignments. I kept it secret for years. Then articles began appearing in other publications, first in the *New York Times,* then in the *Washington Post,* and suddenly everywhere. My secret passion had become grist for the mill; I worried that I had missed my chance. I sent the proposal to my agent Doe Coover, but she said nothing, nor did I. You never knew where the salt police might be lurking. Maybe she thought I had slipped off the shore: *a book on salt and pepper?*

A few months passed and I saw another article. "Sell it," I said, and she did, almost instantly. That was two, maybe even three, years ago and the fervor for salt grows daily. Nor should we ignore its sultry spouse, pepper, the sneaky one of the duo; interest in it, too, has been on the rise. But salt is always stealing the spotlight from pepper. Salt tap-dances naked on your table, makes you blush with delight. Pepper taps you on the shoulder and invites you behind closed doors. Both are shameless in the endless pleasure they impart.

As I was leaving New York for San Francisco one winter morning, my dear friend Peter handed me a small present.

"It's for your Muse," he said, aware that I was heading home to begin the book in earnest. It was an exquisite gift, one of the most precious I have ever received: a crystal cross carved of salt, carried all the way from the Wieliczka salt mines in Poland. I wrapped it carefully in a small cloth and carried it on the plane, tucked into the pocket of my velvet jacket, where I ran my fingers over its hard smooth surfaces every now and then. I never licked it, *I swear.*

I have since become a magnet for salt. I have a tiny wooden salt box full of a fragile flakes, salt that a friend gathered from a natural brine pool off the Sonoma County coastline. In my kitchen, there's a tiny pile of salt made by a photographer who collected salt water near her home in Maine, boiled it to concentrate the brine, then waited patiently for the liquid to evaporate and the crystals to form. I awake to find gifts of salt on my porch; stories about salt arrive by fax and e-mail and post (one in Japanese, which I cannot read). My daughter Nicolle brings me a present, *Salt Hands,* the story of a deer who came to lick salt out of a young girl's hands.

I worked all summer (but who could tell the time of year, here in my quiet study where I am surrounded by salt and pepper, not the sun) to complete the manuscript. One day a phone call came: Would I like to join a press trip to Poland? an unfamiliar voice inquired. Yes, Wieliczka is on the itinerary, I am told. I shiver. It is the Salt Muse, calling me home. As I print out the last pages of *Salt & Pepper,* I have just enough time to pack.

salt & pepper

magical salt

"I love you more than salt," the mythical young princess says to her father. Her older sisters, articulate in their hyperbole—more than gold, they tell the king, more than my own life, as much as God— are rewarded with riches and kingdoms of their own. The arrogant king, devastated to be so poorly valued by his favorite child, condemns her to a life of loneliness and poverty in exile.

The king's next meal is flat and tasteless, and so is the next, and the next, and the next. For thirty days, his food lacks flavor. You might conclude that it is sadness and loss that eclipse his pleasure, but it is not. He summons his chef and demands an explanation.

"You value salt so little, your majesty," the chef explains coyly, "that I no longer use it in your food."

You can see where this is going. The princess is returned from exile, reunited with her secret fiancé—the wily chef, of course—and given a lavish wedding and riches that far surpass those granted her sisters. The king's food sparkles with taste and savor once again.

I was told the story by a cooking student, a woman from India who remembered it from childhood, when she had likely heard it from an English nanny; there are many versions of this tale throughout Europe. Common salt is more essential than we like to admit, each version cautions us.

Another scene: It is Halloween, the eve of el Dia de los Muertos, and a young Mexican girl is boiling an egg. After it is cooked, she runs it under a cool spigot, holding the hot egg even as it burns her impatient hands. When at last it is cool, she removes the shell and carefully breaks the egg in half, revealing the round yellow yolk, the kernel of life at the core, which she quickly discards. She lifts the lid of a nearby box of salt and takes as big a pinch as her fingers can hold, depositing it in the hollow of the egg. She continues, pinch after salty pinch, until the center of the egg is filled. She fits the halves together and tiptoes silently to the bedroom she shares with her sister, where she awaits the stroke of midnight.

Eventually, the hour comes, she puts the egg with its hidden seed, its talismanic treasure, into her mouth, chewing and swallowing quickly so that the jewel of salt does not burst and leave her parched, for she must not take a drink. Her sister wakes and calls her name, but she pretends to be asleep. To speak would break the spell. Who will it be? Who will appear in her dreams and offer her a quenching drink of water? Her life's mate, the story goes, and she falls asleep imagining his face.

Ah, magical salt. It seasons our tales, and spices up our language, each word, every phrase a nod to a single truism: Life is tasteless without salt.

"My little salt box," a pretty young girl in Andalusia might be called by her suitor.

"The salt of the party," Arabs say.

Early Christians rubbed newborn babies with salt. Asians, confronted with a dull youth, shake their heads and whisper, "He was not salted when he was born," a statement so precise and so evocative that I believe we should adopt it immediately.

"Somebody forgot to salt the popcorn," I imagine one friend whispering slyly to another as a third bores them to tears.

To say there is salt between us indicates a bond that must be honored. Trespass not against the salt, the Greeks warned. In Iran, to be disloyal or ungrateful is to be untrue to salt. While we were visiting the salt mines in Wieliczka, Poland, Mariusz Moryl, marketing manager for the Polish National Tourist Office, told me that in his country old friends say they've eaten a lot of salt together. Those same friends might complain about a salty bill when the tab at a restaurant or pub is higher than expected. An indolent employee has long been described as not worth his salt, a reference to Roman soldiers who were paid a portion of their wages—that is, their salary—in salt or with extra currency to buy salt. *Salt of the earth* surely is a compliment, if a rather patronizing one these days.

The spilling of salt is a bad omen, both literally and figuratively. "The Romans are said to have led victims to execution with salt balanced on their heads," Sallie Tisdale tells us in *Lot's Wife*. "When it spilled, so did their blood." Spilled salt foreshadows loss of friendship, a broken heart or bone, a shipwreck, a death. Throw a little over your shoulder, my mother warned me whenever I knocked over the salt shaker. This ritual, so automatic to so many of us, began as an appeasement to the demons said to hover at our left, awaiting a moment of weakness that would give them access to our souls, clumsiness apparently a chief means of entry. Throwing salt, it seems, stopped them in their invisible tracks.

It was European Christians who figured this out; salt, for a time, was their domain. Alleged witches, thought to be worshipers of Satan, were said to hate it; a meal without salt, an unholy affair, became known as a "witch's supper." Heavily salted foods were thought to ward off demons.

In recent times, we have believed exactly the opposite. Salt, we have been cautioned, is an open invitation to the demons we fear the most: high blood pressure, death by stroke and heart attack, cancer. For decades, salt has been

what is salt, anyway?

Salt is a simple chemical made up of just two components. Salt, that is to say, sodium chloride or common salt, the chemical symbol for which is NaCl, forms when sodium, a soft metal, and chlorine, a gas, share electrons in what is called an ionic bond, one of the strongest chemical bonds there is. Once these two elements share electrons, they become magnets, the sodium positively charged and the chlorine negatively charged. The magnetic force holds the sodium and chlorine together in an intricate array of sodium ions surrounded by chlorine ions in turn surrounded by sodium ions, ad infinitum. It takes a great deal of force to separate the two once they have joined. Dissolving salt in water does not loosen the bond, nor does heat or time erode it. The specific configuration of these ions, which creates four 90-degree angles in each molecular bond, and their endless repetition create the perfect crystalline structure of salt, and account for the fact that salt can be cleaved into ever smaller crystals that retain their smooth, angular surfaces. The enormous crystals that can be seen in salt museums are called halite, a term that accurately applies to all rock salt. Some halite seems to glow with colorful inner lights, usually blue from suspended cobalt and red from suspended iron. It was rock salt colored in this way that is said to be the reason that the ground near Sodom turned red just before Lot's wife looked back and met her fate.

our demon lover, our secret culinary paramour, the kinky pleasure we pretend not to crave. But it's a ruse. We have always craved salt.

The story of salt and our craving for it is inseparable from human history. After we crawled out of the sea and wandered inland, we were able to do without extra salt for a time because we got what we needed from the raw meat we ate. But as we grew more and more civilized, cooking our food and learning to farm, our need for salt began to rise, growing into an insatiable hunger if unsatisfied for long.

This hunger must have led us to the nearest salt licks, likely already polished smooth by the tongues of a thousand zebras, giraffes, deer, or elk. Perhaps we followed them to the salt licks, as we later followed the buffalo of North America to natural outcroppings of salt. We've learned something in the process: Today, we leave manmade salt licks in the wild and build observation tents on hills above them, knowing that eventually the wild beasts will come for the salt. (Don't worry, we want to see the animals, not hunt them.)

Those of us who obeyed salt's call lived to reproduce and passed our salt literacy onto our children. Those of us without a taste for salt, those of us who didn't care, died out eons ago. You wouldn't be here if your ancestors had forsworn salt. What is this salient thing, salt, that we need so badly?

Salt is a rock, an inorganic mineral composed of 40 percent sodium and 60 percent chloride, joined by one of the strongest chemical unions there is, an ionic bond. It is a perfect fit; the molecule is often used in chemistry texts to illustrate the principles of attraction and union. When a salt crystal grows without interference—that is, without interlopers (magnesium, calcium, all those other substances that might go along for the ride) intruding on the sodium and the chloride—it is perfectly and exactly square.

Sodium, dissolved in the extracellular fluid that assists with the transportation of nutrients, is one of the main components of the body's internal environment. Sodium functions as an electrolyte, as do potassium, calcium, and magnesium, all of which regulate the electrical charges within our cells. Chloride supports potassium absorption, and helps oversee the body's acid and base balance. It enhances carbon dioxide transportation, and is an essential component of digestive acids. We need it, and so we crave it. It's that simple, and that complex.

common salt, common sense

Today, we believe that we eat much more salt than we ever have. "It's all that processed food," people say, usually preening with superiority as they add that they never use salt. Ho hum. I feel sorry for them, and wonder what else besides good food they deny themselves, but I try to keep quiet, unless too many of them appear at once. Then I get awfully cranky and start citing statistics and talking about Americans' annoying bias against pleasure. I lost my patience with the salt police along about the time a boyfriend took the shaker out of my hand and told me that, henceforth, *he* would decide what foods I would be allowed to salt. (The next one considered putting a salt lick next to the bed, to keep my spirits up, he said; I kept him around a bit longer.)

Yes, we certainly have a penchant for munching salty snacks, but in fact we consume much less sodium chloride than our ancestors did. In the Middle Ages, foods were bathed in salt. Meat and fish preserved in it were the common centerpieces of a meal—this was before refrigeration, before manmade ice, how to preserve the kill, if not with salt?—and more salt was added at the table, cascading off the tips of knives dipped into the elaborate salt cellars that graced the tables of the wealthy. (Status, it should be noted, was revealed by where one was seated in relationship to the salt cellar; to be "below the salt" was an indication of low status or an intentional insult.) Twenty grams a day—about two tablespoons of coarse sea salt—or more were commonly eaten.

In the past century and a half, our consumption of salt has remained fairly level— between about six and eleven grams (between $1\frac{1}{4}$ and $2\frac{1}{4}$ teaspoons of table salt) a

i o d i z e d   s a l t

As you have no doubt noticed, most salt sold in supermarkets is labeled "iodized," which indicates that the salt has had iodine added to it, usually in the form of potassium iodide. This practice began in the 1920s and was developed, in response to research by David Marine and his staff at the Michigan State Medical Society, to prevent thyroid goiter, which was epidemic in certain regions of the United States and particularly among children in the Midwest. The program to encourage families to use iodized salt spread throughout the country, and within thirty years, 76 percent of American households used only iodized salt. The epidemic of goi-

ters virtually disappeared. Today, more than half of all table salt sold contains the micronutrient. Seafood as well as sea salt contains iodine naturally, and the supplement is not necessary if there are sufficient quantities of either in one's diet; we require less than 225 micrograms of iodine a day. But in those developing countries where seafood is rarely if ever eaten, iodine deficiency remains a serious health problem today. In 1990, the World Summit for Children named it their top health priority and stressed that salt is still the most efficient means of combating the deficiency.

day is the world average—with little if any fluctuation in response to the good news and bad news that has been circulating, like a salty brine, for decades.

A cookbook won't put the controversy to rest, but I must add my voice to the choir. I simply can't conclude that anything as essential to our well-being as salt, anything that provides such primal pleasure and delightful satisfaction, is bad. To believe this would be to believe the world itself is made wrong. I believe the world is right and wise (not to mention delicious), and that our true cravings lead us where we should go. There are a thousand ways we can eclipse our body's wisdom, but, still, it cries out for salt.

"The amount of sodium ions [is] so critical," according to Thomas Moore, writing in *The Washingtonian*, "that the concentration of dissolved salt in the blood is

a fist of salt

Mahatma Gandhi captured the attention of the world and invented modern civil disobedience when he gathered a fistful of salt, a commodity that was controlled and heavily taxed by the British government.

"In India's hot climate, [salt] was an essential ingredient in every man's diet. It lay in great white sheets along the shorelines. . . . Its manufacture and sale, however, was the exclusive monopoly of the state, which built a tax into its selling price . . . for a poor peasant it represented, each year, two weeks' income.

"On March 12, 1930 . . . Gandhi marched out of his ashram at the head of a cortege of seventy-eight disciples and headed for the sea, 240 miles away. . . . The weird, almost Chaplinesque image of a little old half-naked man clutching a bamboo pole, marching down to the sea to challenge the British Empire, dominated the newsreels and press of the world day after day.

"On April 5, at six o'clock in the evening, Gandhi and his party finally reached the . . . Indian Ocean near the town of Dandi. At

dawn . . . the group marched into the sea for a ritual bath. Then Gandhi waded ashore and, before thousands of spectators, reached down to scoop up a piece of caked salt. . . . He held his fist to the crowd, then opened it to expose in his palms the white crystals, the forbidden gift of the sea, the newest symbol in the struggle for Indian independence.

"Within a week all India was in turmoil. All over the continent Gandhi's followers began to collect and distribute salt. . . . The British replied with the most massive roundup in Indian history, sweeping people to jail by the thousands. . . . Before returning to the confines of Yeravda prison, [Gandhi] managed to send a last message to his followers.

" 'The honor of India,' he said, 'has been symbolized by a fistful of salt in the hand of a man of nonviolence. The fist which held the salt may be broken, but it will not yield up its salt.' "

—Larry Collins and Dominique Lapierre
Freedom at Midnight

not allowed to vary by more than 1 percent." If everything is working as it should, our kidneys serve as the regulator of salt: Eat more than we require, and more is excreted; eat less, and our bodies, via our kidneys, hang on to what we already have.

Our bodies hear salt's call and respond with longing if something goes haywire. Salt craving—a desire that drives salt-starved children to dip every morsel of food into a pile of salt, and can compel us, in extremis, to eat dirt to extract its smidgen of salt—is the body's way of acquiring life-sustaining salt. If we cannot hold on to our salt, if our body squanders it in excretion, an overpowering craving will eclipse every other impulse; we will become our body's salt servant, or we will die.

Studies completed in the late 1980s and early 1990s indicate that, indeed, salt is not the killer it has been declared to be. The war against hypertension, which began in the 1930s and kicked into high gear during the Nixon administration in the early 1970s, attacked salt; for decades it has been considered a major culprit, declared guilty without a fair trial. Yet new studies show an increased risk of death among those with the *lowest* sodium levels, and they show a large population (between 75 and 80 percent) unaffected by salt. (Salt yea-sayers point to Japan, where consumption is about double ours. Life expectancy there is eighty years; here it is seventy-six.) And no studies show that salt increases blood pressure; rather, certain studies demonstrate that some hypertensives (about 8 percent of the general population) can reduce an already elevated blood pressure by reducing the amount of salt they eat.

The vast majority of people who drink alcohol do not become alcoholics, or even problem drinkers. Some do, but does this mean that everyone should become a teetotaler? Likewise, if some people with hypertension can reduce their blood pressure by reducing salt, should we all follow suit? There are those who would answer yes to both questions—better safe than sorry, they argue, and with straight faces— but scratch a zealot and you'll find a Puritan singing to the tune of, "if it tastes good, it must be bad." *Of course* advice given to a symptom-specific group should not apply to the general population. Common sense and common salt should join hands, make up and go steady, reignite their romance. *Come over here, give me a salty kiss.*

You may already suspect my conclusion: If you have a medical condition that requires you to limit the quantity of salt you eat, that is indeed unfortunate, but it is not a reason to impose similar restrictions on everyone else.

There is yet another side to this controversy. Salt, once so dear, is in modern times plentiful and cheap, easily taken for granted. Having salt was once proof of

s a l t

status; today to abstain is proof of virtue, of taking the high road. Since the early 1980s, many Americans have boasted that they "never eat it," as if those of us who do are somehow lax, indulgent, common, *as common as salt.* "I love you more than salt" falls on deaf ears. *So what?* they think.

Yet these same salt snobs seem to forget about the fast foods on which they rely, the pickles, popcorn, and lunchmeats, the Big Macs and Whoppers, the prepared entrées from the freezer compartment of the neighborhood market. Most prepared foods are laden with salt because food manufacturers know an essential detail of its nature: Salt dissolves only in the desire for more. It makes otherwise bland foods taste good, and it makes good foods taste even better. Its absence can render potentially wonderful things tasteless. Given the hysteria of recent times, we might have seen a proliferation of low-salt and no-salt packaged foods, but you know what? They don't sell, because no one likes them.

If you need to cut down on salt, where do you think you should start? By denying yourself a sprinkling of tasty crystals on your summer tomatoes? By refusing to salt the pasta water, or the grilled eggplant, or that lovely batch of pesto you have just made? Or by leaving lean cuisine entrées and bottled salsa on the grocer's shelf? You know my answer.

Governments all over the world have attempted to impose a heavy tax on salt. The French salt tax, the *gabelle,* wasn't repealed until after World War II, and at least one writer blamed the dearness of salt in France for the country's falling birthrate (cows had recently been shown to suffer compromised fertility when there was insufficient salt in their diets). Today, salt is treated as a food product and as such is rarely taxed.

the flowering sea

I stand on the edge of a vermilion pool, a saturated virgin pickle whose frothy shores resemble pink rock candy. Five years ago, this was saltwater in the San Francisco Bay; today it is a soupy scarlet brine—colored by the algae that bloom red at the specific salinity of this pond—the last stage before it becomes salt. After a summer of wind and sun, most of the salt will have crystallized.

On the midsummer day of my visit, the calm crimson pool is speckled here and there with tiny seed crystals, California's equivalent of *fleur de sel,* though it will not be harvested as such. Instead, larger crystals will grow on the seeds of salt until they fall of their own weight to the bottom of the shallow pool, a foot, sometimes two feet, deep. In the fall the salt will be harvested—in a good year, nearly a million tons of it from seventeen hundred acres of red crystallization ponds—and added to a nearby salt mountain, ninety feet high and nearly a thousand feet long, to await further processing. Eventually, it will be washed in a saturated brine, redissolved, dried in a kiln, and sent through a mill to crack it to size. By next year, it will be sold as table salt, sea salt, iodized salt licks, rock salt for softening water and melting icy roads, and industrial salt, all of it from this same sea source.

barefoot farmers

French sea salt may be sexy, but there is another side to the story of the romantic salt farmer. An Indian folk song moans, "Oh, mother, why did you marry me to a salt worker?" A salt farmer in India has a hard life. Salt is cheap and a family may spend several days harvesting a single ton of salt, which in 1998 brought less than four dollars. In the monsoon floods of that year, thousands of salt workers and their families, living in fragile shacks along the coast near Kandla in the state of Gujarat, were killed by a tidal wave, a cyclone, and subsequent floods. Even in the best conditions it's a dangerous occupation; the harsh Indian sun reflecting off the white mountains of salt is hard on the eyes. Constant exposure to the salty brine can lead to skin lesions which can become gangrenous—when there's too little salt, wounds can't heal; when there's too much, they won't. What are those Frenchmen thinking, not wearing shoes?

—*Time* magazine, 29 June 1998

Salt has a long history in San Francisco Bay. For centuries native Ohlone tribes gathered it from natural brine pools along the southern end of the bay until the Spanish explorers came along, built their missions, and declared the salt (and almost everything else) their own. In 1854, a German immigrant known as John Johnson founded California's modern salt industry; it is one of the state's oldest continuously operating industries.

Salt processing was lucrative when there was a single producer; Johnson's salt was soon fetching fifty dollars a ton, but it was, of course, only a matter of time before competitors came along. Less then twenty years after Johnson founded the industry, there were eighteen salt companies along the bay, a number that declined as prices dropped in response to overproduction.

From 1936 until its sale to Cargill Incorporated in 1978, Leslie Salt Company was the dominant producer, with holdings of forty thousand acres of salt ponds

salt

ringing the bay. Cargill maintains the familiar name of Leslie as a brand, along with nearly a hundred other custom-labeled brands, from Hain Sea Salt to Safeway Iodized Table Salt, all the same salt from the same source, but with various additions made according to the customer's specifications. The company has reduced the area devoted to salt production (but not the yield, because of improved crystallization and harvesting techniques), and sold and donated ten thousand acres for marsh restoration to the California Department of Fish and Game.

Planes at San Francisco International Airport roar above the glassy patchwork of saline ponds, and when passengers glance down on the green, blue, and blue green, rust red and bright red, slate gray and pitch black ponds, their gaze rarely lingers. Industrial salt, they might think, if they think of salt at all. Who cares about California salt, no matter how beautiful the ponds that are its source? It's French salt that's sexy.

For cachet and for mystique, it's hard to beat *fleur de sel,* flower of the sea. As a commercial product *fleur de sel* is a modern conceit, a product of northwestern France—Île de Ré, Noirmoutier, and Guérande are the regions of production—virtually unheard of before the 1980s. It is a by-product of *sel gris,* the Celtic gray sea salt that in the late 1990s became so popular.

Fleur de sel blossoms on the surface of the saline pools that give us gray sea salt. When the conditions are just right, when the sun is hot and the wind is up, the salt blooms, crystallizing out of a saturated brine. Nearly instantly it forms a fragile skin over the salty liquor. For decades, the *sauniers* (salt farmers) broke up the veneer of crystals as they raked the bed of salt; left intact, it forms a shield that slows evaporation. But by the 1980s, French chefs had discovered *fleur de sel* and farmers were only too pleased to fill the new demand; *fleur de sel* is the world's most expensive salt, commanding prices in the United States of more than thirty dollars a pound.

care for a sandwich?

Although the sandwich is utterly familiar to us as that famous dish consisting of two slices of bread with something wedged in between, the suffix "wich" has a long history in England indicating a village where salt was produced. Such places as Droitwich in Worcestershire and Northwich, Nantwich, and Middlewich, in Cheshire, all produced salt. The term seems originally to have indicated the group of buildings where salt was made, as well as the wich-houses, where brine was evaporated. The word "sandwich" as it applies to food is said to have been named for John Montagu, fourth Earl of Sandwich, who once spent twenty-four hours at a gambling table and ate nothing but roast beef between two slices of bread, something he could hold with one hand while he continued to play.

salt

Salt farming has become a popular profession in France. In each of the regions, there are new training schools with more applicants than positions. In America, in the early 1970s, young people headed to rural areas to live closer to the land and escape increasingly corporate sources of food. In France, young people flock to the west coast for the same reasons, for the innocence and rhythm of farming salt. It adds to the perceived romance of the salt itself; photographs show beautiful young men (*Frenchmen,* at that), clad in nothing more than denim shorts, long hair tousled by the coastal winds, raking piles of glittering crystals from aquamarine pools. *What about that salty kiss?*

Condiment salt. Perhaps it was inevitable that the term would be coined, and coined it was. I don't know who first used the phrase, but by the mid-1990s salt lovers, salt sellers, and salt farmers were all using it to refer to *fleur de sel* and a few other specialty salts. *Fleur de sel* is the premier condiment salt, like *aceto balsamico tradizionale* or the finest extra virgin olive oil. The cream atop the milk, it has been called, the caviar of salt. Its flavor is delicate, yet full and round in your mouth; it does not sear the tip of the tongue as some salts do; there is no bitterness, no sharpness. The most important characteristic is its texture; it crunches pleasantly between your teeth, and because it is crystalline rather than flaky, it dissolves slowly: Sprinkled on summer tomatoes, it lingers, salty jewels for the tongue to savor.

If *fleur de sel* leads the pack of artisan salts when it comes to reputation, Celtic gray sea salt isn't far behind. As late as 1996, it was a well-kept secret, praised by food writers, coveted by chefs, and loved by anyone who had visited the marshes of Brittany and tasted the salt that is sold, so casually and cheaply, alongside the road and at the outdoor markets of the area. But it was pricey (in some instances, well over ten dollars a pound) and uncommon in the American kitchen. In 1997, Holly Peterson Mondavi, a chef in the Napa Valley wine country in California, founded her company Sea Stars and began importing and packaging an elegant, coarse crystal from Guérande in France. By 1998, Celtic gray sea salt was everywhere. There are several importers and the price is much lower than it was even a year ago. You'll still find the pricey stuff, but reliable mail-order sources offer the real thing for as little as $1.25 a pound.

Just two hours from Paris (via the high-speed train), windswept Brittany has a wild, ancient feel. The region has a unique cuisine, shaped in part by its signature salts. Here in Brittany locals prefer salted butter, the only region in France where this is true. Lamb raised on these salt marshes is called *pré-salé,* that is, "next to the salt" (not presalted), and praised for its succulence and flavor. And then there are Brittany's prized oysters, so enduring and abundant for centuries, like its salt, yet so fragile and threatened today.

salt, salt everywhere

Artisan salt farming is not a French monopoly. In Portugal, a natural artesian well feeds the salt ponds of Rio Maior, an inland village, where for centuries families have raked and harvested their sun-dried salt using traditional methods. Here, houses are made entirely of wood—walls are joined by wooden dowels; even locks and keys are made of wood. Salt corrodes metal (if you live where it snows you know this; it was news to me, a child of the California sun), and does so quickly, yet it preserves wood for centuries.

Farmers are barefoot in Rio Maior, too (a practice that prevents them from accidentally kicking dirt and rocks into the delicate salt), but not bare-chested, bare-headed, or bare-handed. They wear traditional knit hats to protect themselves from sun and salt, and use hand-carried baskets to transport the salt from the crystallization ponds to nearby piles of fresh salt. The salt—smallish crystals with a clean, briny flavor—is sold through local cooperatives.

The Mediterranean Sea is saltier than the Atlantic Ocean, as inland seas always are. The increased concentration shortens the time required for the water to evaporate and the salt to crystallize. The quieter tides make salt farming an easier task than it is along the Atlantic or Pacific coasts. Most Mediterranean salt, such as La Baleine, a popular French sea salt now owned by Morton's, the American company that made "when it rains it pours" a household slogan, is refined in modern facilities.

Trapani, on the northwestern tip of Sicily, is different. Salt has been farmed there since the time of the Phoenicians, and it seems as if little has changed. Ancient windmills are still the only power, save the sun. These enormous windmills—each is named and most are several centuries old—power the pumps that transport the sea water into the drying pans, and also turn the stone wheels that grind the salt crystals. No barefoot farmers here, though; the workers wear tall black rubber boots. The pure white salt with its angular crystals is extremely hard, dry, and slow to dissolve; it's a good salt to use in salt mills and for salting the water for pasta.

Being sent to the salt mines is not, by any measure, a pleasant employment opportunity. The work was extraordinarily rigorous and dangerous before modern equipment made the process easier and safer, and both prisoners and slaves have been forced to extract rock salt from underground mines. When they were able—away from the watchful eyes of their bosses, or else in their favor—a few of the workers left their marks in carvings of salt along the many tunnels in the mines. These were often religious carvings, which provided a place of worship for workers who often remained underground for some time; they also were thought of as guardians to protect the miners from disaster. Some of the most famous carvings are in the Royal Wieliczka Salt Mine near Krakow, Poland. Little chambers, small chapels, and one huge cathedral are filled with small and large religious statues and bas-relief tableaus, all carved out of the rich black salt of the mines. In many of the underground rooms, elaborate chandeliers made of beads carved of white salt are suspended overhead and fitted with electric lights. As the mine has become increasingly popular as a tourist attraction, newer carvings have been added;

some depict various Polish folk tales and myths, some historical figures such as Copernicus; others celebrate the long tradition of working in the mines, which have been in operation for over seven hundred years. There's a café, a small shopping mall that sells souvenirs of salt in various forms, and a dance hall that can be rented for concerts, weddings, and other private events. Rock salt is no longer extracted from this mine; today, all the salt mined here is extracted as brine and evaporated above ground in vacuum pans. So much salt has been removed over the centuries that to dig more out would present the risk of weakening the ground and causing the town of Wieliczka to collapse into the deep caverns, something that *has* occured in other parts of the salt-world, in Northwich, England, for instance.

In Wieliczka, a vast quantity of salt is dissolved in underground salt lakes, which bloom a brilliant emerald green when they near saturation. Curved bridges and steep wooden staircases, underwater lights, and wave machines that move the water and throw rippling reflections on cavern walls have been added to enchant visitors even more.

Ō-shima island is a forty-five minute plane trip off the coast near Tokyo in Japan, a country where the government still taxes salt and oversees its production. Here, salt is made by using a fast, modern process that concentrates the brine before pumping it into ponds for final crystallization. Darrell Corti, a grocer in Sacramento, California, describes Oshima Island Red Label salt as remarkably sweet and recommends it as a condiment salt. Although I always try to defer to Darrell's superior palate and greater experience, and even though I cower at the prospect of disagreeing with him publicly, I confess that I detect no sweetness at all in Oshima Island salt, and find its small fluffy crystals impractical in a salt cellar (salt spoons don't work, and it wedges itself under my fingernails) and impossible in either a mill or shaker.

The United States sits upon a huge salty empire, enormous underground deposits left by ancient seas that stretched across the Great Lakes region, the Midwest, the Gulf, the desert. In Utah there's the Great Salt Lake, which we all know, and in Louisiana, Avery Island, a better kept secret that is home not only to massive salt mines but also to Tabasco Sauce, one yummy place indeed.

In 1887, Ben Blanchard accidentally discovered that Kansas was sitting on top of a vein of salt that turned out to be about 30 miles wide, 150 miles long, and 325 feet thick. He had been drilling for oil. (Usually it's the other way around, you find salt first, in the form of a natural salt dome, and where you find one there's a good chance there's oil.) At the height of the industry that Blanchard launched, there were eighteen salt producers in Hutchinson, but most were bought out by Morton Salt Company, the first company in the United States to package table salt.

So much salt; salt everywhere, too much salt to tell you everything, too much salt even to know. From the high plains of Peru and the salt lakes of the Himalayas to the beaches of Bali and Baja; from ancient salt mines in Africa to the deep caverns of Germany, Austria, and Poland, there is so much salt, more than we will ever, could ever, use. It's heartening to know, isn't it, that something we need so desperately, so absolutely, is ours in such abundance?

red rocks, crimson crystals

A saturated brine pond turns red because the protoplasm of *Dunaliella* algae develops a red pigment as salinity increases; tiny brine shrimp add an aura of orange. Rock salt (from Utah and coastal France, to name two sources) is studded with trace amounts of reddish-tinged iron. In Hawaii, there's a pale orange salt that occurs naturally along the shores of both Kauai and Molokai; red clay, or alae, is responsible for the color. For centuries a deep reddish brown salt, mixed naturally with dirt, sand, and iron-rich clay, was gathered for both daily and ceremonial use. Today, some red clay is already present in the evaporation ponds of Kauai, but most is introduced to create Hawaii's signature salt. The bond is weak; dissolve a spoonful in a glass of water, and a band of red clay settles to the bottom while the sodium chloride vanishes into solution. Hang a thread in the water and pure white salt crystals migrate up it, a chemical expression of two's-company-three's-a-crowd.

Native Hawaiians use their salt in ceremonies and rituals, such as the blessing of the canoes, when a few grains are sprinkled on the tongue. Red salt is also used in *poke* (cubed raw fish) and to finish cooked fish dishes.

"It is special because it comes from the other islands, because it was once so hard to get," explains Jim Medeiros who lives on the Big Island (Hawaii) and whose great-great grandmother was one of King Kamehameha's mistresses. "It isn't used as everyday salt."

Some do use it daily, saying that the minerals in it are good for you, and taste good too. Why would you use any other salt? they wonder. Unlike many specialty salts, Hawaiian alae salt is inexpensive, selling in supermarkets in Hawaii for about two dollars a pound, slightly more in California. But will the low prices last as Hawaiian salt is discovered? Probably not. In mid-1998, high-end markets and catalogues were adding it to their product lines, at considerably higher prices.

one with the wind, but saved in the salt

Underground salt caverns are valued for their unwavering temperature and humidity. Underground Vaults and Storage, a rental facility in Hutchinson, Kansas, leases hundreds of storage units in its underground facility housed in an old salt mine. Thousands of irreplaceable cultural treasures are stored here, such as the original prints of thousands of films, including, it is rumored, *Gone with the Wind* and *The Wizard of Oz*. The formula for Classic Coca-Cola is also reported to be kept in one of those salty vaults.

salt's mystery

"Salt," I said, writing to Harold McGee, "heightens the flavors of virtually everything, but I'm hoping to answer the question of exactly why and how it does this. Is it enough that salt draws out the moisture and thus the flavor of an ingredient, and then, as we eat, additional salt dissolves slowly on the tongue, thus bringing flavors to the palate and creating a harmonious finish among them?"

"I'm afraid that your question is indeed more complicated than it seems," the well-known food scientist and curious cook responded in an e-mail message written in France. The function of salt "in fact is the subject of much ongoing research.

Pretzels and chips and freshly salted foods aside, the salt in food is already dissolved . . . and in equilibrium with the water and other constituents. Since there are only a few genuine 'tastes'— sensations registered on the tongue, not the nose—certainly salt contributes to the overall complexity and balance of flavor.

"In addition to that, the concentration of salt in a food helps determine chemically how many of the other flavor components are going to behave: that is, how available they are to our senses. But this effect varies among the many hundreds of flavor components in a given food, so it's hard to generalize: except to say that salt contributes more than saltiness to flavor.

"Sorry there's not a neater answer, though maybe it's good to retain some mystery in such a basic matter."

Taste, like love, defies reduction. And just as love is indispensable to the savor of life, so salt is essential to the enjoyment of food. Salt is flavor's midwife; grains scatter across our tongues and melt like tiny stars, enchanting and mysterious, inseparable from taste itself. Savory foods do not reach their full flower without its skillful application; sweets blossom with a judicious sprinkle of salt crystals. Professional chefs identify salt as the single most important ingredient in their kitchen, insist that their new sous chefs learn immediately how to salt properly the foods they cook.

jewish barbecue, the best bacon, and other salty miracles

The mysterious ability of salt to affect flavor beyond adding its own character may be best revealed in dry-salting and brining. Short-term brining adds flavor to bland foods and juiciness to normally dry cuts of meat. Long-term brining transforms both taste and texture, and preserves foods as well. Dry-salting intensifies natural flavors, contributes new ones, and preserves; it is often used on foods that will be smoked.

salting the ritz

Ed Walsh, a chef in northern California, comes from a long line of restaurant workers. His parents met at the Hotel Ritz in Paris, where they fell in love and ran off together. As a young man, Ed went to Paris, too, where he worked in the dining-room kitchen (there were other kitchens for room service) of the Ritz Hotel in the late 1960s. Every night, Ed remembers, the floors of the kitchen were covered with a thick layer of rock salt to keep out rodents and cockroaches. Every morning the salt was swept up, and reused that night.

salt

Brines and dry-salt rubs are used extensively in commercial meat curing. Both brines and salt rubs penetrate meat at the rate of about an inch every seven days, but today brine is commonly injected directly into meat to mimic, however ineffectively, the slower process of making bacon, ham, corned beef, pastrami, and the other products that rely on salt curing for their characteristic flavor and texture. Authenticity and quality are both compromised by this faster method, but it has become so common that many people have never tasted the real thing. You won't find much of the real stuff in major markets, but there are plenty of mail-order sources for meats cured the old-fashioned way. It is easier to find authentic dry-salted smoked bacon, than it is to find true country ham. Many of the producers are in Virginia and Kentucky. (For a detailed description of several companies and their products, try to get a copy of the spring 1997 issue of *The Art of Eating,* Edward Behr's elegantly opinionated newsletter; see resources, page 216.)

When a box of bacon, hog jowls, and ham arrives from R. M. Felts Packing Company of Virginia, it's like my birthday, which conveniently comes in the summer, just about the time the first backyard tomatoes ripen. The first BLT of the year is always a sacred ritual, a lusty Bacchanalia, and it took a leap heavenward when I discovered Felts's bacon in *The Art of Eating.* I must agree with Ed; I've never tasted better bacon.

Felts's bacon is pork and salt, nothing more. The rind is intact, and the bacon comes attached to the ribs or removed; it's a bit of a trick to cut it off the rib yourself, but there is very tasty, lean meat tucked between the ribs that is lost when the ribs are cut off mechanically. (Bacon lovers will get the hang of it in no time.) The bacon produced at this Virginia farm, operating since the 1930s, is rubbed with salt and left for not quite two weeks, during which time the

the saltmen of tibet

For thousands of years, a few nomads have made an annual journey to a Himalayan lake in northern Tibet, where they rake and gather salt, pack it into sacks, sew them shut, and load them onto the yaks (nearly two hundred of the animals) that accompany them. Ulrike Koch tells their story in a two-hour film, *The Saltmen of Tibet,* that was released in 1998. The documentary was taped surreptitiously when the Chinese government denied permission to film. (The nomads had their own restrictions; Koch, a woman, was not allowed on the final days of the journey; her male assistants went on without her.) The nomads sing and chant, communicate in a secret salt language, and mold small animal salt-sculptures in the salt lake before they begin their return journey. The somber, elegiac tone of the movie is underscored by the presence of ramshackle trucks—the first commercial harvesters of the sacred salt—at the lake when the nomads arrive.

salt penetrates right through the meat, which is then washed, smoked for three days, and air-dried in a warm room for another week. *Et voilà!* it is bacon. Before it is sold, Felts's bacon is rubbed with crushed black pepper.

Felts's principal product is dry-salted smoked ham, intensely flavored meat that bears no resemblance to the watery ham sold in supermarkets. It is as close a thing as we have to the prosciutto of Italy and the *Jamón serrano* of Spain, and it is probably best to think of it in this way, rather than as most of us think of domestic ham. A big slice with red-eye gravy and mashed potatoes is likely to be too intense, too salty, for all but the most hard-core devotees. Boiling the ham leaches out much of the salt, but I think it's better in small portions, served raw as an appetizer or used to flavor cooked greens, beans, and stews. Scalloped potatoes flavored with this ham are sensational.

"Pastrami is Jewish barbecue," John Harris, the author of *The Deli Book* tells me, "and what makes it good is salt, pepper, fat, garlic, and spices." The four basic food groups, some might say, plus spices.

Pastrami refers to a process rather than to a specific product. It can be made with duck, turkey, lamb, venison, and wild boar, though classic New York pastrami is made from a tough piece of meat near the belly of a cow known as the plate, or navel. It is a cheap cut, tough and fatty, that needs long slow processing to tenderize it and leach out some of the fat.

Corned beef and pastrami begin with pickling—or corning, after the large salt crystals called "corn" in England—in a salty brine. Corned beef is brisket, a less-fatty piece of meat closer to the chest of the animal, that, after pickling, is ready for sale, though it must be boiled for several hours before being eaten. Pastrami goes through further processing, beginning with a spice rub. Some manufacturers use lots of garlic, others cloves and coriander; some emphasize black pepper. Next, the pastrami is hot smoked; it is fully cooked when you buy it, but tastes best after lengthy steaming, which further tenderizes it.

Of course, it is not only flesh that may be preserved with salt and in salt. Caviar is between 3 and 4 percent salt, and without a proper and careful salting, it's . . . well, it's just fish eggs. Sauerkraut is simply (and miraculously) fermented cabbage and salt. Cucumbers become pickles in a salty brine, as do a host of other vegetables. Without salt, there would be no Korean kimchi. Although some olives are made without salt, most rely on salt either to leach out their bitterness or to add flavor when something else has done so.

Salt is crucial in bread baking; it controls the activity of the yeast, slowing it down so that the flavors of the flour have time to develop. Salt also firms the texture of dough, tightening the gluten. Many French bakers and an increasing number in this country swear by Celtic gray sea salt, but not all bakers agree that there are differences in the way salt influences the taste of bread. Craig Ponsford of Artisan Bakers in Sonoma, the baker who won the 1996 World Cup of Baking for the U.S. team, likes both fine sea salt and kosher salt because they dissolve quickly; subtle differences detected between salts on the tongue, he says, do not create different tastes in bread. I tend to agree. Some (but not exclusively, as Ponsford's scrumptuous breads clearly demonstrate) of the bakers who use Celtic gray salt do, indeed, make superior bread, but I've not been able to identify salt as the single most crucial variable. Rather, it seems to be an overall dedication to excellent ingredients and a special care taken with all of the steps in the process that give superior results.

Cheesemaking the world around would be vastly different were there no salt, which flavors curds, regulates aging, and inhibits or stops the growth of bacteria. Cheeses may be treated with dry salt or a salt brine.

Feta, the traditional sheep's milk cheese from Greece and Bulgaria (France and the United States also produce feta, often using goat's or cow's milk), is probably the best known of the brined, or pickled, cheeses. For classic feta, fresh curds of unpasteurized sheep's milk are ladled into molds, packed, drained, and returned to the whey after it is seasoned with salt. Two weeks later, the cheese has a pleasantly salty taste.

In Poland's Podhale Valley, a region known as the Highlands, sheep's milk and salt are combined to make a delicious fresh cheese called Bryndza; it is creamy in texture,

salt

almost like a fresh ricotta. Another sheep's milk cheese, Oscypki, is pressed into molds, most of them cylindrical but some whimsically shaped into hearts, animals, and toy drums. Some of this cheese is sold merely aged, but most of it is lightly smoked first. The smoked cheese is frequently sliced, fried, and served as an appetizer.

Some cheeses, such as Italy's Taleggio, are washed with brine, which gives the cheese a thin, pliable rind. Rubbing cheeses with dry salt encourages the formation of a harder, tougher rind, Parmigiano-Reggiano being the classic example. In many cheeses, salt is mixed directly into fresh curds; this is the case with Cheddar, Monterey Jack, and most goat cheeses. Some cheeses, such as Emmentaler, are soaked in a brine before being sent to the aging room.

Each of these methods of introducing salt to the cheesemaking process is essential. Attempts to make salt-free cheeses have been largely unsuccessful (as have attempts to make low-fat or nonfat cheese, but that's another story); the cheeses lack character, distinction, and taste, which cannot be created by adding salt to cheese at the table, when it is too late for it to work its transformative magic.

Salt preserves food, among other things, by drawing out moisture not only from the material to be preserved but from the cells of the bacteria that left to their own briny devices would hasten spoilage. Sausages, especially those made of fine emulsions such as bockwurst and bratwurst, also rely on salt to help maintain an even distribution of ingredients. Without salt, there would be no andouille, pepperoni, chorizo, linguiça, or kielbasa, no knockwurst or liverwurst. There would be no turkey jerky for hikers to stuff into their backpacks.

Salt can be a sneaky conspirator; hollow crystals readily absorb and hide the

band of black gold

If salt is essential in cheesemaking, peppercorns, though not crucial, add a savory flourish, a definitive character, to certain regional cheeses. Italian pepato (also made in Latin America and the United States), a sheep's milk cheese just a peppercorn away from pecorino, is studded with both cracked and whole peppercorns. Sicilian pecorino has a band of black peppercorns running through its middle. Several Greek cheeses include peppercorns, such as Métsovo from the village of that name in the Pindus mountains. Kopanistí, a blue-veined cheese, is kneaded with salt after the mold has grown but before the cheese is aged; as it ripens, it develops a mild peppery flavor, the result of interaction between the salt, cheese, and mold, rather than of introduced pepper. One of the classic new American goat cheeses, produced first by Laura Chenel and now by countless small and large cheesemakers, is a five-ounce log of chabis coated with crushed black pepper.

fat in potato chips, tortilla chips, and other prepared foods that have an outer layer of salt. "Greaseless," we are told, and it's true, though deceptive. The fat is still there.

Pepper, too, is a principal ingredient in prepared and preserved foods. Spices were once primary ingredients in preserving foods (spices kill nearly all foodborne bacteria, hence their popularity before the age of modern refrigeration), but today most spices, including pepper, are used primarily for the flavor and aroma they contribute. The food packaging industry is the major consumer of pepper in this country. In fine-ground, light-colored sausages such as bratwurst, ground white pepper is used so that the meat will not be speckled with black. Pastrami, bacon, gravlax, and other cured meats and fish often have an outer layer of cracked black peppercorns.

koshering and kashering

When it comes to meat, the process of *kashering*—preparing foods according to Jewish dietary laws and traditions, that is, making foods kosher—includes the removal of any blood that lingers in the flesh of the animal. Kashering begins with meat from an animal slaughtered by an approved method, though this does not, of course, involve our topic, salt. Salt is a key ingredient in a step further along in the process and its importance has given us the common term "kosher salt," which Rabbi Jonathan Slater of Santa Rosa, California, explains is a bit of a misnomer. Kosher salt is merely coarse salt; it is more accurately called "koshering salt."

Kashering is sometimes done at home, and sometimes at the butcher shop before the meat is purchased. For example, kosher ground beef will have been salted and soaked before being ground; delicatessen meats begin with kashered meat, as well, and no further processing is necessary once they have been purchased. A steak, a roast, or a leg of lamb, however, likely will not have been kashered. If a piece of meat

salt

is to be broiled or roasted, it does not need to be salted; the blood will drain away as it cooks. Meat for stews, soups, and sometimes roasts may need to have the blood removed before cooking, which is achieved by soaking the meat in water, draining it, and then covering it with a layer of salt and letting it sit for thirty minutes or so, during which time a coarse salt, rather than dissolving as granulated salt does, draws out blood and other impurities. The meat is then soaked in cool water for a few minutes and dried; it is then ready to be cooked. Poultry must undergo a similar process. If you keep a kosher kitchen, you don't need me to tell you what is done. But if, like me, you've only heard of kosher kitchens and been intrigued by the practices, perhaps I've clarified the mystery. Kosher salt is not like holy water— it is not blessed by a rabbi and it is not imbued with magical powers. Rather, it performs a specific, tangible function.

the pork barrel

When a politician hands out the pork, what exactly is being given away? Salt pork. For the pioneers traveling west, it was one of just a few staples. Europe had bread; young America had pork belly preserved in a barrelful of salty brine. Salt pork sustained soldiers during the Civil War, and when Northern troops destroyed a new salt mine on Avery Island in Louisiana, Confederate soldiers faced a debilitating salt famine. Lack of salt, and salt pork, is said to have won the war.

Salt pork is used today—in collard greens braised with salt pork, for example—but it's no longer ubiquitous. Faith Willinger, an expert on Italian foods and cooking, considers salt pork better than the pancetta available in the United States. Rub it with cracked peppercorns, she advises, wrap it in plastic, and use it in recipes that call for pancetta. I find the pancetta in my local Italian market just fine, but I use salt pork, too, peppered, just as Faith says. When it comes to preserved meats, the more the merrier.

snowflakes on the windshield

Professional chefs differ when it comes to the salts they prefer. Some don't care (I've been in those kitchens, seen the tin shaker on a rack above the range, watched as a shower of table salt mixed with powdered black pepper rains onto virtually everything); some prefer what they perceive as the more complex flavor of sea salt, even when they aren't quite sure exactly what sea salt is (and even when it's the same product as that table salt).

A lot of chefs like kosher salt, by which they mean the coarse salt sold under the Diamond Crystal brand (now owned by the large Cargill Corporation), which is

salt

22

easy to grab between your fingers, the classic "pinch" of salt. There are other kosher salts on the market, made using different techniques, but Diamond Crystal is unique. It is my salt of choice for cooking, my default salt, the one I carry in my purse or pocket in a discreet little wooden box, just in case. It *is* different, and its qualities and the method by which it is produced are worth a look.

It was a continuing debate with my friend Daniel Patterson, an extraordinarily talented chef with a palate I admire and envy, about our favorite salts (he prefers a French sea salt for general cooking) that set me on the trail of kosher salt's story. It wasn't long before I knocked on the door, electronically

a taste of sin

In France, reports Waverley Root in his remarkable book *Food,* the profession of "sin eater" flourished for a while. When a family member died, a saucer of salt and a piece of bread were placed on the chest of the deceased before a practitioner of this singular trade was summoned. The sin eater arrived, ate the bread and salt, and thus, it was believed, the sins of the departed, saving the loved one from a long stay in purgatory or even eternal damnation. The flaw, at least in this world, was that sin eaters were despised and the profession died out for want of practioners. This symbolic function, that of salt absorbing unwanted material, has a correspondence in the real world—salt draws out and absorbs liquids and soluble impurities, making it effective in the process of koshering, preserving, and embalming.

speaking, of Skip Niman, a chemist who began working for Diamond Crystal in 1959. He is probably the world's leading expert on the Alberger method of producing the coarse crystals we call kosher salt.

"It will be easiest for you to understand important differences between kosher salt and table salt if you look at the two under a magnifying glass," Skip suggested just a few minutes into our first conversation. I followed his instructions, and urge you to do the same. Place small separate piles on a dark surface—a black plate or a piece of construction paper is perfect. Look at each through something that will magnify it a little. The table salt looks like a pile of perfectly shaped ice cubes. Now, think of what happens when you drop ice cubes on a car windshield. They slide down, melting very slowly, leaving a trail of water in their wake. That's how granulated salt acts in food and on your tongue.

The Diamond Crystal kosher salt crystals are uneven and jagged, not unlike snowflakes. What happens when snowflakes fall onto a windshield? They melt instantly (don't argue about frozen windshields and icy buildup; you know what I mean), which is what kosher salt does—it dissolves in a burst of flavor. (If you have another brand of kosher salt around, take a look at that, too. The crystals may be solid and flat, as if run over by tiny steamrollers; or they may be a piles of little cubes, flattened and fused together.)

Most food-grade salt, including much sea salt, is dissolved (or redissolved, in the case of solar-evaporated salt) and dried in an enclosed vacuum pan; the result is granulated salt, those little cubes you saw so clearly under the magnifying glass. The uneven crystals known technically as grainer and casually as kosher salt are made by heating saturated brines, thus hastening evaporation and crystallization, which occurs on the surface of an open pan. The salt grows downward in the brine, forming hollow pyramids with thin sides known as hopper crystals. Because of the cost of fuel, very little true grainer salt is produced today; Alberger salt, a patented technique developed by J. L. Alberger in 1889 and owned today by Diamond Crystal, has replaced it.

Alberger salt is made by dissolving and extracting underground deposits of salt. Sodium hydroxide and sodium carbonate added to the brine cause the most common impurities—calcium, magnesium, and sulfate—to precipitate out of the solution, leaving behind a semipurified brine, which is pumped through a series of pressurizers and heaters that increase the temperature to 290°F.

At this point, it is a rolling, boiling stew of salt, a supersaturated brine that is pumped into a long, cylindrical container called a graveler, filled with large lake stones. Baffling plates force the brine up and down through the graveler, and as it washes over the stones, calcium sulfate, already looking for solid ground, clings to the handy rock surfaces as the brine continues on to the next stage, a series of flashers in which the temperature and pressure are gradually reduced.

sacred salt, psychic pepper

If you need peace and quiet in a noisy house, grind together some salt, sugar, and Dragon's Blood palm, place it in a closed container, and hide it in the house. If there is negativity or a lack of harmony in the home, soak a branch of rue in salt water and shake it throughout the troubled area. To protect your home from being struck by lightning, toss some salt into a fire. Add pepper (a masculine plant, ruled by Mars) to amulets to protect yourself against the evil eye (and your own envious thoughts). Mix pepper with salt and scatter the mixture outside to dispel evil. If you're troubled by ghosts, carry salt in your pocket to render them invisible. If you have an exorcism scheduled, don't forget the pepper, an essential ingredient in the ancient ritual of casting out demons.

—*Cunningham's Encyclopedia of Magical Herbs*

salt

Tiny seed crystals of salt form instantly as the brine is pumped from the last flasher into an open pan shaped like a huge figure eight with the middle part gone. Hopper-shaped crystals begin to form on the salt seeds and sink as they grow heavy. Paddles keep the brine circulating and when the salt has completely precipitated, the slurry—that is, the crystals and the remaining liquor, called bittern—is pumped into a centrifuge (picture a large washing machine). The liquid is spun off, the bottom of the centrifugal basket drops out, and the salt cascades onto a conveyor belt that takes it through a dryer. The dry salt is screened and graded into sizes, the coarsest of which becomes kosher salt.

Alberger salt has a lighter bulk density than granulated salt has: Equal amounts by volume are not equal amounts by weight. Simply put, this means that there is less salt in a teaspoon of kosher salt than there is in a teaspoon of granulated salt. Qualities such as bulk density, rate of solubility, and blendability (dry ingredients mixed with Alberger salt will stay in suspension in a uniform blend; granulated salt will separate out and fall to the bottom, or, in an oily blend, leave striations) are important to food producers, but of little concern to home cooks.

What you need to know is that the saltiness of a specific quantity of salt will vary depending on the type of salt. If you taste as you cook and use your fingers instead of a measuring spoon, you will get the hang of perfect salting quickly. (If you're the curious type, you might enjoy knowing that a pound of granulated salt has 5,370,000 crystals and a pound of coarse Alberger salt a mere 1,370,000, or that it takes 9 minutes to dissolve 1,000 grams of granulated salt, 3.6 minutes to dissolve the same quantity of coarse flakes.)

versatile salt

Salt has more than fourteen thousand uses; less than 4 percent of all salt produced each year goes into food. It is the second most important element—sulfur is the first—in the chemical industry, and is used in the manufacture of fabrics, glass, cosmetics, and ammunition. It is crucial to agriculture and has dozens of uses in the home that have nothing to do with eating, or at least not directly. You can polish copper by rubbing it vigorously with salt and lemon juice; you can extinguish a grease fire by covering it with salt. Salt water poured down a drain will sweeten it. Salt is probably the most effective method to reduce the damage done by red wine spilled on a rug, tablecloth, or other fabric: Cover it immediately with a thick layer of salt (kosher absorbs liquid the fastest), which will draw out the wine and reduce the chance of a permanent stain. In the oven, sprinkle salt on food as soon as it spills; cleaning up after the oven has cooled will be much easier.

—The Salt Institute, *Facts About Salt*

salt

The chef and cookbook author Bruce Aidells, who is known among his friends as The Sausage King, is one of many advocates of brining meats to add flavor. It is particularly effective in adding succulence and juiciness to today's leaner meats, Bruce explains, especially pork; anyone who has gnawed on a rock-hard pork chop will appreciate the technique. When Bruce and his wife, the well-known chef Nancy Oakes, use brine for flavors, they use much less salt than is used in brines for preserving; they add other ingredients, too, including black pepper and other spices, vinegar, maple syrup, mustard, and, in one of Nancy's signature savory recipes, vanilla.

Ed Walsh, the executive chef at Kendall-Jackson Winery in Sonoma County, soaks all meat (except rabbit, which doesn't have enough fat) and poultry in brine before cooking. Brining removes the adrenaline that is released into an animal's tissues when it is killed, he explains, and creates a much cleaner flavor. He begins with one cup of salt (the same proportion as Bruce and Nancy use) to each gallon of ice water and may add juniper berries, peppercorns, onions, and parsley. He brines pork for three days, and chicken for an hour and a half; for the latter he changes the brine every thirty minutes. Brining also improves the flavor of goose, duck, squab, and most game, he adds.

Ed grew up watching his parents salt almost everything that arrived in the kitchen of their restaurant on Long Island. Dried pasta was washed in brine to re-

rejuvenating salt

Salt invigorates our bodies as well as our taste buds. Add several handfuls of sea salt to a bath (or simply soak tired feet) and you'll feel revived. Several cosmetic companies, as well as the Grain & Salt Society, (see resources, page 216) sell non-food-grade sea salt, some already mixed with aromatic oils and fragrances, for this purpose. Salt rubs and salt facials are even more rejuvenating— sea salt moistened with a little oil (almond, jojoba, or olive oil is best) and rubbed vigorously over the skin with a loofah leaves your skin feeling as soft and dewy as a newborn's. An exfoliant, salt removes dead skin cells, revives tired ones, and stimulates circulation. Some say that the minerals in French sea salts draw out toxins. For an exfoliating facial, mix equal parts of sea salt (crushed, not large crystals, which can cut) and olive oil, massage gently in upwards strokes from the neck to the forehead, and leave on for ten to fifteen minutes. Rinse thoroughly with cool water and then apply a moisturizer.

salt

move excess flour; produce was rinsed to extend its life; even seafood was washed in a saltwater bath.

It was from Ed that I first heard the story of *seppuku,* a method of suicide among poor people and women in Japan. Traditionally, poor people did not have knives and women were not allowed to touch them. Instead of committing hara-kiri, a person would eat a pound of salt and die within a day.

pepper

the king of spice

Salt is indispensable. The earth is cloaked in salt; a salty tide moves within us, too, every moment lapping at the edges of our cells. Without it, we die.

Pepper is superfluous. Salt's culinary spouse is expendable, entirely unnecessary for existence (the ideal marriage, one partner frivolous, one keeping the house afloat). It is a gift, a luxury that we have come to take utterly for granted. "Saltandpepper" is nearly a single word in our kitchen vocabulary and the thought of doing without the pepper part is all but inconceivable. But should something occur to put pepper absolutely out of reach, we could live. We would mourn its loss, and with every bite be aware of its absence. But we would live.

In the end, we might get over the loss of pepper without too lengthy a struggle. We have no innate physical longing for it, as we do for salt. We delight in the presence of pepper in our food, but the memory of its taste would fade in a single generation; we cannot pass sensory knowledge to our children, we can only entice them with descriptions, always inadequate when it comes to taste, completely ineffective when it comes to smell. No one would believe our stories. If pepper vanished, it soon would become myth, an enchanting mystery, a tale of the King of Spices who one day walked off into the wilderness and vanished, the Atlantis of spice, nothing more than a tantalizing rumor. Sure, they would think, and what is the moral of this tale? The King would be replaced by . . . allspice? long pepper? coriander? All have been used as we now use pepper—that is, in almost everything—at one time or another.

But don't worry about pepper vanishing—there is plenty, millions of vines

Two varieties of pepper, *Piper vestitum* and *P. grande,* are found in the wild. Both bear small clusters that grow up, rather than down as *P. nigrum* clusters do. The berries of *vestitum* are light golden brown and black; *grande* berries are red. Both are hot but lack the complexity of cultivated pepper.

of it wrapping themselves around the earth, a savory circumference, an equator of savor and taste and heat, a lusty belt around our middle. Pepper—green, black, and white peppercorns—is the fruit of a perennial vine, *Piper nigrum,* that thrives within fifteen degrees of the equator. It flourishes in tropical heat and monsoon rains. Native to the Malabar coast of southern India, pepper vines were introduced into Southeast Asia hundreds of years before the birth of Christ, and much more recently to Brazil, Micronesia, Madagascar, and Nigeria.

Although pepper vines can grow to thirty feet or more, most commercial plants are kept at between nine and twelve feet to make harvesting easier. Some farms keep vines to six feet to make ladders unnecessary during harvest. Each vine is trained around a central pole, or in some areas, a tree whose leaves shield the pepper from too much direct sunlight and whose roots fix nitrogen in the soil. A pepper farm resembles a Christmas tree farm, vines stretching upward like fast-growing pine trees.

Peppercorn berries grow in small clusters up to about three inches long; they resemble diminutive bunches of Cabernet Sauvignon grapes, loose and narrow rather than tight and plump. There may be fifty, sixty, eighty, one hundred berries per cluster, and the clusters do not all ripen at the same time. A single vine must be picked many times in a season to harvest all its fruit; all pepper everywhere is picked by hand.

Black pepper is the most common form of pepper, and for two reasons. It is the easiest to produce, and it has the fullest range of flavor and aroma.

Green peppercorns are harvested several weeks before black pepper is, an advantage if you're worried about pests or disease, when the berry is still soft throughout, its hard core not yet formed. But the flavors are not fully developed at this point, either, and it is hard to keep the young berries green as they dry. Some are pickled in vinegar and some preserved in brine, both wonderfully flavorful in many recipes but not exactly versatile as a spice. Until recently, freeze-drying was the only other method of preserving green peppercorns, but new techniques make it possible to air-dry green berries. To prevent them from turning black (for then they would merely be black pepper without its full range of flavors), they are soaked in vinegar or brine first. Green peppercorns have a mildly tart, fresh taste, full of the characteristic heat of black pepper, but lacking in its complexity and depth. Their flavor fades quickly once they are crushed or ground.

Black peppercorns are harvested when the fruit is still green, but nearing ripeness, about the time a single berry shows a blush of yellow. The clusters are threshed to remove them from their tiny stems, and then they are set out on straw mats in the hot sun, where the outer layer shrivels and turns black as it dries. (Sometimes they are dried on their spikes, then threshed.) The peppercorns take many days to become completely dry; they are combed with a wooden rake each day. Once dry, they are packed into sacks and sold to exporters, who trade them on the world market.

Fruit for white pepper is picked about a week after fruit for black pepper. It is a little more ripe—maybe a few berries show that yellow blush, maybe a single berry has turned reddish orange—but not fully red; to wait that long, pepper farmers tell me, is to extend an invitation to the birds who love the ripe berries. After the almost-ripe berries are picked, they are tied in big sacks and thrown into the nearest body of water (pond, lake, stream, or river), where they soak for several days. Soaking rots the outer mantle of the peppercorn, the skin that otherwise turns black; what hasn't already come off when the wet peppercorns are emptied from the sack is rubbed off before the peppercorns are spread on straw mats, raked, and dried in the sun, just as black peppercorns are. White peppercorns are traded similarly to black peppercorns, through exporters and traders on the world market.

There are two other pepper products that deserve note. Sometimes the dark skin of black pepper is removed to produce something that resembles white pepper visually, but not in taste. This pepper is called decorticated black pepper (and, occasionally, decorticated white pepper) and it tastes like other black pepper, yet is not as aromatic. Sometimes small quantities of immature pepper spikes are harvested before the peppercorns begin to grow; these spikes are preserved in brine. You occasionally see them in Asian markets.

pepper

Pepper is classified according to the country in which it is grown. Thus, Malabar pepper is grown all along the Malabar coast of India, in the state of Kerala. Tellicherry, the name of the port that was once the origin of most pepper shipments, indicates a different grade of Indian pepper, larger berries with a greater quantity of volatile oils and piperine and a distinctly floral aroma. Pepper is assumed to be indigenous to this region (although some sources point to the East Indies, currently Indonesia, as the native home of *P. nigrum*). Today, India is the leader in quantity, producing about sixty thousand tons of pepper (most of it black) a year, half of which is consumed within the country, the rest exported.

Indonesia sells the most white pepper, twenty thousand tons annually; it also produces fifteen thousand tons of black pepper. Much of the pepper is grown on the island of Bangka, off Sumatra, and is shipped through two ports, one of them Muntok, hence the name Indonesian Muntok, which refers to all white pepper from this country. Indonesian black pepper bears the name of Lampong, the port city on the island of Sumatra. Most Indonesian pepper is exported. With the political and economic instability of the late 1990s, prices have increased and consistent delivery has been in doubt.

Malaysia produces about twenty thousand tons a year (fifteen black, five white), an amount that will increase substantially as newly planted vines come into production. Malaysia exports the bulk of its pepper, primarily to Japan and western Eu-

faux peppercorns

Although not true peppercorns at all, pink peppercorns turned up in the late 1970s on trendy menus and in gourmet markets everywhere, an affectation of the *nouvelle cuisine* frenzy. But by the early 1980s, reports of adverse reactions eclipsed their brief, chic status; for a time, their sale was prohibited, but the restriction was rescinded through the efforts of French producers, backed by their government, determined to reopen the market for pink peppercorns from the French island, Réunion, in the Indian Ocean, the source of nearly all of the small, brittle berries. Pink peppercorns come from a tree (*Schinus terebinthifolius,* sometimes called the Brazilian pepper tree) native to South America. A papery outer layer—hot pink, hence the name—shields a small, hard seed with a mildly sweet, mildly aromatic flavor that does not resemble true pepper in the least. Many spice companies include them in four-pepper blends, but they make little if any contribution to the flavor of food. They add color, but nothing more (except for an annoying texture if more than a few are added to a single dish).

rope, though increasing quantities are imported into the United States. Brazil, where pepper was first planted in the 1930s, has been producing about fourteen thousand tons a year for export, much of it to the United States. Brazilian pepper is farmed in the state of Para, with plantings along the Amazon River. In recent years, the quality has been poor and the number of farms and farmers is declining.

China consumes nearly all of the ten thousand tons of pepper it produces each year; recently, the United States has allowed some Chinese pepper into the country. Sri Lanka (the pepper is known as Ceylon, former name of the island-country) produces about five thousand tons a year, shipped from the port of Colombo.

Vietnam, fairly new to the pepper trade, has been producing an increasing amount, approaching twenty thousand tons a year. The quality has been poor but is expected to improve as farms mature and techniques improve. Micronesia has a very small industry, harvesting less than one hundred tons a year, but it fills a unique niche. The pepper is grown on the outermost island of the chain, Ponape, and is not traded on the world market. Some is sold to Australia, but much of it is packaged and sold to tourists in Micronesia as well as in airports in the Pacific. Madagascar, Thailand, and Nigeria produce small quantities, very little of which makes it into the United States. The major producers are members of the International Pepper Community, an organization that in 1998 was expanding its membership to include both countries that consume pepper and trade organizations.

the question of quality

India may be the world's largest producer of pepper, but the United States is its biggest consumer. We imported nearly 134 million pounds of pepper (21 million of ground pepper, 13 million of white peppercorns, and 100 million of black peppercorns) in 1997, primarily through spice traders working for large companies that deal in vast quantities of spices to keep major sellers such as McCormick and Schilling supplied. In that year, nearly 45 percent of the pepper imported into this country came from India. Eventually, between 30 and 40 percent of this pepper will be sold retail, much of it as ground pepper; the rest will be used in the fragrance and beverage industries and in food processing.

White pepper and black pepper are sold as commodities, like corn and pork, according to Marty Goldsmith, a broker with Mueller Company, Inc., of New York

City. He buys pepper through exporters, who in turn buy pepper from the farmers who grow it. Its sale is seasonal. For example, in January through May, Indian pepper is traded; in May and June, most Malaysian pepper is on the market. The crucial considerations are price, consistent availability, and timely shipment.

"Quality absolutely does not come into play when U.S. traders buy pepper. Cleanliness is an issue but quality is not," he says, confirming what I had heard from other sources, that the United States is not a good market for premium pepper (Japan and Germany are the best markets for high-quality pepper). By cleanliness, Goldsmith means an absence of stems and other plant material that might be mixed in with the peppercorns. He adds that all pepper is sterilized upon arrival in the United States and that some is irradiated, at the request of the large seasoning companies who purchase pepper from brokers.

To say that U.S. traders are not concerned with the quality of pepper may sound more alarming than it is. In a sense, pepper is pepper, as salt is salt, its major characteristics of heat and aroma always present with only subtle variations. Quality is more a matter of degree and intensity. Volatile oils contribute pepper's heady aromas; the alkaloid piperine oleoresin accounts for the heat and flavor. These elements become stronger as the clusters of berries hang on the vine (to a point, that is; left too long, they begin to fade), so if a farmer is willing to be patient and take the risks involved with later harvest, the pepper will be more peppery, more itself. The aroma and flavor of pepper can be eclipsed, too, if it is contaminated with bacteria and the toxins they produce.

There is another aspect to the story of peppercorns than the one demonstrated by major spice traders. Smaller companies, some of them mail-order suppliers, some of them selling wholesale to the public, do search for high quality and sell spices that are neither chemically sterilized (the United States is the only country in the world still using ethylene oxide to sterilize spices) nor irradiated. A few even manage to locate spices that have been grown without chemical fertilizers and pesticides, no easy task with products from the tropics, where farmers are reluctant to risk losing crops to the pests and viruses that thrive in a humid climate. Organic farming is a very new endeavor in developing countries, though several countries, including Malaysia and Sri Lanka, are devoting considerable resources to the organic farming of both pepper and other spices.

"It's easier to find out what's going on in Malaysia," Bill Penzey of Penzeys Ltd. tells me while I'm working on this book, adding that there are interesting developments that will make Malaysian pepper increasingly important in the coming years. I've visited southern India already and understand well the physical and cultural challenges I would encounter if I pursued the pepper trail along the Malabar Coast. I welcome the chance for discovery, and I recognize the name Borneo from long-ago Sunday school classes. (But where is it exactly? I ask myself.)

"You should stay at the Holiday Inn," he continues. "Room service makes a great steak au poivre with fresh green peppercorns."

Two months later, I arrive in Kuching, the capital of Sarawak, one of two Malaysian states on the island of Borneo (the largest portion of which belongs to Indonesia). In front of the hotel is one of several large cat sculptures in this city whose name means "cat," this one showing a litter of playful kittens surrounding two adult felines. The city celebrates its namesake not only with whimsical statues but also with the world's only cat museum, where T-shirts and tea towels proclaim Kuching "Cat City." Other cities in Sarawak pay tribute to signature agricultural products—Serian has a statue of the infamous durian (the "King of Fruits" they say, and it must be seen, tasted, and most of all, smelled, to be believed) in its town square; Sibu, in the heart of pepper farm country, has a statue of a pineapple, also an important crop.

The next morning, I head to the Pepper Marketing Board, a federal agency, founded in 1972, responsible for grading and certifying all pepper exported from Malaysia. It also markets the spice, and processes between 10 and 15 percent of the pepper grown in the country. Modern pepper cultivation was underway in 1875 in Sarawak, then a British colony; by the 1930s, it was producing a significant quantity of the spice. It wasn't until the 1950s, however, that quality and production became consistent.

am i making you hungry?

Pepper is an important ingredient in the fragrance industry. Through distillation, volatile oils are extracted from peppercorns (almost always black; occasionally white). It contributes to a perfume's middle notes (those that dissipate within two or three hours; top notes vanish within about twenty minutes; bottom notes linger for five or six hours), providing a warm, earthy element. Polo includes black pepper; Modern Eau de Parfum, released by the Banana Republic in 1998, uses white pepper.

pepper

Tropical air, heavy and saturated, is a fragrant soup of aromas, some appealing, some staggeringly aggressive and offensive until you become used to them. As I approach the Kuching office of the PMB, the seductive aroma of black pepper mingles with the other smells. The air is thoroughly intoxicating and suddenly, I'm thinking of lunch.

"Black pepper stimulates appetite, making you salivate," Anandan Abdullah, the general manager of the PMB volunteers, perhaps reading my mind or maybe simply aware of the nature of the commodity he has overseen for more than two decades.

As he shows me through the warehouse where pepper is received, packaged, and shipped, the aroma of black pepper eclipses everything until I am frantically, savagely hungry. "Feed me now!" I think, but I'm quiet, a polite visitor. (Could black pepper oil be used to stimulate the appetites of anorexics and cancer and AIDS patients, I wonder. I've not found an answer.)

Anandan apologizes for spiders I don't see. They remove webs once a week, he says, but let the spiders live; they are very successful at controlling mosquitoes and other insects. Cats, currently sleeping out of sight, keep the facility free of the rats who would eat the jute bags that contain the pepper. Environmental sensitivity appears to underscore everything here.

I taste several types of pepper, crunching into whole peppercorns with abandon, then cringing as their heat sears my palate. Organic black pepper, from a small test farm, is remarkably fragrant, sweet, and fresh tasting. Creamy White Pepper, with its large, evenly sized berries and a uniform pale color that does indeed resemble cream, is exceptional and is sold as one of two value-added peppers for which the PMB is trying to create a consistent market so that when the price heads downward from its present high, farmers will have a safety net.

In the summer of 1998, world pepper prices are high and farmers are happy; prices have been rising for several years. But pepper prices fluctuate in eight- to ten-year cycles, and they are bound to fall sometime soon. When the price is low, as it was in the early 1990s, fewer farmers are motivated to grow pepper. Some replant with more lucrative crops; some stockpile their pepper hoping for a price increase; some ignore their vines because the compensation is so meager. Gradually, supply decreases, there is not enough pepper to fill world demand, prices begin to rise, and farmers become interested again. They clean out the warehouse and plant new vines (which take a year and half until their first harvest, three years to hit their stride); increased production moves slowly and for a while prices continue to rise. If the PMB can create a market for Malaysian pepper, specifically for Creamy White Pepper and Naturally Clean Black Pepper, farmers will be able to ride out these economic cycles.

The next morning, I begin the long, winding ride to Sibu, 462 kilometers northwest of Kuching, on the Rajang River in the heart of the Sarikei Division (that is, county), where 40 percent of Sarawak's pepper is grown. First, we stop at Serian to observe the process of making Creamy White Pepper.

Creamy White Pepper begins with large berry clusters; the PMB pays a premium for quality fruit. Instead of being tied in sacks and placed in a stream or river, the peppercorns are placed in large plastic barrels (covered), where fresh water from a nearby mountain spring circulates through them for close to two weeks. After they are drained, rubbed clean, and thoroughly dried, they are sorted to remove dark, small, and light (by weight) berries. Most of the pepper is sold to Japan and western Europe.

"The U.S. is not a good market for high quality," Anandan explains. "It is a bulk market, the biggest user of pepper in the world. Most white pepper is used by sausage makers and food packers; they want consistency and are not looking for high quality." (ASTA, the American Spice Trade Association, specifies moisture content, cleanliness, and allowable percentage of light berries; Malaysia packages a Brown Label pepper—to meet these requirements.)

There are forty thousand hectares of pepper farms in Sarawak, and forty thousand pepper farmers. The average farmer has between two and three hundred vines, which are planted six hundred to the acre. A good vine produces between four and six pounds of peppercorns a year, a great vine as much as ten or twelve pounds; it will remain at peak yield for fifteen to twenty years. As we drive through the Sarikei Division towards Sibu, the hillsides are studded with small farms, some with mature vines in full production, some with tiny new vines covered with dried ferns to shield them from the sun.

Bintangor is a small agricultural town near Sibu. It is the location of the first modern processing plant in Malaysia for Naturally Clean Black Pepper, the other value-added pepper developed by the PMB. Here, fresh peppercorns arrive one day and by the next are ready to be shipped. What normally takes weeks is condensed into twenty-four hours.

Sarikei pepper farmers deliver their pepper in the early morning, before the heat of the day. The Pepper Marketing Board buys the pepper, stalks and all, before it is threshed, with the requirement that it is delivered to the facility within twenty-four hours of picking.

Shortly after its arrival at the facility, the pepper enters the first stage in a semiautomated process, a double thresher that removes virtually all plant material before sending the berries through a cold-water bath to wash away dirt and dust. The washed berries go into a one-minute hot-water rinse to kill microbes and are then carried up a conveyor belt into an enormous flat-bed stainless-steel tank, where huge fans blow hot air over them for twenty to twenty-four hours, during which time their skins wrinkle and turn black.

When I visit the center late on a hot June morning, the fans have recently been shut off. I stand on my tiptoes and poke my head into the dryer, whose doors are open to cool the pepper, breathing in the luscious dark aromas. *When's lunch?* I think instantly.

Once cool, the dried berries enter another conveyor system, passing through a blower that separates the dust from the berries on their way to being packed in twenty-kilo plastic sacks that will be slipped inside three-ply paper bags and labeled. The pepper will be sent to the Kuching facility to be shipped. (It is a confirmation of the increasing popularity of pepper that the dust, once discarded, is now sold; it makes an excellent mulch and fertilizer in your garden, I am told. I wish I could get some back home.)

Wong Hoon Sing, grading inspector for the PMB, tells me this is the best pepper in the world, an assessment I don't feel qualified to confirm. The newly dried pepper looks beautiful—clean, without stems or dust, evenly sized—and smells clean, earthy, rich, and erotic all at the same time. I crack a peppercorn between my teeth and my mouth is flooded with heat and flavor. I have never had better pepper, but then, I have never tasted it this fresh, nor seen it in this quantity before. Is my judgment eclipsed by my exotic surroundings?

At this time in history we look toward old, traditional methods of food production as superior to our modern, industrialized techniques. We search out the hand-crafted, the sun-dried, the pure and simple. We want heirloom vegetables, artisan cheeses, condiment olive oils from small farms, range-fed organic beef from steers who get weekly massages. Yet here, on the edge of the rain forest on the island of Borneo, I am enchanted by pepper made in a completely new, technologically sophisticated method. Most pepper is sun-dried by the farmers who grow it, raked with the same wooden rakes they've used for decades, for centuries. What is the story?

In fact, the alliance between the PMB and the local farmers seems to be an extremely successful union between the old world and the new. The PMB has a vested interest in the success of the farmers, and the agency seems to make a farmer's life easier—they are paid a premium for good farming practices that result in quality fruit, and they can deliver their crop shortly after harvest.

There is another element to consider. All pepper is tested for bacteria, including salmonella and *e. coli,* its two most likely contaminants and the main reason pepper is sterilized or irradiated. Pepper is particularly vulnerable to such conta-

mination because it sits for several weeks on those straw mats on the ground in front of the family home, where chickens run free and birds fly overhead. If the wind comes up, as it always does at some point, dirt, chicken droppings, and a multitude of other pesky little things sweep right over the drying pepper, some inevitably dropping into it. As resistant strains of bacteria develop, there could be a serious threat of dangerous contamination.

Certainly, bacteria are killed during sterilization, but by then toxins released by bacteria may have already altered the flavor of the pepper. Chemical sterilization has the added liability of introducing harmful chemicals into the environment. By processing the pepper before bacteria contaminate it, the potential for flavor damage is eliminated; the water bath kills bacteria and the pepper needs no further sterilization.

For pepper that does not meet the requirements for Naturally Clean Black Pepper, the FAQ (Fair to Average Quality, the world standard) pepper, which the PMB also processes, there is a new steam sterilization plant at the Kuching facility. The single drawback is that steam sterilization is expensive; the chemicals used in sterilization are inexpensive (but only in the short run, and only because the companies that produce them want them used.) Other countries have similar plants, but the total amount of pepper (and other spices) processed this way is small, less than 10 percent of world production.

pepper

The population of Sarawak is about 51 percent Iban, a colorful native tribe with centuries of history on the island. (Their traditional festival costumes, dances, and music are among the most beautiful and compelling I have seen anywhere.) Today, many Iban are pepper farmers who live in longhouses, traditional structures (in some cases built with modern materials; in some cases with thatch, bamboo, and wood from the rain forest) with a dozen or more families sharing a single extended roof.

Before we begin the long drive back to Kuching, we visit Kotak ("box") long-house, not far from the PMB's Bintangor processing plant. The small porch leading to the main house is crowded with black and green peppercorns drying in the sun; more are on the ground outside the house. Inside, the common area, which stretches the length of the twenty-two-door structure (a longhouse is measured by its number of doors, each of which leads to a single-family apartment), is deserted.

The chief greets us and slowly a few residents join him, curious about their red-headed visitor. Older men smile and stare; young men laugh. Women approach more slowly, bringing sweet snacks but always hanging back, never joining the cir-cle where we sit with the chief. A young man pours me a glass of rice wine, a tradi-tional beverage made by each family; if I were here on a feast day, it would be rude not to accept (and drink) a glass from each family. The wine is smooth and refresh-ing, but deceptively potent.

One of the snacks is a large, airy thing of grain and sugar resembling a crescent moon made of spun gold. When I hold it up as if in the sky, everyone laughs and it feels as if we have bridged a cultural gap, the inevitable uncomfortableness between strangers. We've all watched a crescent moon rise in the night sky, we all recognize it for itself. They laugh again when I accept a second glass of wine. They ask, through Wong, if I would like to spend a night; an overnight stay at a longhouse is a popular tourist activity; some build special guest houses to encourage the additional source of income. My spontaneous yes draws another shared chuckle. I am so obviously enchanted by my hosts, I am sorry when it is time to go.

Each family here has a pepper farm. Before leaving, we walk to the nearest ones, just across a road that is both muddy from daily rains, and dusty from baking in the sun. The noon sun is so hot I feel faint, but soon I am partially shielded from its full intensity by towering pepper vines, currently under harvest. A sack half full with just-picked pepper clusters lies between two rows. I pluck off a berry and chew it; it is spicy hot, aromatic, and pleasantly crunchy. It tastes just like black pepper, only greener, brighter, more urgent. Here, too, the air is a thick stew of peppery aromas. Unlike, say, vanilla, pepper does not need processing to develop its qualities; they are present from the start.

Two farms border a pond where white pepper is soaked, protected from the muddy bottom by wood platforms. If I listen carefully, I can hear water from a nearby stream trickling into the pond.

Some Kotak farmers sell their pepper to the PMB, others dry it themselves and sell to exporters. Transportation is not a problem here; this longhouse is close to Bintangor and Sibu, but not all pepper farms are so conveniently situated. Hundreds are several hours away and farmers must travel first by boat and then by car, toting their harvest, to deliver their pepper. The PMB employs teams of traders who visit remote farms, buy the pepper, and bring it back to be processed. If a farmer can sell his pepper easily, he is more likely to keep growing it.

Interestingly, pepper doesn't play much of a role in the local cuisine, Iban or otherwise. Whenever I comment on what seems to me an unusual omission, I receive the same response: "Our food is so fresh and so good, we don't need pepper." The

an aromatic aphrodisiac

In the master bath of the Marilyn Monroe Suite in the Legend Hotel (where Windows 95 was launched, by the way) in Kuala Lumpur, Malaysia, there is a small ceramic aromatherapy bowl, set over a votive candle. When the lid is removed, the air-conditioned room is filled with the mingled aromas of tangerine, black pepper, and sandalwood. Near the black-tiled sunken tub, there's a beautiful bar of soap scented with patchouli, black pepper, and ylang ylang; it's called "Sexy." (Other blends are known as "Uplifting," "Refreshing," "Relaxing"; which would you choose?)

It is coincidence that I am here, here being an aromatherapy seminar conducted by two certified practitioners from Culpeper Ltd., a small company based in London that produces aromatherapy oils, massage oils, soaps, and a few other luxurious products for skin and spirit. Black pepper, they emphasize, is very strong and is used only in small amounts in two blended massage oils, one to relieve sore muscles, and one with the same name as that soap, Sexy. Black pepper, like many substances that stimulate the senses, is believed to be an aphrodisiac. I return to California with both oils as well as pure black pepper oil, which I burn in my aromatherapy pot, an attempt at inspiration, an urgent call to my Muse. It works, apparently; you're reading the results.

pepper

Malaysians I spoke with think of pepper as something to add flavor when flavor is lacking (and as a source of income, of course), and to some degree, as a preservative. When they use pepper, it is usually white, finely ground into a powder. There are exceptions, of course. A multicultural country, Malaysia has substantial Indian and Chinese populations, as well as Nyonyas, as those of native Malay and Chinese ancestry are called. Indian cuisine makes substantial use of black pepper, as does Chinese, though to a lesser degree. Nyonya cuisine includes a number of traditional recipes that rely on black pepper as an important ingredient.

In 1991, the PMB launched the annual Pepper Festival, held in October in Kuching and supported by the city's hotels and hotel chefs, who develop special pepper recipes. The board also is attempting to increase the use of pepper through the development of a number of commercial products, including candy made with black pepper oil. During my stay at the Holiday Inn, I found a piece of pepper candy on my pillow each evening, as sweet and spicy as a goodnight kiss, or almost.

a brief history of the world

Exploring the history of pepper is akin to taking a refresher course in the lessons of elementary school. The names and stories are so familiar. There's a confused Christopher Columbus stumbling onto the West Indies, there's Magellan and Marco Polo, trade routes, and overland spice trails. There's Portugal's famous navigator, Vasco da Gama ("For Christ and spices!" he is said to have shouted upon landing in India), and the Dutch East India Company. And there are all those annoying pirates too—pirate-infested waters, one writer puts it, as if they were sharks or rats—tripping them up at every unexpected jut of land, every swell of the sea. How did they ever make it?

And weren't we told they did it all for *spices,* especially for black pepper? That's taking the short view, don't you think? There are no spices on the moon, but we couldn't resist making that effort, could we? If it hadn't been spices, it

peppercorn rent

In England, rent was paid with a pound of pepper, a payment occasionally made today as a symbolic recognition of property rights; Prince Charles receives peppercorn rent from Wales. British contracts still contain a "peppercorn" clause, and the gesture is considered an acknowledgment of ownership.

would have been something else. Both the exploration and the spices were inevitable. It was merely a matter of time.

Sanskrit texts refer to pepper as the first spice, though it took a while to make it to Europe. Homer doesn't mention it, but by the fourth century B.C., Theophrastus, a Greek philosopher, described both *Piper nigrum* and *P. longum,* the long pepper that was initially more popular in Europe than black pepper was. Pliny the Elder, writing in Rome in the first century A.D., reports that long pepper cost four times as much as black pepper did. When Rome imposed a duty, it was on white pepper and long pepper; black pepper was spared, apparently not fashionable enough to warrant the effort.

An elaborate spice market was built in Rome, and the road which led to it was Via Piperatica, Pepper Road. Spices, so expensive and so sought after, were heavily guarded. From Rome, all three peppers (white, black, and long; there was no green then) spread throughout western Europe.

It is not clear exactly when black pepper overtook long pepper in popularity, but peppercorns were used abundantly in Rome to season everything from sauces to desserts. By the time the Visigoths conquered the city in 408 A.D., black pepper was so dear that they demanded three thousand pounds of it as part of their tribute (the rest was in gold and silver). You could say it served the Romans right, surrendering all that pepper. After all, they're the ones who, upon destroying Carthage (on the north coast of Africa about ten miles east of the modern Tunis) in the second century, covered the city in salt, rendering it uninhabitable, as they left. You reap what you sow.

After Rome fell, Europeans frittered away their time for several centuries and pepper became scarce once again. And, like so many rare things, its value grew and grew and grew, surpassing any reasonable price you might normally pay for a seasoning. Pepper became so valuable, so desirable, that you could use it as money to negotiate any debt. It was considered to be even more stable than gold, because the gold on coins could be scraped off by the unscrupulous. Just as balsamic vinegar would be a few centuries later, peppercorns were passed on through dowries and the estates of the wealthy.

In the medieval world, wealth often was expressed not by the amount of gold in one's vaults but by the amount of pepper in one's pantry. It is said that both rents and salaries were paid with peppercorns and that a slave could buy freedom with a pound of them, though you might wonder where the slave would get the peppercorns in the first place. In France, pepper was a customary bribe to judges, and "pepper bags" a derogatory moniker in Saxony for noblemen who married commoners for their money.

There is more to the story of pepper at this time than high prices; great mystique surrounds it, and plenty of misunderstanding too. My favorite story is one told by Waverley Root in *Food*. "Pepper ripens in the heat of the sun," a fourteenth-century friar is reported to have explained, "and serpents defend the woods where it grows; to pick it, the trees are set on fire [to drive the serpents away] and the pepper becomes black." (It was centuries later that the American nutrition fanatic Sylvester Graham claimed that excessive use of pepper would cause insanity.)

Eventually the Crusades would get Europeans up and moving, but when it came to spices, the fervor was fueled by economic competition and religion more than the pursuit of flavor. (If it had been merely a pursuit of flavor it's hard to imagine how they ever got beyond Italy and its white truffle.)

During this period, Venice (having secured its position and fortune with salt, harvested from nearby marshlands) controlled trade within Europe. The Venetians sailed to Alexandria in ships filled with soldiers and returned loaded with spices, including pepper. The missing

"care for a little freshly ground pepper?"

Who hasn't been trapped in a plane (economy class, of course) with its cramped seating, bland food, and teensy packages of salt and pepper? And what about pricey restaurant dishes prepared by a chef who has bowed to current salt-phobes? You can spice things up (both food and conversation with nearby strangers on a plane) by carrying your own seasonings. William Bounds, Ltd. produces a salt mill for travelers, a small plastic grinder with adjustments for grain size and a handy little flap on the bottom to keep salt from spilling out until you need it; it comes in a black velour carrying pouch. Atlas has a three-inch brass pepper mill that comes in a classy velvet pouch; it produces a consistent, medium-coarse grind. The Grain & Salt Society sells tiny cherrywood salt boxes that fit discreetly into the palm of your hand, perfect for surreptitiously slipping a few grains of salt over an otherwise sensational dish without insulting the chef.

link was how the spices got to the Holy Land in the first place. The Arab spice monopoly had been in place at least since 950 B.C. and Arabs had been successful at keeping their overland trails and sea routes secret, but European explorers became determined to make their own way to the cache of tasty barks, berries, and seeds in the tropics.

Genoa, also a thriving port but a greater distance from Alexandria than was Venice, posed the only competition until the Portuguese reached India by sea in 1498. Then all bets were off; the Europeans were no longer dependent on the Arabs for peppercorns or other spices. The Portuguese remained dominant for a time, reaching the East Indies, including the Spice Islands, before others. Then the Dutch wrested control from Portugal, and eventually the British usurped their power. Spain competed briefly, but found the gold in North America more alluring than spices; they sold their rights along the spice trail to Portugal.

By the late 1700s, the United States was involved. Elihu Yale was the first colonist to get into the pepper trade, and the fortune he made went to establish Yale University. In 1778, when Jonathan Carnes of Salem, Massachusetts, acquired direct trading partners in Southeast Asia, including some in Sumatra, then the source of the world's best pepper, Salem became the Venice of the New World. America's role in the spice trade grew, and for a time the taxes raised from imported pepper paid 5 percent of all U.S. government expenses. In 1805, we reexported 7.5 million pounds of black pepper. In spite of the difficult journey—the route from Salem to Sumatra and back was twenty-four thousand miles by sea—the industry thrived. In 1873, U.S. ships made a thousand round trips.

By this time, the transcontinental railroad had been completed. It became customary in the dining cars to offer pepper at the table, in pepper grinders, so that diners could see that it was indeed black pepper, and not bits of coal, seasoning their food. There was reason to be suspicious of unidentified black specks. The popularity of ground pepper in Europe had inevitably given rise to unscrupulous suppliers. In England in the 1700s and 1800s, ground black pepper was often adulterated with a variety of cheap materials, from ground olive pits and date pits to crushed dried leaves and the ground hulls of black mustard. White pepper was mixed with ground rice. By 1900, James Trager tells us in *The Food Chronology,* most ground pepper sold in London contained very little pepper. The adulteration was so common that actual pepper might be returned to the market as too strong. So much for the pursuit of flavor.

pepper

a salt & pepper cookbook

seasoning to taste

The quantity of salt and pepper added to most recipes (except for baking) has been left, since the earliest cookbooks, to individual taste. The casual simplicity of the suggestion is appealing and for the most part good advice. Certainly, the balance of salt and pepper in most savory dishes should be adjusted just before serving. A flat sauce will perk right up with a little salt; a dull soup will blossom with flavor when the right quantities of salt and pepper are added. Virtually everything is improved when it is seasoned properly.

For foods to reach their peak flavor, you need to add salt as you cook, as well—the onions as they sauté, for example. Think of a recipe as a construction project; each step needs to be completed properly before you go on to the next. Add salt and pepper lightly in stages, and then taste the finished dish. It is easiest to become comfortable with this process if you salt using your fingers—you will quickly develop an intuitive feel for what is the correct amount. A sturdy pepper mill is best for adding pepper at the cooking stage. If you build flavor in this way, your cooking will improve.

Vegetables should be blanched in salted water, and the water for boiling them should be salted, too. Pasta cooked in unsalted water will never be as flavorful as that cooked in salted water, no matter how tasty the sauce or how much salt you add at the table.

In the United States, we usually think of white pepper as pepper without the color; we use it in pale sauces to avoid the black specks. White pepper is almost always more expensive than black. In Europe, the reverse is true. White pepper is often less expensive, and it is considered the all-purpose pepper for cooking. Black pepper is added at the table, as a condiment.

There is an element of wisdom in the European tradition, though I don't believe the differences are so significant that they warrant using the more expensive pepper. The crux of the difference is that there are more volatile oils in black pepper, and those oils dissipate as the pepper is exposed to heat. If black pepper is expensive, it makes sense to conserve it rather than let an important element of its character vaporize.

Good white pepper has a particular taste that results from the lengthy soaking that removes its outer coat. It's a deep, almost caramelized flavor that some describe as winy. Because of this almost-sweet character, white pepper goes well with ginger and other aromatic spices. But so does black pepper, whose full range of aromas and flavors makes an essential contribution to most dishes.

A word of caution is in order. Although salt improves the flavor of almost everything, neither it nor its pungent companion pepper can disguise poor ingredients. Much has been made lately of a return to an almost elementary style of cooking. Paul Bertolli, the chef of Oliveto in Oakland, California, praises the simple goodness of grilled meats seasoned only with salt and pepper. In an article in the *Wine Spectator,* the author heaps praise upon a chef daring enough to season salmon with nothing more than sea salt. *Please,* I want to add, let's keep things in perspective. If you begin with a wonderful piece of meat or fish, a silky heirloom tomato, or an eggplant lovingly nurtured every step of the way, plucked at precisely the right moment, and served instantly, the simplest preparation in the world will produce sensational results, especially if they are seasoned with a deft hand. Indeed, they will need nothing more than a little good salt, a bit of fresh pepper. (Witness the phenomenal and enduring success of Chez Panisse, a restaurant in which the cooking is based upon this principle: ingredients first and ingredients last.)

If, however, you are using poor quality ingredients, you cannot expect miracles just because you change the type of salt or pepper you are using. My best advice is this: If you have banned salt from your kitchen, bring it back (and hurry up!) and make sure it's a good one, not table salt. If your pepper comes in a big tin and already ground, toss it and start over with whole peppercorns. But pay attention to other ingredients, too. Shop for seasonal produce at farmers' markets and forget about such things as tomatoes, peaches, and apricots in January. Get to know your baker, fishmonger, and butcher; find out who sells the best cheeses and start talking to them. (And definitely find a source for good inexpensive wine.) It is remarkably easy to cook well if you begin with a kitchenful of good things. Without good ingredients to begin with, you're fighting a losing battle that salt cannot help you win.

the shaker dilemma

When you make the switch from granulated table salt to kosher salt or another salt with larger flakes or crystals, your shakers become useless. How do you make the salt easy to use, both at the stove and on the table? In the kitchen, I prefer a rectangular wooden box with a hinged lid; I use one made of maple that holds about eight ounces of kosher salt (see resources, page 216). At the table, salt cellars with tiny silver spoons (Restoration Hardware sells them in blue velveteen bags) are perfect at a formal dinner party, but for everyday use, something casual is better; those tiny spoons are a bit effete and impractical. Small ramekins work well, as do the small, shallow condiment dishes available in Asian, especially Japanese, stores.

In response to the increasing popularity of coarse salts, several manufacturers have added sturdy salt grinders to their lines of pepper mills. This newer generation of salt mills is an improvement over earlier models, which ground the salt to a fine powder; the new ones have adjustable grinding mechanisms and easily produce coarse flakes. Although I appreciate the increased efficiency, I prefer to use my fingers to add salt both during cooking and at the table. I usually keep a salt grinder as well as salt cellars on my table so my guests have a choice.

As you would expect with something as recently liberated as salt, there has been no end to the silliness surrounding its use. (But, hey, better exuberance than persecution.) You can now find both articles and recipes that warn you that salt, like pepper, must be freshly ground for optimum flavor. This is ridiculous. Salt is a rock. There is no organic material to deteriorate, no volatile oils to dissipate. Very dry salt might absorb a little moisture in a humid atmosphere; moist sea salt might dry out a bit in a dry climate. But its flavor does not change. There is absolutely no benefit to grinding salt immediately before using it.

An alligator in sunglasses; a kangaroo and its joey, both in tuxedos; a gospel quartet; a rising sun; a full moon; a crescent moon and star; cows in a convertible Cadillac; a jukebox; a gas pump; a burger and fries; Elvis and his guitar; Betty Boop in red shoes; Mount Rushmore; Bakelite cherries with sterling silver leaves; a bride and groom, who, when viewed from the back become an angry couple, her bouquet transformed into a rolling pin. What do these images have in common? All of them are salt and pepper shakers, sitting on collectors' shelves, crammed into glass cabinets with thousands of other pairs, transported with extreme care to annual conventions all over the country. They are photographed for web sites, and books are devoted to them. They are rarely filled with salt and pepper.

There is a substantial subculture of salt and pepper shaker collectors: specialists in Victorian shakers, early American shakers, shakers from the 1930s, or 1940s, or 1950s. Salt and pepper shakers are not only the domain of retro kitsch. In 1997, The Clay Studio in Philadelphia held a show of fine-art salt and pepper sculptures. A company in Oregon shapes beautiful, delicate shakers of blown glass, some of them attached to elaborate glass pedestals wound around with glass serpents. There's something about these two-piece evocations of culture that is endlessly intriguing.

freshly ground pepper

In most cases, peppercorns must be cracked, crushed, or ground before being added to a recipe. There are many ways to accomplish this task, the easiest of which is to purchase ground pepper, though I don't recommend it. Once crushed, peppercorns lose their aromatic quality fairly quickly; for the most flavor, you should use whole peppercorns. (I do keep a small quantity of commercially ground pepper around for use in Cajun cooking; it seems to add crucial character.)

Cracking is easiest in a *suribachi,* a *molcajete,* or with a large mortar and pestle. For best results, place no more than two teaspoons in the container and then press down firmly and directly onto some of the peppercorns until you feel them crack. Continue until they are all evenly cracked. You can also crack pepper by placing it between two sheets of wax paper, cooking parchment, or the folds of a tightly woven tea towel, and then rolling over it with a heavy rolling pin or pounding it with a meat tenderizing mallet until the peppercorns are *just* cracked. In a pinch, you can use a hammer, carefully.

In general, when grinding by hand it is best to avoid small containers, because the peppercorns will simply jump out. There is one exception. Mason Cash, an English company that manufactures a variety of ceramic products for the kitchen, makes a small, narrow mortar with an almost cylindrical pestle. Because the sides of the mortar are vertical, you can grind small quantities of peppercorns and other spices without their leaping onto the counter and floor.

Crushed pepper indicates a coarse texture, smaller than cracked but not as fine as ground. Commercial pepper mills do an excellent job, but you can also use a *suribachi* or other hand grinder. Just continue to grind until the peppercorns are the size you prefer. For ground pepper, fairly fine but not quite a powder, most commercial mills do a good job in not too much time, but again, you can easily do it by hand. For very finely ground pepper, grind the peppercorns by hand or use an electric spice grinder (or converted coffee grinder, either electric or hand-cranked, on the lowest setting).

the best pepper mills

Those ridiculously long pepper mills waved by many an overeager waiter (*Wait! Let me taste my food first!*) have a single function, to reach across the table to the customer in the far corner. In selecting a mill for home use, longer or bigger is not necessarily better (though you do want a large enough capacity that you're not refilling it every other day). Several articles rating pepper mills have appeared in the past few years, and two are worthy of note. *Cook's Illustrated* (March/April 1996) and *Good Housekeeping* (May 1997) both rate the Unicorn Magnum Plus the best mill. It grinds quickly (five seconds to grind half a teaspoon according to *Good Housekeeping;* ten seconds, according to *Cook's Illustrated*), produces a wide range of grinds, holds one and a half cups of peppercorns, and is very easy to fill.

A ten-inch maple wood mill sold by Chef Specialties placed second in both evaluations. *Good Housekeeping* also recommended the Zassenhause grinder, which *Cook's Illustrated* did not test. Olde Thompson's Manor pepper mill was also recommended by both publications. If you stick to any of these brands, you'll have good results grinding pepper. I also like my wooden Peugeot mill, but admit that it is difficult to fill without spilling peppercorns. I use a brass Atlas grinder for white peppercorns; I like its appearance and its hard metallic feel in my hand. It produces a consistent medium-coarse grind, but it's not easy to adjust (you need a screwdriver, often an impossible hurdle), so it has limited possibilities for all-purpose use. I don't recommend novelty grinders that offer high-concept designs and technical gymnastics. None improves on the conventional design of a good grinding mechanism made of stainless steel and a sturdy hand crank or bulb.

repetitive pepper syndrome

At first sight, the new electric pepper mills seem ridiculous. I first saw one at the San Francisco Fancy Food Show in 1997, when Chef Specialties, Olde Thompson, and Peugeot were exhibiting battery-operated pepper grinders. The mills all operate on the same principle—there is a push switch on the top, easily pressed by the thumb, which turns the grinding mechanism and at the same time illuminates the cascade of ground pepper and the food to be seasoned. I started to laugh, but then I thought of my ex-mother-in-law's painful arthritis, a colleague's carpal tunnel syndrome, a culinary student whose movement is limited to a few weak hand motions. All three have sophisticated palates, but are limited in what they can actually do in the kitchen. The electric pepper mill—which seems so frivolous that I can't imagine them buying it for themselves—offers an easy and tasty solution to one of a myriad problems. It's a thoughtful gift for anyone with limited hand or arm movement. The sturdiest, called A Touch of Pepper (see resources, page 216), is pricey but comes with a battery charger and a lifetime guarantee.

a pound of pepper

Recipes often call for five peppercorns, or ten, or thirty. It's helpful to know how those numbers may be translated into standard level measurements. The ranges account for the smaller peppercorns, Malabar, Muntok White, and Sarawak, and the larger, Tellicherry. There are about twenty-five hundred medium-size berries in a cup of whole peppercorns. A pound of peppercorns contains between nine thousand and fifteen thousand berries.

⅛ teaspoon	5 to 7 peppercorns
¼ teaspoon	13 to 18 peppercorns
½ teaspoon (1 gram)	22 to 37 peppercorns
1 teaspoon (2 grams)	34 to 60 peppercorns
1 tablespoon (6 grams)	106 to 189 peppercorns

*Think of an appetizer as an invitation, a proffer, an enticement
to make us ready—that is, hungry—for the meal to come. Fine
restaurants often serve complimentary* amuses gueules—*the Muses
of the meal, as it were, come to bless our pleasure—tiny single bites
of savory morsels that tickle and delight our palates. Salt may be the
most important element of an appetizer; like a kiss, it dissolves on
the tongue and leaves us longing for more. A regular culinary Don
Juan, salt is an effective seducer. Pepper plies a randy trade as well;
even its aroma makes us salivate, which in turn increases our hunger.
Appetizers needn't be complex, nor bountiful. A few salted nuts, a
bowl of olives, crisp radishes with butter and salt, or a little cheese is
sufficient before a hearty meal. More elaborate appetizers can be
good, too, as long as you keep the main goal in sight—tempt your
guests, but don't sate their appetites.*

salted almonds

Salted nuts—peanuts, walnuts, cashews, pecans, and Brazil nuts, as well as almonds— are among the most common appetizers in the world, and with good reason. The salt perks up the appetite and makes us hungry; the nuts, almost always eaten in small portions, do not fill us. In addition, nuts contain excellent micronutrients and in small quantities, the perfect appetizer serving, for example, are extremely beneficial to our health.

Juice of 1 lemon

1 teaspoon sugar

1 cup (4 ounces) almonds, shelled, skins on

1 tablespoon kosher salt

In a small bowl, combine the lemon juice and sugar. Add the almonds, toss, and set aside for 30 minutes. Stir the almonds every few minutes.

Preheat the oven to 300°F. Drain off any lemon juice in the bowl of almonds, add the salt, toss quickly, and spread the almonds on a sheet pan. Bake for 25 to 30 minutes, stirring occasionally, until the almonds are lightly browned and give off their aroma. Do not let them burn. Remove from the oven, cool, and store in a sealed container until ready to serve.

makes 1 cup

perfect
deviled eggs

It's important to know how to make perfect deviled eggs, a classic American appetizer and picnic dish. A purist, I eschew additions such as pickle relish, capers, minced onions, or olives, but think a strong jolt of aromatic black pepper is essential. Once you've mastered the purity of these flavors, there are, however, some delicious variations, one in which green peppercorns are used along with black, and one made with the intoxicating smoked salt imported from Denmark. Because the egg whites tend to wobble on their rounded bottoms, it's best to serve them on top of greens, such as a bunch of flat-leaf parsley, spread over the plate, or a bed of arugula.

6 large fresh eggs

1/3 to 1/2 cup mayonnaise

3 tablespoons Dijon mustard

Dash of Tabasco Sauce

2 teaspoons black peppercorns, crushed

3/4 teaspoon kosher salt

Place the eggs in a single layer in a medium saucepan and add water until it is at least 1 inch above them. Set over medium heat, bring to a boil, and cook for 12 minutes. Remove from the heat, let cool for 2 or 3 minutes, and then transfer the eggs to a cold-water bath, changing the water two or three times as it warms. When the eggs have cooled to room temperature, carefully peel them, rinse them, dry them on a tea towel, and cut them in half lengthwise. Scoop out the yolks and set the whites on a platter.

Press the yolks through a potato ricer into a bowl or place them in the bowl and mash them with a fork. Mix in 1/3 cup of the mayonnaise, the mustard, Tabasco, pepper, and salt. If the mixture seems a little dry, add the remaining mayonnaise. Fill the centers of the egg whites with the egg yolk mixture, cover with plastic wrap, and refrigerate for at least 30 minutes before serving.

variations

Dissolve 1/2 teaspoon smoked salt (see resources, page 216) in 1/2 teaspoon lemon juice and use it in place of the kosher salt.

Reduce the quantity of black peppercorns to 1 teaspoon, add 1 teaspoon crushed dried green peppercorns, and 1 teaspoon green peppercorns in brine (drained); top each stuffed egg with 2 or 3 brined green peppercorns.

serves 4 to 6

fresh soybeans
and sea salt
edamame

As I worked on Salt & Pepper, *a local farmer harvested a crop of soybeans and began selling them at the weekly farmers' market where I shop. Having never found fresh soybeans in the market before, I was thrilled to be able to make this traditional Japanese appetizer for myself.*

1 pound fresh soybeans in their pods

2 tablespoons coarse sea salt, and more to finish

Toss the soybeans with the salt and let them sit for 15 minutes. Bring 2 quarts of water to a boil, add the soybeans, return the water to a boil, and simmer for 2 to 3 minutes. Drain thoroughly, place the beans in a bowl, season with a little more salt, and serve hot or at room temperature. To eat the soybeans, pinch off one end of the pod and squeeze the beans into your mouth.

variation

For a more formal presentation, refresh the drained beans in ice water and drain thoroughly. Shell the beans. Just before serving them, plunge them into boiling, salted water for 30 seconds. Drain thoroughly, toss with $1/2$ teaspoon kosher salt or Japanese sea salt, place in a small bowl, and serve immediately.

serves 4 to 6

pineapple with black pepper

A few wedges of pineapple make a wonderful appetizer either before a rich main course, such as Kalua Pork (page 122) or Black Pepper Crab (page 110), or on a very hot night. The kosher salt adds a bit of zing to the pineapple, and the black pepper adds a sultry flavor and aroma. To serve fewer than six people, use half of the pineapple and reserve the other half for another recipe, such as the Pineapple Granita with Black Pepper (page 190). The challenge in this simple recipe is in finding excellent pineapple, no easy task unless you're in an area where pineapples are grown. The pineapples sold in Hawaii, for example, are vastly better—more tender, less tart, and much sweeter—than those that are shipped to the mainland. When purchasing pineapples in domestic markets, look for those that have an intense, fruity aroma.

1 large ripe pineapple

Kosher salt

1 tablespoon black peppercorns, coarsely crushed

Place the pineapple horizontally on your work surface. Use a heavy, sharp knife to cut it in half lengthwise, cutting through the crown and stem as well as the fruit itself.

Cut each half of the pineapple in half again, lengthwise. Use a paring knife to cut out the core at the top of each quarter, inserting the knife at one end and pulling it along to the other. Lift off and discard the core.

Using a sharp, somewhat flexible knife, cut each quarter wedge of flesh away from the skin; leave it in place. Cut each wedge into slices about 3/4 inch thick, being sure not to cut through the skin.

Set the wedges in their skins on a serving platter. Using your fingers and holding your hand several inches above each wedge, shower the pineapple with a generous pinch of kosher salt, followed by a heavier sprinkling of black pepper. Cover lightly with plastic wrap and chill for 30 minutes before serving.

serves 6 to 8

spanish toast

In restaurants all over Spain, it's common to find a plate of tomatoes and garlic already on the table when you sit down. Then, after you have placed your order, a basket of toast arrives. Spaniards know what to do, but I've seen Americans eat the tomatoes, and even the whole cloves of garlic, before the waiter even arrives. A light sprinkling of salt over the tomato pulp and olive oil is essential to bring the flavors together.

8 to 12 thick slices sourdough or other country-style bread, toasted or grilled until golden brown

6 large garlic cloves, unpeeled and cut in half lengthwise

6 small (2-inch-diameter) ripe tomatoes, cut in half through the equator, not through the poles

Best-quality extra virgin olive oil

Kosher salt, Celtic gray sea salt, or Hawaiian alae salt

Black pepper in a mill

Have the bread hot, in a basket and covered with a tea towel. Place the garlic and tomatoes on a plate, and have the olive oil in a bottle or cruet from which it is easy to pour.

Set a piece of bread on a plate and rub one side of it with the cut side of a half clove of garlic, pressing firmly. Next, rub a half tomato into the same side of the bread, pressing firmly so that the pulp of the tomato is deposited on and in the bread. Discard the skins of the garlic and tomatoes. Drizzle a little olive oil over the bread, add a generous sprinkling of sea salt and one or two turns of black pepper. Eat and repeat.

serves 4 to 6

olives

"When I ate my first olive, I knew instinctively I was tasting the heart of the world" (a comment made to Mort Rosenblum and recounted in his book *Olives*). If an olive is the world's heart, its life-giving blood is salt. Salt effectively leaches out an olive's bitter flavors and it's only after this leaching that we can enjoy them. Salt also returns flavor to those olives stripped of every nuance and distinction by lye, which leaches out bitterness more quickly than salt does (twenty-four hours rather than weeks or months) but takes everything else along with it, leaving the olive tasteless. Lye-cured ripe olives, baptized in a salty brine, become the ubiquitous California-style black olives. A bowl of olives—a mixture of green and black, dry-cured and brine-cured, seasoned with lemons, oranges, chiles, herbs, or nothing at all—is an effortless appetizer that is always pleasing and always appropriate, no matter what is to follow.

crostini with olive and artichoke tapenade

If you have a wood stove for heating, as I do, you can toast crostini on top of the stove; just remember to wipe the surface free of ash and dust before you begin. Although crostini are basically bite-sized bruschetta, there are traditional toppings for each. Chicken livers sautéed with sage are frequently served with crostini but rarely with bruschetta; most commonly bruschetta are topped with diced tomatoes, salt, pepper, and olive oil. Traditional olive tapenade also is a common topping for crostini. These days countless new versions have emerged as Italian cuisine becomes ever more popular. You can also serve crostini with Sarawak Sambal (page 180), Yogurt Cheese (page 185), and Raisin, Onion, and Green Peppercorn Chutney (page 181).

1 crusty Italian baguette, sliced into ³/₈-inch-thick diagonal slices
Peppercorn oil (page 169) or olive oil
1¹/₂ cups Olive and Artichoke Tapenade (page 174)
5 ounces fresh chèvre (such as chabis)

Preheat the oven to 375°F. Brush the bread on both sides with a small quantity of olive oil, set the slices on a baking sheet, and bake until crisp and golden brown, about 20 minutes. Remove from the oven and cool. (The crostini may be stored in a sealed plastic bag for a day or two before serving.)

To serve, spread each slice of bread with chèvre and top with about ³/₄ teaspoon of tapenade. Serve immediately. Alternatively, place the tapenade in a small bowl, set the chèvre on a plate, surround with the crostini, and serve immediately.

makes about 30 to 36 pieces

bruschetta with sautéed greens

"You will see how it tastes of salt, the others' bread," Dante, one of the world's most famous Tuscans, wrote in The Divine Comedy. *In his newsletter "The Art of Eating," Edward Behr describes—which is not to say explains; no one really knows why—the tradition of unsalted bread in Tuscany, of the Tuscans' expectation that bread dough not be salted. Inevitably, salt appears, of course. In the simplest version of bruschetta, called* fettunta, *bread is toasted, drizzled with good olive oil, and topped with salt. Although not the traditional salt of Italy, Celtic gray sea salt has a robust flavor that is excellent with any type of bruschetta: with just olive oil and garlic, with diced tomatoes, or with sautéed greens, perfect in the spring before tomatoes are in season. In the summer, combine the two (see Variation).*

3 tablespoons olive oil

2 or 3 garlic cloves, minced

½ pound greens (such as beet tops, Swiss chard, kale, or spinach), large stems removed and leaves sliced

8 slices of country-style bread

3 tablespoons extra virgin olive oil

Celtic gray sea salt or kosher salt

Black pepper in a mill

Heat a stove-top grill or prepare a fire in a charcoal grill. When the grill is ready, prepare the greens. Heat the olive oil in a sauté pan or wok, add the garlic, and sauté for 15 seconds, stirring constantly. Add the greens and cook, stirring and tossing them continuously, until they are completely wilted and tender. Set aside and keep hot. Toast the bread on the grill until it is well browned on both sides. Place the bread on a platter, drizzle each piece with about a teaspoon of extra virgin olive oil, and top with some of the greens. Sprinkle a little Celtic gray sea salt over each piece, grind black pepper over all, and serve immediately.

variation

Dice 1 large ripe tomato, toss it with two minced garlic cloves, and spoon it on top of the greens before adding salt and pepper.

serves 4

onandaga
salt potatoes

One afternoon, an e-mail message arrived from Valerie Jackson Bell, who is the curator of the Salt Museum in Onandaga County, New York. "Don't forget about our 'salt potatoes,' " she said, adding that according to local folklore, back when the salt factory was in operation, kids would toss small white potatoes into the pots of boiling brine, a salty saturated brew that was about fifty times as salty as sea water. Locals still cook succulent little potatoes in the same way, though on top of the stove and not in an outdoor cauldron, Valerie wrote, and serve them dripping with melted butter. You will be amazed just how succulent and flavorful the potatoes become in the brine. For the best results, choose tiny potatoes and don't skimp on the butter. A saturated brine is 26.4 percent salt, which equals 2.64 pounds of salt per gallon of water. The water in this recipe is not saturated, but there is enough salt in it to flavor the potatoes.

1 1/2 cups kosher salt or unrefined sea salt

2 pounds very small new white potatoes

6 tablespoons unsalted butter

Black pepper in a mill

Fill a medium pot with 2 quarts water, add the salt, and set over high heat. Stir to dissolve the salt, add the potatoes, and bring to a boil. Reduce the heat to medium-low and simmer the potatoes until they are completely tender when pierced with a fork, about 15 to 20 or 25 minutes, depending on the size of the potatoes. Drain thoroughly, place in a large bowl, add the butter, and toss lightly until the butter is melted. Serve immediately, and pass the pepper mill.

serves 4 to 6

a salt & pepper cookbook

grilled figs with prosciutto and black pepper

Jack McCarley of Green Man Farms in Healdsburg, California, who grows excellent figs, tells me that this is one of his favorite ways of enjoying his crop. They make a yummy fall appetizer (serve some salted almonds alongside), and an excellent accompaniment to chicken, duck, pork, and game, too. To serve as a first course, set them on a bed of greens such as arugula and drizzle balsamic or sherry vinegar over them before adding plenty of black pepper.

10 black Mission figs, firm-ripe (not too soft)

10 slices (about ¼ pound) prosciutto, cut in half crosswise

20 bamboo skewers, soaked in water for 1 hour

Black pepper in a mill

Prepare a fire in a charcoal grill at least 1 hour before grilling the figs.

Cut the figs in half lengthwise, wrap each half in a slice of prosciutto, and secure it with a bamboo skewer, breaking off any extra length of skewer and discarding it. Grill the figs for 3 or 4 minutes on each side, transfer to a platter, grind black pepper over them, and serve immediately.

makes 20 pieces

shrimp roasted
on rock salt

*Shrimp roasted on a bed of hot salt are suc-
culent, tender, fragrant, and not at all salty;
the salt serves to transfer heat efficiently, not
to flavor the shrimp. They can be served
simply, with just a squeeze of lemon, or with
this sweet-and-sour sauce studded with
peppercorns.*

2 to 3 pounds rock salt

12 large shrimp in their shells

3 tablespoons unsalted butter

2 tablespoons honey

2 teaspoons crushed black peppercorns

1 tablespoon lemon juice (more or less,
   to taste)

Pinch of salt

Lemon wedges, for garnish

Preheat the oven to 400°F. Select a heavy pan with a lid that is large enough to hold the shrimp in a single layer. It should be at least 2-inches deep. Add rock salt to form a 1-inch bed in the pan. Set the pan in the oven and heat for 30 minutes. When the salt is very hot, set the shrimp on top, cover, and roast for 2 minutes. Turn the shrimp, cover the pan again, and roast for 2 minutes more, until the shrimp turn pink and are hot and sizzling. Meanwhile, melt the butter in a small saucepan, and add the honey, peppercorns, lemon, and pinch of salt.

Place the shrimp on warmed serving plates, drizzle each portion with a little of the butter, and serve immediately, garnished with lemon wedges.

serves 4

taramosalata

Caviar probably best demonstrates the ability of salt to transform the edible to the delectable. From the highly prized osetra and beluga caviars to the humble salmon and mullet roes, it is salt that makes a culinary delicacy out of a sack of messy fish eggs. In the traditional Greek dish, dried bread and olive oil soften an intensely salty roe (traditionally, mullet or carp), creating a delicious condiment that perks up the palate and stimulates the appetite. I prefer a version made with potatoes, also traditional if not as common.

One 7-ounce jar *taramá* (mullet roe) or other
    inexpensive caviar
Half a small red onion, minced (about ¼ cup)
2 medium russet potatoes, baked and riced
    (see note)
1 tablespoon minced lemon zest
Juice of 2 lemons
²/₃ cup extra virgin olive oil
2 tablespoons minced fresh flat-leaf parsley
1 baguette, thinly sliced
2 bunches small radishes, cleaned and
    trimmed
1 cucumber, thinly sliced
½ cup olives of choice

Using a large *suribachi,* grind together the *taramá* and onion until fairly smooth. Use a rubber spatula to fold the potato purée and the lemon zest into the mixture. Add the lemon juice slowly, mix until completely incorporated, and then add the olive oil, a small quantity at a time, mixing well after each addition. Add the parsley, taste, and add a little more olive oil if the mixture is too tart. Cover with plastic wrap and chill for at least 1 hour before serving.

Preheat the oven to 300°F. Place the baguette slices on a baking sheet, brush with a little olive oil, and toast until golden brown, about 15 minutes. To serve, place the toasts in a small basket. Transfer the taramosalata to a serving bowl, set it on a plate, and surround with the radishes, cucumber slices, and olives. Serve immediately, with the basket of croutons alongside.

note

Pierce scrubbed, unpeeled potatoes in several places with a fork and bake at 375°F until tender, about 40 minutes. Let them cool until they are easy to handle. Use both hands to break each potato in half, and then place the halves, one at a time, into a potato ricer with the interior part of the potato facing into the ricer. Press the potatoes through (as you would garlic through a press), open the ricer, and remove and discard the skin. Repeat. There is no substitute for the light, uniform texture of riced potatoes; mashing results in a more dense and less even mixture.

serves 6 to 8

Gravlax is usually made with two large fillets of salmon coated in a salt mixture and then pressed together. Two full-length fillets make a lot of gravlax and I experimented to see how effective the process would be using a single piece. It works perfectly and is a great way to produce a smaller amount of gravlax. I often serve gravlax with Green Peppercorn Mustard (page 170) and thin slices of toasted rye bread. It is also excellent served in the traditional fashion, with minced red onion, sieved hard-cooked egg, capers, and sour cream alongside. Spicy Salt Egg Sauce (page 179) also makes an ideal accompaniment.

1 salmon fillet, about 1³/₄ to 2 pounds, skin on

2 tablespoons Pernod or *pastis*

¹/₄ cup kosher salt

2 tablespoons sugar

1 teaspoon coarsely crushed green
   peppercorns

1 teaspoon coarsely crushed white
   peppercorns

1 teaspoon coarsely crushed black
   peppercorns

1 teaspoon white mustard seeds

Be sure the scales of the salmon are removed. Use needle-nose pliers to pull out the pin bones. Place the salmon, skin-side down, in a glass container in which it can lie flat and pour the Pernod over it. Combine the salt, sugar, peppercorns, and mustard seeds. Spread the mixture over the salmon, adding more where the fillet is thickest. Cover the salmon with a piece of plastic wrap and place a heavy weight on top. Cover the entire dish with plastic wrap and place in the refrigerator. After 1 day, remove the salmon from the refrigerator and unwrap it. Spoon the juices over the salmon and then turn it skin-side up. As before, cover it, weight it, cover the dish, and return to the refrigerator. Repeat this daily for up to 4 days (3 will suffice), by which time the flesh of the salmon will glisten. Remove the fish from the brine, wrap it tightly in clean plastic wrap, and refrigerate. Kept wrapped tightly in clean wrap, the gravlax will keep for 8 to 10 days.

To serve the salmon, cut several thin slices, cutting down to, but not through, the skin. Arrange them on a plate and serve with condiments (see headnote).

serves 8 to 10

a salt & pepper cookbook

halibut
gravlax

Halibut cured in the same way as salmon produces delicate, delicious gravlax, with a brighter flavor than salmon. Most supermarkets sell halibut steaks rather than fillets, but if you have a specialty fish market or wholesaler near you, you can usually order fillets (though you might have to purchase an entire fish).

2 halibut fillets, about 1³/₄ pounds each, skin on

2 tablespoons vodka

¹/₂ cup kosher salt

4 tablespoons sugar

2 teaspoons toasted, crushed, and sifted Sichuan peppercorns (see note)

2 teaspoons coarsely crushed black peppercorns

Be sure the scales of the halibut are removed. Use needle-nose pliers to pull out any pin bones. Place one of the halibut fillets, skin-side down, in a glass or stainless-steel container in which it can lie flat and pour the vodka over it. Set the other fillet on a clean work surface. Combine the salt, sugar, and peppercorns. Spread half the mixture over each fillet, adding slightly more where the fillet is thickest, and rubbing slightly to insure that the mixture sticks to the fish. Invert the fillet that was lying on the work surface and set it on top of the fillet in the dish. Cover the halibut with a piece of plastic wrap and place a heavy weight on top. Cover the entire dish with plastic wrap and place in the refrigerator. After 1 day, remove the fish from the refrigerator and unwrap it. Spoon the juices over the halibut and then reverse the fillets, placing the one that had been on top on the bottom. Always keep the skin-side facing out, with the inner part of the fillets touching each other. As before, cover and weight the fish, cover the dish, and return to the refrigerator. Repeat this daily for up to 4 days (3 days will suffice), by which time the flesh of the halibut will glisten. Remove the fish from the brine, wrap it tightly in clean plastic wrap, and refrigerate. Kept wrapped tightly in clean wrap, the gravlax will keep for 8 to 10 days.

To serve the halibut, cut several thin slices, cutting down to, but not through, the skin. Arrange them on a plate and serve with condiments (see headnote on page 65).

note

Unlike true peppercorns, Sichuan peppercorns, sometimes called fagara, *have hard, tasteless seeds in their centers that should be sifted out and discarded after toasting and grinding.*

serves 16 to 20

a salt & pepper cookbook

brandade

de morue

Depending on where in the United States you live, salt cod either is ubiquitous—as it is in Rhode Island, where the Italian and Portuguese communities keep the demand high—or impossible to find. Because of health department regulations in some states, California, for example, you won't see it hanging above the deli cases. It will be refrigerated, often in a special compartment in the back, so if you don't see it, ask. In order to leach out excessive salt, salt cod needs to be soaked in a water bath that is changed every few hours; I have found that twelve hours is usually sufficient; occasionally, a longer soak is a required. Should you be distracted, your cod will still be okay after three days in its bath. Once soaked, salt cod is no longer salty, and the finished dish will need to be properly seasoned before it is served. Brandade de morue *is a classic French bistro dish, generally served as an appetizer or first course, with toasted croutons alongside.*

1 pound boneless, skinless salt cod, soaked
   for 1 to 2 days (see headnote)
2 or 3 russet potatoes (about 2 pounds),
   baked until tender and riced while hot (see
   note on page 64)
10 garlic cloves
1 teaspoon kosher salt
2/3 cup heavy cream

2 to 3 teaspoons black peppercorns, crushed
2/3 cup best-quality extra virgin olive oil

Remove the salt cod from its last cold-water bath, place it in a large sauté pan, cover with fresh cold water, and set over medium heat. When the water boils, remove the pan from the fire, and cover it. Let the cod sit for 15 minutes, drain it thoroughly, and cool. Break the fish into small pieces and pick out any pieces of bone. Set aside.

Using a *suribachi* or a mortar and pestle, crush the garlic with the kosher salt until it is nearly liquefied. Combine the cream and 2 teaspoons of the black peppercorns in a small saucepan and scald over medium heat. Set aside.

Place the salt cod in the container of a food processor, add the garlic, and pulse several times. With the machine running, pour in the olive oil in a slow drizzle, followed by the hot cream. When both are completely incorporated, transfer the mixture to a medium bowl. Use a heavy wooden spoon or wooden spatula to fold in the riced potatoes. Taste the *brandade* and correct the seasoning with the remaining teaspoon of pepper. Serve with toasted garlic croutons.

serves 6 to 8

lemon pepper
chicken drummettes

If you don't want to go to the trouble of making the drummettes yourself (although it doesn't take long), you can usually purchase them at a good meat market. If you have homemade preserved lemons (see page 182 for a recipe) made with lemon juice (rather than brine), you can use some of the liquid from those lemons in this dish. Otherwise, use fresh lemon juice in which you've dissolved a tablespoon of kosher salt.

2 or 3 lemons, very thinly sliced

1 dozen chicken wings

2 tablespoons olive oil

1/2 cup liquid from preserved lemons
or 1/2 cup fresh lemon juice mixed with
1 tablespoon kosher salt

1 tablespoon freshly cracked black
peppercorns

Fleur de sel or *sel gris* for garnish

Preheat the oven to 375°F. Spread the lemon slices over the surface of a baking dish large enough to hold the wings in a single layer.

To make drummettes, cut the chicken wings at each joint. Reserve the wing tips for stock. Place the drummettes in a large bowl and toss with the olive oil. Add the lemon juice and toss again; add the black pepper and toss once more. Arrange the drummettes in a single layer on the baking dish, setting them on top of the lemon slices. Bake until tender and lightly browned, about 20 to 25 minutes. Place the lemon slices and drummettes on a serving platter, sprinkle with a bit of *fleur de sel,* and serve immediately.

serves 6 to 8

peppered
dried plums

For months I'd seen dried plums—which are another variety different from the familiar prune plums—at my local farmers' market and although I'd eaten plenty, I hadn't cooked with them. Then I came upon an enchanting recipe by Rosemary Barron, a highly respected expert on Greek cooking. The moment I saw her recipe for Peppered Dried Figs, I was inspired. I bought some dried plums and assembled this version of Rosemary's recipe, adding orange peel because it goes so nicely with plums, and waited impatiently, for three days, then four, then five, until the plums were finally fragrant enough to serve with feta cheese and olives. If you can't find dried plums, you can use moist dried apricots from Turkey or, as Rosemary recommends, the fleshy dried figs from southern Greece.

8 bay leaves

18 moist dried plums

2 tablespoons freshly crushed black peppercorns

2 tablespoons candied orange peel

Place 3 bay leaves on the bottom of a half-pint glass jar. Press three or four plums firmly into the pepper and then place them in the jar on top of the bay leaves. Sprinkle a little additional pepper and one quarter of the orange peel on top. Continue, adding a few bay leaves now and then, until all of the plums have been packed tightly into the jar. End with the last few bay leaves. Close the jar and set in a cool, dark pantry for 5 days. The plums will keep for 4 to 6 weeks.

makes ¹/₂ pint

Signing books at a trade show, I was approached by a young woman who wanted to tell me that although she had seen several recipes for soup in one of my books, she never made it because her soups did not turn out as well as her mother's did. She explained that she used the best ingredients she could find to make stock, but still her soups were bland and flavorless. When I inquired about salt, she looked horrified. "Salt? I never, ever use salt in anything."

Soup without salt is bland. Garlic soup from Provence or Mexico will taste insipid. Without salt, chilled avocado soup is flat; properly salted, it is a voluptuous delight. Japanese soups rely on mildly salty seaweed stock (dashi) for flavor, but other broths and stocks require an addition of salt for both flavor and balance. Often, all a bland soup needs is a proper salting and it perks right up.

Pepper, too, is an important ingredient in virtually every soup in the world. From restorative chicken broths to the rich soup topped with dumplings and known as Philadelphia Pepper Pot, pepper adds depth and character, completeness, you could say, to soup. Black pepper can serve to balance the sweetness of certain ingredients, too, such as carrots and sweet potatoes, vegetables that make excellent soups but need a savory component.

Both salt and pepper play leading roles in many soups. In India, a broth heavily seasoned with black pepper is served as a digestive; in Malaysia, a similar soup is served with certain noodle dishes and can be poured directly over the noodles.

seaweed
stock
dashi

Sea vegetables concentrate the aroma of sea water, the essence of which is salt, into highly nutritious bundles of flavor, sometimes with such intense flavor that if you are unfamiliar with them you'll find them unpleasant. They take some getting used to, and a soup using a seaweed stock is a subtle way of introducing these good flavors to the novice. Dashi, a simple stock made of giant kelp and dried fish, is a critical building block of Japanese cuisine; you cannot achieve essential delicate flavors without it. It's remarkable that it's so easy to make. Because I live close to the Pacific Ocean, many types of seaweed are readily available, much of it gathered, dried, and sold by the Mendocino Sea Vegetable Company. There have been times when I craved some miso soup, had no konbu, but did have nori and dulse. I've made stock using them, and although the results are not absolutely traditional, I was pleased and fortified by my soup. You can find both seaweed and dried bonito in many health food stores and most Asian markets.

1¹/₂ ounces konbu (giant kelp)

1 ounce dried bonito flakes

Pour 2 quarts cold water into a large soup pot, add the konbu, heat the water very slowly, and just before it boils, turn off the heat and cover the pot. Let sit for 1 hour. Test the *konbu* by pinching it with a fingernail; if it is tender, remove it from the pot; if it is still tough, let it sit for another hour. (Reserve the konbu for making a secondary stock; see Note below.)

Add the bonito flakes to the *konbu* stock, slowly bring the liquid to a boil, and remove immediately from the heat. Let the pot sit without moving it for about a minute as the flakes settle to the bottom. Skim off any foam that has formed, and then strain the stock through 3 or 4 layers of cheesecloth; save the bonito flakes for secondary stock. Use immediately, or cool to room temperature and store, covered, in the refrigerator for up to 4 days.

note

To make a secondary dashi, fill a soup pot with 2 quarts water, add the reserved konbu and bonito flakes, bring to a boil over medium heat, reduce to a simmer, and cook, partially covered, until reduced by half, about 20 to 25 minutes. Stir in ¹/₂ ounce of dried bonito flakes, remove from the heat, let settle for 1 minute, skim off any foam, and strain through cheesecloth. Cool and refrigerate. Use secondary dashi for thick soups, noodle soups, or as a stock for cooking vegetables.

makes 2 quarts

red miso soup with garlic, ginger, and noodles

Miso is a thick fermented bean paste, sometimes salty, sometimes sweet, used to make the clear, delicate soup that is almost always served before sushi. Miso also is used to make many dressings and sauces, and miso soup is a common breakfast dish in Japan, in part because it is so easy to make, in part because it is very high in protein, about 37 percent.

There are several kinds of miso. White miso is mild, delicate, and sweet. Yellow miso, which includes rice mold, is salty and tart, and is the easiest to find in the United States, although other kinds are increasingly common. There are several types of red miso, but virtually all include rice and barley in addition to beans. Red miso is salty, full-flavored, and excellent for soup. Dark brown miso, generally made with just beans, is the most robustly flavored; it is intensely salty.

4 cups Dashi (page 71)

2 slices fresh ginger

4 garlic cloves, sliced

1/2 teaspoon crushed red pepper

4 tablespoons red miso

2 tablespoons *mirin* (sweetened sake, for cooking)

3 ounces *sōmen* (thin white wheat noodles), cooked and rinsed

3 scallions, white and light green part, trimmed and cut into thin rounds

In a soup pot, bring the dashi to a boil, add the ginger, garlic, and chili flakes, cover, and remove from the heat. Let steep for 15 minutes. Use a small strainer to remove and discard the ginger and garlic. Place the miso in a small bowl, add 3 or 4 tablespoons of the hot dashi, and stir until smooth. Return the dashi to the heat, stir in the miso and *mirin,* add the noodles, and when the soup is just hot, remove from the heat. Divide among 4 small soup bowls, using tongs to distribute the noodles evenly. Top each portion with some of the scallions and serve immediately.

serves 4

black pepper soup

In San Francisco, the Mandalay Restaurant on California Street, the city's first Burmese restaurant, serves a wonderfully fragrant black pepper soup. There's more black pepper in the soup than you'd think you could add successfully, yet the soup is not overwhelming or out of balance. After the soup has been eaten, a film of black pepper glistens in the bottom of the bowl, a testament to this robust and unusual dish.

1 bunch (about 10 ounces) red chard, thoroughly rinsed

2 ounces dried Chinese black mushrooms, soaked in ³/₄ cup water for 30 minutes

8 cups homemade chicken broth (see Note below)

1 slice fresh ginger

2 tablespoons freshly crushed black pepper

2 zucchini, sliced into thin rounds

1 pound rock fish fillets, boned, cut into 1-inch pieces

4 ounces rice vermicelli or other thin noodle, cooked and drained

¹/₄ cup fresh cilantro leaves

Trim the stems from the chard and reserve them for another purpose. Cut the leaves crosswise into ¹/₂-inch slices. Set aside.

Strain the liquid from the mushrooms through a coffee filter or very fine strainer and combine it with the chicken broth, ginger, and black pepper in a large soup pot. Set over medium heat, bring to a boil, reduce the heat, and simmer for 10 minutes.

Add the soaked mushrooms, zucchini, rock fish, and chard, and simmer until the fish is cooked through, about 10 minutes. Add the vermicelli, heat through, and ladle into large soup bowls. Top each portion with some of the cilantro leaves and serve immediately.

note

Broth, as distinguished from stock, is made primarily from flesh, rather than flesh and bones. It has little if any gelatin, and hence, little structure, making it inappropriate for sauces. If made with good quality chicken (or duck, beef, or lamb), it is full of flavor and the most appropriate liquid for this soup.

serves 4 to 6

mulligatawny
soup

Tamil Nadu, a state in southern India, is the home of Piper nigrum. Tamil is the language of the native population (also known as Tamil) and it is their expression for "pepper water," molaga-tanni, that gives us the classic English soup, Mulligatawny. As the story goes, a British colonist requested some more of that "mulligatawny," referring to a spicy soup he'd enjoyed. Countless versions have been made since that first awkward request, though the main characteristics—a mild spiciness and heat, a bit of sweetness from apples, and chicken—are constants. In this version, I've used the chicken-apple sausages that have become so popular in the past decade and finished the soup with tender sautéed spiced apples.

2 cups jasmine rice (makes 3 1/2 cups cooked)

2 pounds chicken-apple sausages

1 cup fruity white wine

2 firm sweet-tart apples, peeled and cut into 1/8-inch slices

4 tablespoons clarified butter

2 teaspoons curry powder, commercial or homemade (see page 166)

1/2 teaspoon ground cumin

Black pepper in a mill

One 2-inch piece cinnamon

1 yellow onion, minced

2 carrots, peeled and minced

4 garlic cloves, minced

2 teaspoons grated ginger

2 teaspoons kosher salt

1 teaspoon turmeric

1/4 teaspoon cayenne pepper

4 cups chicken stock

One 14-ounce can coconut milk

Put the rice in a strainer or colander and rinse it under cool running water until the water runs clear. Place the rice in a large saucepan with 3 cups cold water and bring to a boil over high heat. Reduce the heat to low, cover the pan, and cook for 20 minutes without lifting the lid. Remove from the heat and let the rice steam undisturbed for 10 minutes before fluffing with a fork. Fluff the rice, cover, and set aside while you prepare the soup.

Prick the sausages in several places with a fork, place them in a pan, add the wine, cover, set over medium heat, and simmer for 7 or 8 minutes. Remove the lid, increase the heat, and brown the sausages evenly all over. Set aside and let cool. Cut into ¼-inch slices.

Cut the slices of apple in half crosswise. Melt 2 tablespoons of the clarified butter in a large soup pot, add the apples, and season with a pinch of the curry powder, a pinch of the cumin, and several turns of black pepper. Add

the cinnamon stick. Sauté the apples until they are tender and golden brown. Remove from the pot, leaving the cinnamon stick behind, and set aside.

Heat the remaining 2 tablespoons of the clarified butter in the same pot, add the onion and carrots, and sauté over medium-low heat until very soft and fragrant, about 15 minutes. Add the garlic and ginger, and sauté for 2 minutes more. Stir in the curry powder, cumin, salt, turmeric, and cayenne, add the chicken stock and 3 cups of water, bring to a boil, reduce to a simmer, and cook for 15 minutes. Add the sausages and simmer for 15 minutes more. Stir in the coconut milk, add 1 teaspoon of freshly ground pepper, taste, and correct the seasoning. Divide the rice among individual soup bowls, ladle the soup over the rice, top with the apples, and serve immediately.

serves 4 to 6

thai salmon and mushroom chowder with green peppercorns

You can sometimes find clusters of fresh green peppercorns in a few markets in Asia; occasionally, you even see a few scraggly ones—rather the worse for their long journey from the tropics—in ethnic markets in the United States. Because their season is so short and because virtually all pepper is processed after harvest, very few recipes traditionally include fresh pepper. It is used, however, in a few Thai chowders, and if you're in that part of the world and find a pretty little green stem with tiny round berries—they resemble tiny clusters of unripe Cabernet Sauvignon grapes—consider yourself lucky and enjoy them.

2 tablespoons crushed dried green peppercorns

1 tablespoon crushed coriander seeds

2½ teaspoons kosher salt

1 teaspoon crushed black peppercorns

3 or 4 crushed cardamom seeds

1 pound fresh salmon, boned, skinned, and cut into 1-inch cubes

4 tablespoons clarified butter

1 large yellow or white onion, thinly sliced

4 garlic cloves, minced

2 serrano peppers, minced

2 tablespoons granulated sugar

1 pound mushrooms, such as oysters or morels

1 tablespoon minced fresh ginger

Black pepper in a mill

2 cups mild chicken stock or fish stock

2 tablespoons fish sauce (see glossary, page 221)

One 6-inch stalk of lemongrass, bruised

One 14-ounce can cups coconut milk

3 tablespoons fresh Thai basil or large-leaf basil, cut into thin strips

3 tablespoons fresh cilantro leaves, torn into small pieces

3½ cups cooked jasmine rice (see page 74), hot

Crushed green peppercorns and whole cilantro leaves, for garnish

Mix together the green peppercorns, coriander seeds, 1 teaspoon of the kosher salt, the black peppercorns, and the cardamom seeds. Place the salmon in a medium bowl, sprinkle half of the spice mixture over it, toss the fish thoroughly, cover, and refrigerate. Set the remaining spice mixture aside.

Melt 2 tablespoons of the butter in a large, wide soup pot, add the onion, season with $3/4$ teaspoon of the remaining kosher salt, and sauté over very low heat until the onions release their sugar and begin to caramelize, about 30 minutes. Do not let them burn. After the onions are cooked, add the garlic and serranos, and cook for 2 minutes more. Taste the mixture; it should be very sweet from the onions; if it is not, add the sugar. Stir in the remaining spice mixture.

While the onion is sautéing, melt the remaining 2 tablespoons butter in a sauté pan, add the mushrooms, season with the remaining $3/4$ teaspoon salt, and sauté over very low heat until the mushrooms are completely limp and have released their liquid. Add the ginger and simmer for 2 minutes more. Remove from the heat and set aside.

Add the stock to the onion mixture and then add the fish sauce, lemongrass, cooked mushrooms, and 2 cups water. Bring to a boil, reduce the heat, and simmer for 10 minutes. Add the salmon and cook for 5 minutes more. Add the coconut milk, basil, and cilantro, and heat through but do not boil. Use tongs to remove the stalk of lemongrass. Divide the rice among individual soup bowls and ladle the soup over. Garnish with a pinch of crushed green peppercorns and a few whole cilantro leaves, and serve immediately.

serves 4

salt cod
chowder

One morning I received a phone call from a woman in her seventies who reads my weekly column in the Santa Rosa, California, Press Democrat and wanted to share recipes from her mother, who immigrated from Portugal in the early 1900s. One of the recipes was for a hearty soup of fresh fava beans, rock fish, and linguiça, which I've used for inspiration for this Portuguese-style chowder. Linguiça is a spicy pork sausage seasoned liberally with garlic, cayenne pepper, black pepper, and a small amount of red wine, which contributes a characteristic acidity. It is widely available in the United States, but if you can't find it, use kielbasa, andouille, Spanish chorizo, or another spicy sausage instead. If you have Portuguese salt, which currently is being imported by a few companies in the United States (see resources, page 216), be sure to use it here for a flourish of authenticity.

$1/2$ pound salt cod, soaked for 1 to 2 days
   (see *Brandade de Morue,* page 67)
1 pound linguiça, or other spicy pork sausage
   cut into $1/4$-inch rounds
1 onion, diced
6 garlic cloves, minced
Kosher salt
1 pound waxy potatoes, such as Yellow Finn
   or Yukon Gold, diced
One 28-ounce can whole tomatoes, with
   juice (preferably Muir Glen brand)
6 cups chicken stock or vegetable stock
3 ounces ($3/4$ cup) cracked green olives,
   pitted and sliced
$1/4$ cup dry Madeira
Black pepper in a mill
8 thick slices of country-style bread, toasted
   and rubbed with garlic
Olive oil

Remove the salt cod from its final cold-water bath, place it in a large sauté pan, cover with fresh cold water, and set over medium heat. When the water boils, remove the pan from the fire, and cover it. Let the cod sit for 15 minutes, drain thoroughly, and cool. Break the fish into small pieces and pick out any pieces of bone. Set aside.

Fry the linguiça in a large soup pot set over medium heat until most of the fat has been released. Using a slotted spoon, remove the linguiça from the pot and set it aside. Fry the onion in the fat until it is limp and fragrant, about 7 to 8 minutes. Add the garlic and sauté

for 2 minutes more. Season with a little salt and return the linguiça to the pot, add the salt cod, potatoes, tomatoes, and stock, bring to a boil over high heat, reduce the heat, and simmer, covered, for 25 minutes, until the potatoes are completely tender. Add the olives and Madeira, and simmer for 5 minutes more. Taste and season with salt and pepper.

Place a piece of toast in each of 4 individual soup plates, drizzle with olive oil, and then ladle the soup over the bread. Serve immediately, with the remaining toast alongside.

serves 4 to 6

ginger beef
noodle soup

The night I arrived in Kuching, Sarawak, on the island of Borneo, I went down to the recently renovated river walkway that each night teems with young people, tourists, and hawkers offering delicious local (and American) foods. The very last stall offered huge bowls of soup, served in the hot clay pots in which it was cooked to order. The soup had big chunks of beef and the broth was redolent of ginger, garlic, black pepper, and spicy chiles. You'll need to start this version the day before serving it, so that you are sure to have a rich and flavorful stock. The amount of actual hands-on work is minimal.

stock

5 pounds beef shanks, cut 2-inches thick through the bone (about 6 or 7 pieces)

1 carrot, cut into 3 or 4 pieces

1 tomato, cut in half

1 yellow onion, cut in quarters

4 or 5 stalks lemongrass

6 large slices of ginger

3 kaffir lime leaves

2 star anise

soup

3 tablespoons clarified butter

1 large yellow onion, diced

6 garlic cloves, minced

One 3-inch piece fresh ginger, grated

1 teaspoon whole white peppercorns

1 teaspoon whole black peppercorns

2 teaspoons kosher salt

$1/2$ teaspoon red pepper flakes

10 ounces rice noodles, $1/4$-inch wide

$1/4$ cup fresh cilantro leaves

1 or 2 limes, cut into wedges

To make the stock, preheat the oven to 375°F. Place all but two of the beef shanks, the carrot, the tomato, and the quartered onion in a large roasting pan, and roast for 45 minutes. Place in a large soup pot, add 12 cups of water, 2 or 3 stalks of the lemongrass, the sliced ginger, the kaffir lime leaves, and the star anise, bring to a boil over high heat, reduce to low, and simmer, partially covered, for about 4 hours, until the meat completely falls off the bone and the liquid is reduced by two thirds. Let cool, strain, and refrigerate overnight. Remove and discard the layer of fat that forms on top.

To make the soup, melt the clarified butter in a wide soup pot, add the diced onion, and sauté until the onion begins to caramelize, about 20 minutes. Add the garlic and grated ginger, and sauté for 2 minutes more. Add the reserved 2 beef shanks and cook until they are nicely browned on both sides. Heat the stock in a separate pot and when the shanks are browned, pour it over them. Add 2 cups of water, the white and black peppercorns, the remaining 2 stalks lemongrass, kosher salt, and red pepper flakes, bring to a boil over high heat, reduce to low, and simmer, partially covered, until the meat is very tender, about 2 hours.

Cook the rice noodles according to package directions and drain. Remove the cooked shanks from the pot, chop the meat coarsely, and return it to the pot. Remove and discard the lemongrass, taste the broth, and correct the seasoning. Divide the noodles among individual soup bowls, ladle the soup over the noodles, garnish each portion with some cilantro leaves and a squeeze of lime, and serve immediately.

serves 4

spicy sweet potato soup
with nutmeg cream

If you find sweet potatoes almost too sweet, as I do, you'll love this recipe; several spicy, tangy elements—garlic, smoked peppers, vinegar, and lots of black peppercorns— mitigate the sweetness of the potatoes and create a deliciously complex yet easily prepared soup. This is an excellent way to begin a fall or winter meal.

3 tablespoons olive oil

1 yellow onion, diced

1 shallot, minced

6 garlic cloves, minced

$^1/_2$ teaspoon chipotle powder

2 teaspoons kosher salt plus more to taste

2 teaspoons crushed black peppercorns
  plus more to taste

3 medium sweet potatoes (about 2$^1/_2$ pounds
  total weight), peeled and thinly sliced

1 medium russet potato, scrubbed and
  thinly sliced

$^1/_4$ cup apple cider vinegar

1$^1/_2$ cups apple juice or apple cider

Nutmeg, whole

Nutmeg Cream (see note)

Heat the olive oil in a heavy soup pot over medium heat, add the onion, and sauté until soft and fragrant, about 7 to 8 minutes. Add the shallot and sauté 5 minutes more, stirring occa-sionally to be sure neither the onion nor the shallot browns. If necessary, reduce the heat to medium-low. Add the garlic and chipotle powder, stir, and sauté for 2 minutes more. Season with about a teaspoon of kosher salt and the 2 teaspoons of black pepper. Add the sweet potatoes, russet potato, vinegar, apple juice, and 3 cups of water. Increase the heat to medium, bring to a boil, reduce the heat, and simmer until the potatoes are tender, about 20 minutes. Add more water if necessary. Purée the soup with an immersion blender or pass it through a food mill and add several grat-ings or grindings of nutmeg (about $^1/_2$ teaspoon total). Add the remaining teaspoon of salt, taste, and correct the seasoning with additional salt and pepper, if necessary. Ladle into soup bowls, drizzle with a little nutmeg cream, and serve immediately.

note

Nutmeg Cream: Mix together $^1/_4$ cup sour cream, 2 to 3 tablespoons half-and-half, $^1/_2$ teaspoon freshly grated nutmeg, $^1/_2$ tea-spoon kosher salt, several turns of black pep-per from a mill set on medium-coarse, and a pinch of sugar. Taste, correct seasoning, and refrigerate, covered, until ready to use.

serves 4 to 6

pasta, rice other grains

Salt is an essential ingredient in coaxing out the flavor of nearly all grains. When making risotto, for example, the onions and other aromatics should be salted before rice is added, and the final dish must be salted, too, or it won't come together. If steamed rice will be served neat, without condiments, the cooking water should be salted.

Most breads include salt, which controls the action of the yeast and adds flavor. The breads of Tuscany are exceptions; Tuscan bread is by tradition unsalted bread, but salt is added at the table, as a condiment. Pepper is used to flavor flatbreads in countries where pepper is grown, including India, where the crispy lentil wafers called pappadums are sometimes spiked with ground black pepper. Botia roti is a fresh flatbread, seasoned with black pepper, salt, and other spices.

Black pepper has become a popular ingredient in fresh pasta and is worked right into the dough before it is kneaded, rolled, and cut. It retains its flavor better than nearly any other of the seasonings and flavorings (the exception is hot chiles) added to fresh pasta.

Perhaps nowhere do we see the essential nature of salt function more clearly than in the cooking of pasta.

The cooking water must be properly salted. You cannot add flavor that fails to develop because of a lack of salt. I add 4 tablespoons of kosher salt to 6 quarts of water and find that with less than this amount, the pasta tastes bland. In some cases (if, for example, your water has a lot of sodium in it), 3 tablespoons might be sufficient.

You must begin with sufficient water if you want your pasta perfectly cooked; it needs room to tumble freely as it absorbs water and expands. If you have one of those handy pasta pots, you won't have questions about size, but if you don't, use the largest pot you have. The best is a heavy stockpot that holds 6 quarts of water with 3 inches of space above the water. This is large enough to cook up to 2 pounds of strand (noodle) pasta or large shapes, or 3 pounds of small shapes, such as *farfalline*.

Allow the water to come to a rolling boil, and add the salt after the water boils; adding it first really doesn't shorten the time it takes to boil the water. Some cooks believe that adding the salt before the water boils causes an aftertaste in the pasta, but I have not found that to be the case and there is no explanation for such a possibility. I add salt just before I add the pasta so that I don't have to remember if I've already added it.

Stir the pasta after putting it in the water, and stir now and then as it cooks to be certain it is not sticking together. Pay attention to the cooking time recommended on the package, but begin tasting it a minute or two before you expect it to be cooked.

Drain the pasta in a large strainer or colander the instant it loses its raw firmness yet retains a bit of resistance, that is to say, when it is al dente. If you will be serving the pasta immediately, do not rinse it. If you are preparing the pasta for a recipe that will undergo further cooking, or for a dish that will be served at room temperature, rinse it in cool water and toss it with a small amount of olive oil to prevent it from sticking. Place pasta to be held until later in a wide bowl so that it is not smashed by its own weight.

spaghetti
carbonara

No book about black pepper would be complete without a recipe for the classic Roman dish, spaghetti carbonara—coal miner's spaghetti—named for the black pepper that punctuates the strands of pasta like bits of black coal. You'll find many versions of this dish, some with cream, others with mushrooms, prosciutto, and olives, a few with barely any pepper at all. I've never had a bad version, though I admit disappointment when the dish arrives with cream, which eclipses the rich, silky texture of the classic version. Then it's a good dish, but more closely resembles fettuccine Alfredo than spaghetti carbonara. As a restaurant critic in Sonoma County, I once took an Italian café to task for serving just such a version while advertising it as classic carbonara. After the review appeared, I received a delightfully defensive letter from the restaurateur who blamed the cream on the presence of American troops in Italy during World War II, who, he claimed, demanded cream in everything. "Cream is communism!" he declared, the great equalizer that renders distinct flavors similar. Everyone demands it these days, he continued, adding a promise to prepare the classic version on my next visit.

1 1/4 pounds dry spaghetti

1 tablespoon olive oil

3 garlic cloves, peeled

1/4 pound pancetta, diced

6 large eggs

4 ounces Parmigiano-Reggiano, grated

2 ounces Pecorino, grated

2 teaspoons cracked black pepper

3 tablespoons minced fresh flat-leaf parsley

Black pepper in a mill

Kosher salt

Bring a large pot of water to a boil, add salt and the spaghetti, stir, and cook until just done. Drain thoroughly but do not rinse.

Meanwhile, heat the olive oil in a small skillet, add the garlic, and sauté, turning frequently, until it is lightly browned. Remove and discard the garlic. Add the pancetta to the pan and sauté until it is almost, but not quite crisp. Break each egg into a small dish, one at a time, and then transfer it to a large bowl. Whisk the eggs together quickly, add the cheeses, parsley, black pepper, and pancetta, and whisk again. Add the hot pasta to the bowl and use two large forks to mix thoroughly; the heat of the pasta will heat the eggs. Season with salt and serve immediately, with additional black pepper on the side.

serves 4 to 6

spaghetti with pepato, black pepper, and nutmeg

I enjoy this dish around the winter holidays, when hectic schedules and rich foods threaten to eclipse our normal lives. Then, I like nothing better than a simple Caesar salad followed by this lean and fragrant pasta. Add a tangy cranberry soup and bottle of Champagne and you have an elegant Christmas Eve dinner that is very simple to prepare. It is important to use freshly grated nutmeg in this dish and there is now an easy way to do so. For years, I skinned my knuckles nearly every time I used one of those tiny aluminum nutmeg graters. Now Zassenhaus, producer of outstanding pepper grinders, has developed a hand-cranked nutmeg mill. It looks nearly exactly like a pepper mill, but with a compartment on the bottom that holds a single whole nutmeg. It is a marvelous invention; you'll never need to buy ground nutmeg again.

12 ounces spaghetti or other thin strand pasta

3 ounces pepato

6 tablespoons extra virgin olive oil

2 teaspoons kosher salt

Black pepper in a mill

Nutmeg in a grinder

Cook the pasta in boiling salted water until it is just done. While the pasta cooks, prepare the cheese. Use a vegetable peeler to make several curls of cheese, set them aside, and grate the remaining cheese, using the fine blade of a grater.

Drain the pasta thoroughly and place it in a medium bowl. Drizzle the olive oil over the pasta and toss thoroughly; add the grated cheese and toss again. Sprinkle with salt, grind generous amounts of both pepper and nutmeg over the pasta, and toss lightly and quickly. Divide among warm plates, top each portion with a few curls of cheese, and serve immediately.

variation

Divide 6 cups mixed young salad greens (such as arugula, cress, nasturtium leaves) among 3 or 4 individual plates. After tossing the pasta with the olive oil, cheese, salt, pepper, and nutmeg, set some on top of each portion of greens. Garnish with the curls of cheese and serve immediately.

serves 3 to 4

linguine with fresh artichokes and feta

French feta is smoother (some might say bland, but I don't) than Greek feta—both are cured in a salt brine—and not quite as salty. The Greek cheese is ideal in a salad of crisp vegetables dressed with a bold vinaigrette, that is, the classic Greek salad, but would overpower the subtle nuttiness of the artichokes in this dish. If you make this in the springtime when young fava beans are in season, add a cup of blanched and peeled favas along with the artichokes.

4 medium artichokes, cooked (see Note below)

1 pound fresh linguine or 12 ounces dried linguine

6 ounces French feta cheese, cut into 1/4-inch cubes

4 tablespoons extra virgin olive oil plus more to pass at table

2 teaspoons black peppercorns, coarsely crushed

1 tablespoon minced preserved lemons (page 182) or zest of 1 lemon, minced

Kosher salt

2 tablespoons snipped chives or minced fresh flat-leaf parsley

Bring a large pot of water to a boil. Separate the leaves of the artichokes from the hearts, cut out the thistlelike choke, and discard it. Cut the hearts crosswise into thin slices, and then cut the slices in half. Using a very sharp knife, cut the meat at the base of each artichoke leaf into a thin julienne. Place the sliced hearts and julienned leaf tips in a large bowl.

Add salt to the boiling water and cook the pasta according to directions on the package. While it cooks, add the feta, olive oil, peppercorns, and preserved lemons to the artichokes, and toss with a fork. Drain the pasta, add it to the bowl, and use two forks to toss it thoroughly but gently. Season with a little kosher salt, scatter the chives over the top, and serve immediately, with extra virgin olive oil alongside.

note

To cook artichokes, fill a large pot two-thirds full with water and add a tablespoon of salt. Pour a teaspoon of olive oil into the top of each artichoke, so that it sinks down into it. When the water boils, use tongs to place the artichokes in the water. Return to a boil, reduce the heat, and simmer, partially covered, until you can easily pull off a leaf, about 15 to 35 minutes, depending on the age and size of the artichoke. Drain the artichokes and them let cool to room temperature.

serves 4

dried gnocchi with lemon, pepper, basil, and ricotta

Two peppers—good black pepper, freshly ground so that it is as fragrant as possible, and tangy green peppercorns in brine—offer a sensual contrast to the refreshing tastes of lemon, basil, and ricotta in this remarkably simple recipe. Ricotta is made from the whey that remains after a firm cheese is made; the whey is cooked with vinegar, which causes soft curds to form and rise to the top. The curds are scooped out, salted or not, and packed in containers, usually with holes in them that allow the cheese to drain. Ricotta is best eaten shortly after it has been made, but it's nearly impossible to find it this fresh outside Italy. It's another thing entirely from the cloying, dense packaged stuff that most of us think of as ricotta. Fresh-style ricotta is available in the United States, most commonly in areas with large Italian communities; do not use standard commercial ricotta or low-fat ricotta.

1 pound dried gnocchi (or other medium-sized pasta shape, not strand)

9 ounces fresh ricotta

Zest from 2 or 3 lemons, minced

4 garlic cloves, minced

1 tablespoon green peppercorns in brine, drained

2 teaspoons freshly crushed black pepper

1 teaspoon kosher salt plus more to taste

¼ cup fresh basil leaves (loosely packed), torn into small pieces

2 tablespoons snipped chives

4 tablespoons O Olive Oil (see note)

4 tablespoons homemade bread crumbs, toasted

Bring a large pot of salted water to a boil and cook the pasta according to package directions. Meanwhile, place the ricotta in a large bowl, add the lemon zest, garlic, green peppercorns, black pepper, and the teaspoon of salt.

Drain the pasta quickly but not thoroughly; you want some of the cooking water to cling to it. Add the pasta to the ricotta, toss thoroughly so that the cheese melts from the heat of the pasta, add the basil, chives, and olive oil, and toss again. Add salt to taste, scatter the bread crumbs over the pasta, and serve immediately.

note

O Olive Oil is made in northern California using ripe Mission olives and organic Meyer lemons, and is available at selected markets and specialty shops in many parts of the country. It is also available through mail order (see resources, page 216). A good substitute is 3 tablespoons extra virgin olive oil mixed with 1 tablespoon fresh lemon juice and 1 teaspoon minced lemon zest.

serves 4

black pasta
with caviar

All salt is ultimately sea salt, the oldest the essence of a long-ago saltwater ocean, the newest freshly evaporated sea water. Caviar, too, evokes the sea, as does squid ink, which is responsible for the deeply colored pasta in this recipe. Until recently, it was almost impossible to find dried black pasta, but now several Italian companies make it. Fresh black pasta retains more of an aroma of the sea, so check with local pasta shops—it is often made around Halloween. Lima sea salt has a purplish gray sheen to it, which is why I have recommended it here; feel free to use kosher salt or a small (not fine or ground) sea salt crystal in its place.

1 pound black pasta

4 tablespoons unsalted butter, at room
   temperature

Unrefined sea salt, such as Lima

Black pepper in a mill

6 ounces American golden caviar

3 tablespoons minced red onion

2 tablespoons minced fresh
   flat-leaf parsley

1 hard-cooked egg, sieved

1 lemon, cut into wedges

Cook the pasta until just done in plenty of boiling salted water. Drain the pasta but do not rinse, and place it in a large bowl. Add the butter, season with salt and pepper, and toss quickly until the butter is melted. Add half the caviar, toss quickly, and divide among serving plates. Top each portion with some of the remaining caviar, red onion, parsley, and egg. Garnish with lemon wedges and serve immediately.

serves 4

harvest pasta
with sungold tomatoes,
haricots verts,
sausage, and feta

You can make delicious fall pastas simply by strolling through the farmers' market and selecting the best-looking vegetables. I developed this one when a farmer gave me a couple of baskets of Sungold tomatoes, intensely sweet, orange cherry tomatoes. Use whatever small tomatoes you have available, but keep in mind the sweeter, the better. If you don't have haricots verts, *use Blue Lake green beans, blanched and cut into 2-inch pieces. Vegetarians can simply omit the sausage; the saltiness of the feta is, however, essential.*

½ pound sausage (such as linguiça,
    kielbasa, or andouille) diced

1 pound gemelli, or other medium-size pasta

6 garlic cloves, minced

6 ounces *haricots verts*

3 cups Sungold tomatoes, halved

4 tablespoons extra virgin olive oil

2 tablespoons minced fresh herbs: oregano,
    flat-leaf parsley, chives, and basil

2 teaspoons ground mixed peppercorns
    (black, green, and white)

4 ounces feta cheese, cut into ¼-inch cubes

1 teaspoon kosher salt

In a large sauté pan, fry the sausage over medium heat until most of its fat has been leached out. Drain off and discard all but about a tablespoon of the fat and return the pan to the heat. Add the garlic and sauté for 1 minute. While the sausage cooks, cook the pasta according to package directions. Drain but do not rinse; place in a large bowl.

Add the *haricots verts* to the sausage and garlic, toss quickly, cook for 2 minutes, add the tomatoes, cook for 2 minutes more, and add the olive oil, herbs, and peppercorns. Heat through and add to the pasta, along with the feta cheese. Toss quickly but thoroughly, divide among serving plates, and season each portion with a generous pinch of the salt.

serves 3 to 4

90

risotto
pepato

Carnaroli *is a variety of rice grown in the Veneto, in northeastern Italy. It produces a creamier, and to my palate, tastier risotto than does Arborio. It is increasingly easy to find in Italian markets. Think of this recipe as a savory canvas for the flavor of peppercorns, in both the pepato, a pecorino-style cheese studded with black pepper, and added to the risotto itself. Use the best quality peppercorns you can find; crushing them shortly before using them is essential to retain their full aroma and flavor.*

2 tablespoons unsalted butter

2 medium leeks, white and pale green parts
   only, trimmed, thoroughly cleaned
   and cut into thin rounds

Kosher salt

1 shallot, minced

3 garlic cloves, minced

1¼ cups Carnaroli or Arborio rice

6 to 7 cups chicken stock, chicken broth,
   or vegetable broth, hot

4 ounces pepato, grated

2 teaspoons freshly cracked black
   peppercorns

2 ounces pepato, in one piece

Heat the butter in a large sauté pan over medium heat until it is completely melted. Add the leeks and sauté until they are completely wilted, about 10 minutes. Season with about ³/₄ teaspoon salt, add the shallot and garlic, and cook for 5 minutes more. Add the rice and stir with a wooden spoon until each grain begins to turn milky white, about 3 minutes. Keep the stock warm in a pot over low heat. Add the stock half a cup at a time, stirring after each addition until the liquid is nearly absorbed. Continue to add stock and stir until the rice is tender, about 18 minutes. Just before the last addition of stock, stir in the grated pepato, add the pepper, taste, and correct the seasoning. Stir in the last of the liquid and ladle the risotto into warm soup plates. Using a vegetable peeler, quickly make curls of the remaining *pepato,* scatter them over each portion, and serve immediately.

serves 3 to 4

risotto with zucchini, green peppercorns, and basil

Green peppercorns retain a bright, fresh taste even when they are dried, a quality that makes them ideal with summer produce such as fresh basil and zucchini.

4 tablespoons clarified butter

³/₄ pound zucchini, cut in ¹/₄-inch dice

1 tablespoon crushed dried green
  peppercorns

2 teaspoons freshly crushed black
  peppercorns

Kosher salt

1 small (about 4 inches) zucchini, cut
  into very thin julienne

2 tablespoons olive oil

1 small yellow onion, diced

1 teaspoon minced fresh garlic

1¹/₄ cups Arborio or Carnaroli rice

6 to 7 cups chicken stock, chicken broth,
  or vegetable broth, hot

1 tablespoon fresh lemon juice

3 tablespoons minced fresh basil leaves

Heat 2 tablespoons of the butter in a medium skillet over medium heat. Add the diced zucchini and sauté it until it is just tender, about 8 minutes. Add 1 teaspoon each of the peppercorns and season with about ³/₄ tea-spoon salt. Transfer the zucchini to a bowl and set aside. Melt a teaspoon of the remaining butter in the sauté pan, add the julienned zucchini and cook quickly until just barely limp, about 2 or 3 minutes. Season with small pinches of green peppercorns, black peppercorns, and salt and set aside.

Heat the remaining butter and the olive oil in a large sauté pan over medium heat. Add the onion and sauté until soft and fragrant, about 8 minutes. Add the garlic and sauté for 2 minutes more. Add the rice and stir with a wooden spoon until each grain begins to turn milky white, about 2 minutes. Keep the stock warm in a pot over low heat. Add the stock half a cup at a time, stirring after each addition until the liquid is nearly absorbed. Continue to add stock and stir until the rice is tender, about 18 minutes. Stir in the diced zucchini, lemon juice, remaining green and black peppercorns, and 2 tablespoons of the basil. Taste, correct the seasoning, and remove from the heat. Quickly reheat the julienned zucchini. Ladle the risotto into individual soup plates, top each portion with some of the julienned zucchini and some of the remaining basil. Serve immediately.

serves 3 to 4

dirty
rice

*Cajun spice mixtures owe their essential
character to dried herbs and finely ground
pepper. In certain recipes, garlic powder and
onion powder add a traditional dimension
that cannot be mimicked by fresh ingredients; it is a certain taste one is searching for.*

cajun seasoning mix

1/2 teaspoon ground cayenne pepper

1 teaspoon sweet paprika

2 teaspoons kosher salt

2 teaspoons finely ground black pepper

1 teaspoon finely ground white pepper

1 teaspoon dry mustard flour (such as
   Colman's)

1 teaspoon ground cumin

1 teaspoon dried thyme leaves

1 teaspoon dried oregano leaves

4 tablespoons salted butter or chicken fat

2 yellow onions, diced

4 to 5 celery stalks, diced (about 1 cup)

1 green bell pepper, diced

6 garlic cloves, minced

1/2 pound chicken gizzards, ground in a food
   processor or meat grinder

1/2 pound ground pork

1/2 bay leaf

2 cups long-grain white rice

3 cups chicken stock, boiling hot

1/2 pound chicken livers, cleaned and ground
   in a food processor

First, combine the spices and dried herbs
for the Cajun seasoning mix. Set aside.

Heat 3 tablespoons of the butter or chicken
fat in a large frying pan over high heat. Add the
onions, celery, green pepper, and garlic and
sauté until they are soft and fragrant, about
15 to 20 minutes. In a small frying pan, heat the
remaining tablespoon of butter, add the gizzards and pork, and sauté, stirring frequently to
break up the pork, until the mixture is thoroughly browned. Add the bay leaf and the seasoning mix, stir, and add this mixture to the
cooked vegetables. Stir and simmer together
over medium heat for about 8 minutes (stirring
frequently from the bottom of the pan so that
nothing sticks). Stir in the rice, add the chicken
stock, reduce the heat to medium-low, cover,
and simmer until the liquid is nearly completely
absorbed and the rice is almost tender, about
15 minutes. Remove the lid, stir in the chicken
livers, cover, and cook until the rice is completely tender, about 5 to 10 minutes more.
Remove the pan from the heat and let the rice
rest, covered, for ten minutes. Fluff with a fork
and serve immediately.

serves 6 to 8

three-peppercorn bread

You don't have to be an expert to make good bread at home; you don't even need to have a lot of time on your hands. This modest dough, which can be used for pizza and bread sticks as well as for a loaf, is simple and forgiving; I make it when I crave the sensual rhythm of kneading as a relief from a hectic schedule. Think of it as BLT bread with the bacon on the inside; the first time I made it, I sliced it while it was still warm, spread it with mayonnaise, and topped it with fresh summer tomatoes, coarse salt, and black pepper. Nothing could be better.

2 teaspoons yeast

1/3 cup warm water

3 1/2 cups all-purpose flour

2 tablespoons crushed black peppercorns

1 tablespoon crushed white peppercorns

1 tablespoon crushed green peppercorns

2 teaspoons kosher salt

4 tablespoons extra virgin olive oil

4 ounces pancetta, minced

4 garlic cloves, minced

Cornmeal

In a large bowl, combine the yeast and warm water and set aside for 10 minutes. Using a whisk, stir in 1 cup water, 1 cup of the flour, all but one teaspoon each of the peppercorns, the salt, and 2 tablespoons of the olive oil. Switch to a heavy wooden spoon and add as much of the remaining flour, about half a cup at a time, as the dough will take. Turn the dough (it will be sticky) onto a floured surface and knead it gently until it is smooth and velvety, about 7 or 8 minutes. Wash and dry the mixing bowl, rub it with olive oil, and place the dough in the bowl. Cover with a tea towel and let the dough rise until it has doubled in size, about 2½ hours.

Turn the dough onto a lightly floured work surface and let it rest for a few minutes. Meanwhile, put 1 tablespoon of the remaining olive oil in a sauté pan, add the pancetta, and fry until it is almost but not quite crisp. Add the garlic, sauté for 1 minute more, and remove from the heat. Add the remaining tablespoon of olive oil and the remaining 3 teaspoons of crushed peppercorns.

Shape the dough into a rectangle and spread the pancetta mixture over the entire surface of the dough. Roll the dough into a log and tuck the ends under. Sprinkle a pizza paddle or the bottom of a baking sheet with cornmeal and let the loaf rise, lightly covered, until it has doubled in size (1 to 2 hours, depending on the temperature of the room).

About 30 or even 45 minutes before you plan to bake the loaf, place a baking tile or stone in the oven and preheat it at 400°F. Just before baking, scatter cornmeal over the surface of the stone and then carefully place the loaf on top of the stone. Reduce the heat to 350°F and bake for between 35 and 40 minutes, until the crust is golden brown. Remove the loaf from the oven and cool it on a rack for at least 15 minutes before slicing.

variation

To make bread sticks, let the dough rest after its first rise. Preheat the oven and two baking tiles to 375°F. Cut the dough in half, then cut each half in half again, and continue until you have 18 equal pieces of dough. Lightly flour your hands and roll each piece between your palms until it forms a rope about 8 to 10 inches long. Set each rope on a floured surface. Mix an egg white with a tablespoon of water and brush each bread stick with the mixture. Sprinkle each bread stick lightly with coarse salt (such as Celtic gray sea salt or Hawaiian red salt; if using kosher, be sure not to oversalt), set on baking tiles sprinkled with cornmeal, and bake until lightly browned, about 12 minutes. Cool on a rack and use within a day or two.

makes 1 loaf

If space were not a consideration, if this were a website, another online publication, or an encyclopedia, a chapter on main dishes in a book about salt and pepper could include virtually every recipe in the world. Where is salt unnecessary? When is pepper not welcome? I can think of very few instances.

In choosing recipes for this section, I focused on techniques, on those traditional methods in which salt is used not as seasoning but as a vehicle for cooking. Crusts and doughs of salt trap moisture, aroma, and flavor. Have you ever had a facial? A mask made of, say, seaweed, dries on your wet skin and forces the moisture into the skin's cells. When the mask is removed, your skin is moist and dewy because the moisture had nowhere else to go. The same is true with the aroma and juices in a salt crust; they have nowhere else to go and so they infuse the foods being cooked.

These techniques originated before gas and electric ovens, when cooking was done over wood or coal, the heat of which is harder to control. A salt crust or salt dough encases the food almost as if it were its own little oven, and the heat is thus distributed more evenly. The technique saves fuel, too; removed from the heat, these salt ovens continue to cook the food inside for an hour or more. Today, the technique might seem cumbersome but I promise that the results—succulent meats, fish, and poultry, full of natural juices and intense flavors—make the effort worthwhile.

The other recipes here are some of my very favorites, and all of them demonstrate the wonderful transformative abilities of salt and pepper.

salted mustard greens
and rice

Salting is a technique used to preserve a variety of greens all over the world; fermented (such as sauerkraut) or not (such as these), they have a tangy spiciness and a crispness that is extremely appealing. Here, they are tossed with aromatic rice for a simple yet satisfying vegetarian dish.

2 cups jasmine rice

3 tablespoons toasted sesame oil

1 tablespoon white (yellow) mustard seeds

1½ cups (packed) Salted Mustard Greens
(page 184), coarsely chopped

Kosher salt

Black pepper in a mill

1 cup (from 1 large or 2 small) chopped ripe
tomato

1 teaspoon Gomashio (page 165)

Put the rice in a strainer or colander and rinse it under cool running water until the water runs clear. Place the rice in a large saucepan with 3 cups cold water and bring to a boil over high heat. Reduce the heat to low, cover the pan, and cook for 20 minutes without lifting the lid. Remove from the heat, let the rice steam undisturbed for 10 minutes, and fluff it with a fork.

Heat the sesame oil in a large sauté pan set over medium heat, add the mustard seeds, and sauté for 1 minute. Add the cooked rice, stir and toss to heat through, add the mustard greens, and continue to cook, tossing and stirring, until the greens are hot. Taste and season with salt and pepper. Divide among individual serving bowls, top each portion with ¼ cup of the tomatoes and a little of the *gomashio,* and serve immediately.

serves 4

variation

When tomatoes are not in season, serve with Spicy Salt Egg Sauce (page 179).

grilled portobellos with black pepper polenta

Portobello mushrooms are so meaty and substantial (and fairly inexpensive, too) that they make a hearty main course not only for vegetarians, but also for anyone—they are definitely not a compromise. Portobellos stand up to bold flavors, such as the vinegar and pepper in this marinade. Although I normally prefer fresh herbs to dried, I made this for the first time using a commercial mixture of bonnes herbes (chives, dill, basil, tarragon, chervil, and white pepper) from Penzeys Ltd., and was very pleased with the results. To use such a mixture, be certain it is fresh and full of good aromas; use 2 teaspoons in the marinade and 1 in the polenta, and continue as directed.

1/2 cup sherry vinegar or white wine vinegar, such as Vinaigre de Banyuls (see resources, page 216)

1 shallot, minced

2 garlic cloves, minced

1 tablespoon snipped chives

4 teaspoons freshly cracked black peppercorns

1 teaspoon minced fresh chervil

1 teaspoon minced fresh tarragon

1 teaspoon minced fresh basil

4 teaspoons kosher salt

4 large portobello mushrooms (about 8 ounces altogether), cleaned and stems removed

1 1/2 cups coarse-ground polenta

1 tablespoon butter

2 ounces (1/2 cup) grated Parmigiano-Reggiano or dry Jack, optional

1 lemon, cut into wedges

Sprigs of fresh herbs, for garnish

In a medium bowl, mix together the vinegar, shallot, garlic, 3 teaspoons of the pepper, $1/2$ teaspoon each of the chervil, tarragon, and basil, and 1 teaspoon of the salt. Set the mushrooms, gill-sides up, in a single layer in a nonreactive container and spoon the marinade over them. Turn 2 or 3 times so that the mushrooms are completely coated. Let them sit for at least an hour.

Prepare the polenta about an hour before you want to serve dinner. Preheat the oven to 350°F and start a charcoal fire or heat a stovetop grill. Put the polenta in a 2-quart container such as a soufflé dish or a rectangular Pyrex baking dish, add the remaining tablespoon of salt, the butter, and 6 cups of cold water. Stir with a whisk and be certain to break up any lumps that form. Bake for 40 minutes, stir in the remaining 1 teaspoon peppercorns and $1/2$ teaspoon each of the chervil, tarragon, and basil and optional cheese, and bake until all the water has been absorbed and the polenta is tender, about 10 minutes more. Remove from the oven and set aside, keeping it hot.

When the fire or grill is hot and the polenta has been cooking for about 20 minutes, grill the mushrooms, tops down, rotating once to mark them, for 10 to 15 minutes, until they begin to become tender. Turn them over and continue to grill, again rotating them once, until they are completely tender, from 10 to 15 minutes more, depending on the thickness of the caps. Transfer to a work surface.

Cut the mushrooms on a slant into $1/4$-inch-thick slices, as you would cut a duck breast or a thick steak. Arrange on a platter, garnish with lemon wedges and sprigs of herbs, and serve immediately, accompanied by the polenta.

serves 4 to 6

artichokes, shallots, and new potatoes roasted on salt

As I worked on Salt & Pepper, *I received a fax from Paula Wolfert telling of a minor salt misadventure ("What? You don't have salt in America?" the postmaster demanded when she mailed salt from the Île de Ré in France to a friend in New York) and sending along a recipe from her book* Paula Wolfert's World of Food. *Potatoes, she said, have been cooked on a bed of moist local sea salt in unglazed clay pots for three hundred years, and develop their characteristic flavor as the heat turns the moisture into salty steam. I've added artichokes, shallots, and whole heads of just-harvested garlic, all of which also become moist and tender in the salty atmosphere inside the pot.*

1 lemon, cut into wedges

1 pound (about 10 to 12) very small fresh artichokes

4 to 6 red shallots

1 large garlic bulb

1¾ pounds (about 2 cups) Celtic gray sea salt

1 pound very small creamer potatoes, scrubbed clean and dried

2 teaspoons unsalted butter, at room temperature

¼ ounce aged Asiago or Parmigiano-Reggiano, grated

Kosher salt

Black pepper in a mill

¼ cup extra virgin olive oil, optional

½ baguette, sliced and toasted

Fill a small bowl with water and squeeze one lemon wedge into it. Using a small paring knife, trim the toughest outer leaves from the artichokes, dropping each trimmed artichoke into the lemon water before moving onto the next. Remove the papery outer skins of the shallots and the garlic, leaving the bulb intact.

Preheat the oven to 375°F. Spread the salt over the bottom of a cast-iron Dutch oven large enough to hold the vegetables in a single layer. Dry the artichokes thoroughly. Arrange the artichokes, potatoes, shallots, and garlic on top of the salt, cover tightly with the lid or with aluminum foil, and bake until the potatoes and the artichokes are completely tender when pierced with a fork or the tip of a wooden skewer, about 40 to 50 minutes. Remove from the oven, pull out the garlic bulb, and replace the lid until you are ready to serve.

Carefully, so as not to burn your fingers, extract the pulp from the garlic by removing the root and then using a fork or the heel of your hand to press out the soft interior of each clove. In a small bowl, use a fork to combine the garlic purée and butter until smooth. Add the cheese, $1/2$ teaspoon kosher salt, and several turns of black pepper. Taste, correct the seasoning, and place in a small serving dish.

Transfer the potatoes, artichokes, and shallots to a serving platter. Serve with the roasted garlic butter and toasted bread, and accompanied with kosher salt, black pepper, and olive oil.

serves 4

a salt & pepper cookbook

pepper-crusted pizza with porcini, fontina, and sage

The recipe for dough on page 94 makes enough for two pizzas. I usually make one pizza, and use the other half of the dough to make spicy bread sticks (see the variation at end of that recipe). You'll have the best results if you bake pizza (or any bread) on a baking stone; you needn't buy an expensive one—unglazed Mexican paver tiles work well and cost about two dollars apiece or less. The highly-prized porcini can be found in many U.S. farmers' markets and specialty stores, but if you can't get them, use chanterelles or, in a pinch, criminis.

Three-Peppercorn Bread dough (page 94),
 taken through the first rise
¼ cup clarified butter
1 shallot, minced
3 or 4 fresh porcini (bolete, about 1 pound),
 cleaned
2 teaspoons snipped chives
Kosher salt
Black pepper in a mill
4 ounces Italian Fontina, thinly sliced
8 to 10 fresh sage leaves
Cornmeal

Cut the dough in half and let it rest, covered, on a work surface.

In a medium sauté pan, heat 3 tablespoons of the butter over low heat until it turns golden brown and begins to give off a nutty smell. Cool slightly, add the shallot, and sauté for 7 to 8 minutes, until soft and fragrant.

Cut the porcini lengthwise into ¼-inch-thick slices; add them to the pan with the shallot, and sauté 3 to 4 minutes, turn, and sauté for 3 or 4 minutes more, until golden brown. Add the chives and season with salt and pepper.

Preheat the baking stone and oven at 475°F for at least 30 minutes before you plan to bake the pizza. Lightly flour a baker's paddle or other work surface and use your hands to shape one half of the dough into a 10-inch round. Melt the remaining tablespoon of butter, brush it over the surface of the pizza shell, and top with the cheese, arranging it in a single, overlapping layer. Arrange the porcini over the top of the cheese, spoon any pan drippings over the mushrooms, and add the sage leaves on top.

Sprinkle the stone lightly with cornmeal and set the pizza on top. Bake for 10 to 12 minutes, until the cheese is bubbly and the crust is lightly brown. Let it cool for 3 or 4 minutes before serving.

serves 4

potato curry

My visit to Malaysia in June of 1998 coincided with the opening of the new international airport at Kuala Lumpur. I was lucky enough to score an invitation to the opening ceremony, which included one of the best catered buffets I have seen anywhere. Traditional Malaysian, Chinese, and Indian dishes were served, a delicious potato curry among them. Accompanying the savory dishes were huge platters of tropical fruits—watermelon, papaya, and pineapple—any of which would make an excellent dessert following this curry, which should be accompanied by steamed rice, yogurt or raita, and chutney.

4 tablespoons clarified butter, hot

3 tablespoons curry powder, such as
   Maharajah

3 pounds medium waxy potatoes,
   such as Yukon Gold or Yellow Finn,
   scrubbed and cut into wedges

1 yellow onion, minced

3 garlic cloves, minced

One 3-inch piece fresh ginger, peeled and
   grated

2 cups raw shelled fava beans, blanched and
   peeled, or 2 cups fresh or frozen peas

1 cinnamon stick

2 teaspoons kosher salt

1 teaspoon whole black peppercorns

1/2 cup coconut milk, optional

1/4 cup cilantro leaves

Preheat the oven to 350°F. In a large bowl, combine 1 tablespoon of the clarified butter and 1 tablespoon of the curry powder, add the potatoes, toss until they are evenly coated, and spread them on a baking sheet. Bake until they are almost but not quite tender.

Meanwhile, heat the remaining butter in a wide sauté pan, add the onion, and cook over very low heat until very soft and fragrant, 15 to 20 minutes. Add the garlic, the remaining curry powder, and ginger, stir, and sauté for 2 minutes more. Add the potatoes, fava beans, and 2 cups water. Stir and add the cinnamon, salt, and peppercorns. Bring to a boil, reduce the heat, and simmer, covered, until the potatoes are completely tender, about 20 minutes. Stir in the optional coconut milk, taste, and adjust the seasoning. Ladle into a serving bowl, top with cilantro, and serve immediately.

serves 4 to 6

salt and
pepper shrimp

Shrimp and other small crustaceans cooked
with spices are common throughout Asia as
well as in the American South. There seem
to be as many versions of this dish as there
are cooks. Some coat the shrimp in a batter
before cooking them, others don't, and many
use either chiles or Sichuan peppercorns instead of black pepper. This version, which I
can't blame on anyone but myself, features
the full range of heat and flavor from several
of the commoner peppers and chiles in the
world: black and white peppercorns, Sichuan
peppercorns, serrano chiles, and chipotles. It is
more Asian than American, its influences are
Thai as well as Chinese, and I encourage
you to fiddle with my version as much as I
have with the originals. The main things to
keep in mind are that the shrimp must be
cooked in their shells (split the back of the
shells to devein them) and that the heat must
be high; otherwise, the shrimp will become
dry and hard.

2 pounds medium shrimp in their shells,
 washed, deveined, and dried
 on a tea towel

1/4 cup dry Marsala, sherry, or *mirin*

2 teaspoons kosher salt, plus more
 as needed

2 teaspoons Sichuan peppercorns,
 toasted, crushed, and strained

1/2 teaspoon ground black pepper

1/2 teaspoon ground white pepper

1/4 teaspoon chipotle powder

6 garlic cloves, minced

2 serrano chiles, minced

One 1-inch piece ginger, peeled and
 diced

2 cups peanut oil

8 to 10 scallions, white and green parts,
 cut into thin rounds

6 cups shredded iceberg lettuce

Dipping Sauce (recipe follows)

Place the shrimp in a bowl, drizzle the Marsala over them, and toss them lightly. Sprinkle with the 2 teaspoons of salt, the Sichuan peppercorns, black pepper, white pepper, and chipotle powder, toss again, and set aside for 10 minutes.

Use a *suribachi* to grind the garlic, serranos, ginger, and a generous pinch of salt to a paste. Drain the shrimp and discard any liquid that has collected in the bowl. Pour the oil into a wok, set over high heat, and when hot, add the shrimp. Cook for 1 minute, tossing and stirring constantly, until the shrimp begin to turn opaque pink. Set a strainer over a bowl, carefully pour in the shrimp and the oil, and lift the strainer to drain the shrimp.

Return 2 tablespoons of the cooking oil to the wok, return to high heat, add the garlic mixture, and cook, stirring constantly, for 30 seconds. Add the shrimp and half of the scallions, toss, and cook for 1 minute. Remove from the heat.

Spread the lettuce on a large serving platter, top with the shrimp and cooked scallions, and sprinkle on the remaining uncooked scallions. Season with a little salt and several turns of black pepper, and serve with the dipping sauce.

serves 4

dipping sauce

¹/₄ cup fresh lime juice (from 1 to 2 limes)

¹/₄ cup rice vinegar

2 tablespoons sugar

1 teaspoon kosher salt

3 garlic cloves, minced

2 serrano chiles, minced, or 1 teaspoon
   chipotle flakes

2 teaspoons fresh grated ginger

2 tablespoons minced fresh cilantro leaves

Combine the lime juice, vinegar, sugar, and salt in a small bowl and stir until the sugar and salt are dissolved. Add the garlic, serranos, ginger, and cilantro leaves, stir, and set aside until ready to serve.

makes about ¹/₂ cup

a salt & pepper cookbook

snapper fillets
baked in salt

You can bake any fish—filleted or whole—in a crust of salt without wrapping it. However, it is easier, especially for the home cook who may use this technique only occasionally, to get the hang of it if the fish is wrapped in something that will shield it from direct contact with the salt. Although the fish itself does not become salty (that is, the salt does not penetrate and flavor the flesh), a substantial quantity can cling to the outside of the fish and it can be awkward to brush off. I suggest protecting both fillets and whole fish from the salt by wrapping them in grape leaves, seaweed, or sprigs of herbs. In addition to making the process easier, it makes a beautiful presentation and, if herbs are used, provides additional elements of aroma and flavor. In this recipe, the salt is combined with egg whites and water, which makes a harder crust than one with just salt.

6 snapper fillets, about 6 ounces each

2 teaspoons crushed black peppercorns

1 teaspoon ground cumin

$1/2$ teaspoon cayenne pepper

3 or 4 pounds rock salt or kosher salt

2 egg whites

12 large grape leaves, blanched or in brine (see note)

2 lemons, cut into wedges

Preheat the oven to 400°F. Set the snapper fillets on a work surface. In a small bowl, mix together the pepper, cumin, and cayenne; sprinkle over both sides of each fillet. In a large bowl, combine the salt, egg whites, and 1/2 cup water, mixing to form a loose, sticky paste. Spread a layer of this salt paste about 3/4 inch thick on the surface of a large baking sheet or other ovenproof container. Put a layer of grape leaves down the center and set the fillets on top of the leaves; cover the fillets with the remaining grapes leaves and add the remaining salt paste on top, completely burying the fish and grape leaves.

Bake for about 20 minutes, testing with a thermometer and removing the fish from the oven when the temperature is about 130°F. Let the fish sit for 5 to 10 minutes, during which time its temperature will rise a few degrees as it continues to cook in its salt oven. Carefully break apart the salt and extract the fish fillets. Serve with lemon wedges and one of the suggested condiments.

note

If using grape leaves preserved in brine, first rinse them under running water for a minute or two and dry them thoroughly. To blanch fresh grape leaves, bring a large pot of water to a boil and add about two teaspoons of kosher salt for each quart of water. Stack 4 or 5 leaves together and use tongs to hold them in the brine for about 30 seconds, until they are completely limp. Remove them from the brine, rinse in cool water, drain in a colander, and dry them thoroughly. Fresh leaves that have not been blanched will crack when you try to fold them.

serves 4 to 6

a salt & pepper cookbook

trout baked in a salt crust

Trout is outstanding cooked in salt. Rock salt is a good choice because it makes the best-looking crust, but you can use whatever is least expensive—flavor, finesse, texture, or other subtle qualities of specific salts are irrelevant when salt is used in this way. Most recipes for salt crust call for the food—a loin of beef, a whole chicken, a fillet of salmon, a peach—to be placed directly on the salt. In a few recipes, the food is encased first in herbs, then in parchment, and lastly in foil before being tucked into its nest of salt. I prefer a middle ground, with something between the salt and the food itself that will both protect it and contribute aroma and flavor. If you happen to grow French lavender, you can use clippings of the greens (not the flowers) in place of the parsley. It will impart a subtle yet appealing flavor and aroma to the fish. You can also wrap each trout in freshly blanched grape leaves or grape leaves preserved in brine (see note, page 107). You may also use fresh cilantro, which is especially good with the Spicy Salt Egg Sauce (page 179).

2 trout, about 1 to 1¼ pounds each, cleaned but not boned

4 slices fresh ginger

3 pounds rock salt

2 egg whites

2 lemons, thinly sliced

1 bunch flat-leaf parsley, with stems

1 lemon, cut into wedges

½ cup Spicy Salt Egg Sauce (page 179), optional

Rinse the trout under cool water and dry on a tea towel. Place two slices of ginger inside the cavity of each trout.

Preheat the oven to 375°F. In a medium bowl, combine the salt, egg white, and $1/3$ cup water. The mixture should be slightly sticky, and without any lumps. Place about a third of the salt on a baking dish or baking sheet in a $3/4$-inch-thick rectangle just slightly larger than the 2 trout. Leaving a 1-inch margin, cover the surface of the salt with half of the lemon slices and set the trout on top. Cover the trout with the remaining lemon slices and cover any remaining exposed skin with some of the parsley.

Tuck parsley sprigs between the trout, tucking them in as tightly as possible. Pack the remaining salt over the trout, enclosing it completely.

Bake the trout for 30 minutes. Remove the pan from the oven and let it sit for 5 minutes before breaking open the salt, which will have hardened, and removing the trout. Use a dry pastry brush to brush off any salt that may have stuck to the trout.

Place the trout on a serving platter, garnish with lemon wedges, and serve immediately, with the Spicy Salt Egg Sauce, if using, on the side.

serves 2 to 4

black pepper
crab

San Pedro's Cafe is a small restaurant near the Portuguese Square, in the Portuguese settlement, a historic community in Malacca in West Malaysia, about 3 hours south of Kuala Lumpur. San Pedro's specializes in the Portuguese-influenced foods of the region, and serves crab half a dozen ways, including this traditional recipe, one of the rare Malaysian dishes that includes a substantial quantity of black pepper.

1/4 cup clarified butter

3 shallots, minced

8 garlic cloves minced

1 serrano chile, minced

2 tablespoons dried shrimp, ground

2 tablespoons freshly cracked black peppercorns

2 tablespoons dark soy sauce

2 tablespoons oyster sauce

2 tablespoons brown sugar

2 large Dungeness crabs, cooked, cleaned, and broken apart

In a wok or sauté pan, heat the clarified butter, add the shallots, sauté for 3 or 4 minutes, add the garlic and serrano, and sauté for 2 minutes more. Stir in the shrimp, peppercorns, soy sauce, oyster sauce, and brown sugar, and mix well. Add the crab, toss to coat thoroughly with the butter mixture, add 1/2 cup water, cover, and simmer for 7 to 8 minutes, until the crab is heated through. Transfer to a platter and serve immediately.

serves 3 or 4

citrus salad

with black pepper

spaghetti with pepato,

black pepper, and nutmeg

shrimp roasted on

rock salt

RYE

pastrami

on rye

lamb loin baked

in a salt crust

salt cross

roasted strawberries

with black pepper

salt cellars, salt shakers, and salt mills

come in a variety of shapes and sizes

rockfish baked in salt

Years ago I was visiting a new friend and when we were hungry, she pulled a few sheets of nori from the cupboard, tore them in half, and toasted them over the flame of a gas burner. They turned black and crisp almost instantly. Next, she poured soy sauce into a small bowl and squeezed the juice of a lime into it. We dipped the nori into the sauce and I thought it was one of the most delicious, refreshing things I'd ever tasted. The memory of that long-ago pleasure inspired this recipe. The nori shields the fish from direct contact with the salt, making its removal all the easier; the sauce couldn't be simpler, and it is perfect with the tender fish. The salt crust in this version is made of salt only, without the water and egg white that are used in the other recipes in this book. This method is simple and direct, and you get excellent results, but the addition of water and egg white does make a more solid crust. Feel free to use that technique if you prefer.

1 rockfish, about 3 pounds, cleaned

3 slices fresh ginger

2 to 3 sheets nori

4 pounds rock salt

$1/2$ cup dark soy sauce

Juice of 1 lime

1 tablespoon grated fresh ginger

1 bunch (about 10) scallions, trimmed and sliced into thin rounds

Preheat the oven to 400°F. Rinse the fish in cool water and dry it with a tea towel. Tuck the slices of ginger into the cavity of the fish. Spread a layer of salt about $3/4$-inch thick on the surface of a large baking sheet or other oven-proof container large enough to hold the fish. Wrap the fish entirely in the nori, set it on top of the salt, and then use the remaining salt to bury the fish completely.

Bake for about 30 to 40 minutes, until the fish reaches an internal temperature of about 130°F (use an instant-read thermometer and poke it through the salt crust into the fish). Remove the pan from the oven and let it rest for 5 to 10 minutes, during which time the fish will continue to cook.

Meanwhile, mix together the soy sauce, lime juice, ginger, and about a tablespoon of the scallions. Carefully remove the fish from its salt bed, set it on a work surface, and remove the nori wrapper. Set the fish on a serving platter, scatter the remaining scallions over the surface, and serve immediately, with the sauce alongside.

serves 3 to 4

salmon with sweet-and-sour peppercorn sauce

Slightly sweet, a little hot, and pleasantly tangy, this sauce provides a creamy and inviting coating for the sweet salmon. If you have it, use the red Hawaiian alae salt to finish this dish; it's the same color as the salmon and will add a beautiful flourish.

1 teaspoon white peppercorns

1 teaspoon black peppercorns

1 tablespoon dried green peppercorns

1 teaspoon kosher salt plus more to taste

4 salmon fillets, 6 to 8 ounces each

3 to 4 tablespoons unsalted butter, chilled

1 teaspoon sugar

1 tablespoon green peppercorns in brine, drained

1/2 cup fruity white wine (such as Viognier)

Juice of 1/2 lemon

Hawaiian alae salt

Using a *suribachi* or heavy mortar and pestle, grind the white and black peppercorns to a medium coarseness. Add the green peppercorns and grind the mixture together until all the peppercorns are uniformly ground to a medium-fine coarseness; add 1 teaspoon kosher salt and mix together. Set the salmon fillets on a work surface and use your fingers to sprinkle the pepper mixture over the entire surface of the salmon, pressing lightly to make it stick.

Melt 1 to 2 tablespoons of the butter in a heavy sauté pan over medium heat, add the fillets skin-side up, and cook until golden brown, about 2 to 3 minutes. Turn the fillets skin-side down, reduce the heat to low, cover, and cook for 5 minutes. Remove the lid and cook until done, about 3 to 5 minutes more, depending on the thickness of the fillets. Transfer the fillets to a serving platter and keep warm.

Increase the heat to medium, add the sugar, brined peppercorns, and wine, and simmer until the wine is reduced by about two thirds. Add the lemon juice and 1 tablespoon of the remaining butter. Swirl the pan as the butter melts, but do not let it boil. Add the remaining butter, swirl until it melts, taste, and add a generous pinch of salt to balance the flavors. Pour the sauce over the salmon, sprinkle each serving with a little Hawaiian salt, and serve immediately.

serves 4

grilled salmon
with shredded sorrel

If you happen to grow sorrel or have a neigh-
bor who does, make this dish using the tech-
nique for Snapper Fillets Baked in Salt
(page 106), using large sorrel leaves in place
of the recommended grape leaves. If not, you
can use grape leaves or you can grill the
salmon on either a charcoal or a stove-top
grill. Whichever method you use, you will be
delighted by the flavors of the sweet salmon,
sour sorrel, and salty seasoned butter.

4 small salmon fillets, about 4 to 6 ounces
    each

Olive oil

Kosher salt

Black pepper in a mill

6 cups shredded sorrel (about 1¹/₂ pounds,
    trimmed)

4 teaspoons Sorrel Butter (page 173),
    optional

1 lemon, cut into wedges

Prepare a charcoal grill or heat a stove-top
grill. Brush each salmon fillet lightly with olive oil
on both sides; use your fingers to sprinkle salt
over the salmon; then grind black pepper over
each fillet. Cook the salmon until just cooked
through (or more or less to taste), rotating it
once on each side to mark it, and turning it
once. It will take about 5 to 6 minutes per side
for a 1-inch-thick fillet.

While the salmon cooks, divide the shredded sorrel among 4 serving plates. Transfer the
grilled salmon to the plates, setting a fillet on
top of each mound of sorrel. Top each fillet with
a coin of Sorrel Butter, if using, garnish with a
lemon wedge, and serve immediately.

serves 4

whole salmon
baked in a salt crust

I used to bury salmon in a pit in the ground, which produces excellent results but is admittedly time consuming; it also requires a place in which to dig the pit, which means apartment dwellers are out of luck. Anyone, however, can encase a salmon, or other fish, in salt, which serves many of the same functions as the underground method; it keeps the salmon juicy, traps aromas, and provides the pleasure of unearthing a cooked treasure. For this recipe, you will need a large pan; what is called a hotel pan (an insert for a chafing dish that is 2-inches deep works well, but not everyone has one sitting around the house). Use the longest pan you have, and if the tail of the salmon hangs over, just wrap it in aluminum foil so that it doesn't burn.

8 to 10 pounds salt

3 egg whites

18 large grape leaves, blanched fresh or
    in brine

One 5- to 6-pound fresh salmon

12 cilantro stems (with leaves)

2 stalks lemongrass, cut into $1/2$-inch pieces

8 garlic cloves

1 red onion, quartered

3 serrano chiles, split

2 lemons, cut into wedges

Preheat the oven to 400°F. In a large bowl, mix together the salt, egg whites, and $3/4$ cup water. Spread a layer of salt about $3/4$-inch thick on the surface of a large baking sheet or other ovenproof container large enough to hold the fish. Put a layer of grape leaves down the center of the salt. Tuck the cilantro stems, lemongrass, garlic, onion, and serranos into the cavity of the salmon, and set the salmon on top of the grape leaves and salt. Cover the salmon with the remaining grape leaves, being sure to tuck the leaves around the curves of the fish. Top with the remaining salt, covering the salmon completely.

Bake for about 50 to 60 minutes, until the fish reaches an internal temperature of about 130°F (use an instant-read thermometer and poke it through the salt crust into the fish). Remove the pan from the oven and let rest for 10 to 15 minutes, during which time the fish will continue to cook.

Carefully break the salt crust and remove the salmon from the salt. Set it on a work surface, remove the grape leaves, and set the salmon on a serving platter. Serve immediately, with the lemon wedges alongside.

variation

After removing the grape leaves, remove the herbs and other aromatics from the cavity, cover, and chill the salmon. Serve it chilled, garnished with lemon slices, and with Green Peppercorn Mayonnaise (page 170) alongside.

serves 4 to 6

a salt & pepper cookbook

grilled swordfish with parsley and green peppercorn sauce

Salt brings together the flavors in this sauce; without it, it tastes flat and sharp. Fleur de sel adds a refined flourish to the finished dish. Although you can make this sauce without the peppercorns in brine, it is worth the effort to find them.

2 garlic cloves, minced

2 cups flat-leaf parsley leaves, minced
   (about ¾ cup minced)

1 tablespoon lemon zest

2 teaspoons green peppercorns in brine,
   drained

¼ cup fresh lemon juice

½ cup extra virgin olive oil

1 teaspoon kosher salt

1 teaspoon crushed dried green
   peppercorns

Black pepper in a mill

4 swordfish steaks, about 8 ounces each

2 teaspoons *fleur de sel,* Celtic gray sea salt,
   or other finishing salt

Lemon wedges and parsley sprigs,
   for garnish

Combine the garlic, minced parsley, lemon zest, and brined green peppercorns in a small bowl. Stir in the lemon juice, olive oil, kosher salt, dried green peppercorns, and several turns of black pepper.

Place the swordfish steaks in a shallow dish large enough to hold them in a single layer, spoon half the sauce over them, and turn them once so they are coated with the sauce. Cover and refrigerate for at least 1 hour and up to 3 hours. The unused sauce may be set aside, covered, at room temperature for up to 2 hours.

Heat a stove-top grill or prepare a fire in a charcoal grill. When it is ready, grill the swordfish steaks until they are just cooked through, about 4 to 5 minutes on each side for 1-inch-thick fillets. Set the steaks on a serving platter or on individual plates, spoon some of the remaining sauce over each fillet, and season lightly with *fleur de sel.* Garnish with a lemon wedge and parsley sprig, and serve immediately.

serves 4

chicken alla
diavola

You find pollo alla diavola *in traditional Italian restaurants, those homey, turn-of-the-century eateries often in a basement and frequently decorated with photographs of famous Italian actors and politicians on the walls. Sometimes, the dish includes mustard, a French rather than Italian addition. (For a delicious Asian twist, see the variation at the end of the recipe.)*

Please note that the chicken is rinsed to remove any lingering liquids that might influence the taste, not to remove bacteria from the chicken. Obviously, when a chicken is washed under running water, there should be nothing—no salad greens, no other ingredients whatsoever—underneath the flow of the water to become contaminated by the run-off.

1 large free-range chicken, cut into pieces

3 tablespoons black peppercorns,
   coarsely crushed

2 to 3 teaspoons kosher salt

¹/₃ cup fresh lemon juice

¹/₂ cup extra virgin olive oil

2 lemons, cut into wedges

Rinse the chicken pieces under cool water and dry them with a tea towel. Place the chicken in a single layer in a glass baking dish.

Sprinkle the black pepper over the chicken, turning so that both sides are coated. Sprinkle 2 teaspoons of the salt over the chicken, then drizzle with the lemon juice and the olive oil. Cover and let the chicken marinate in the refrigerator for 4 hours or overnight, basting occasionally.

To cook the chicken, prepare a charcoal fire. When the fire is ready, set the rack about 5 inches from the fire, set the chicken skin-side up on the rack, and broil for 15 minutes, or until the chicken is lightly brown. Baste the skin side with the marinade (for an added element of flavor, use large stalks of rosemary or sage for the basting), turn, and baste the cooked side. Continue to grill, rotating the chicken to mark it evenly, and basting occasionally. Turn a final time and cook until the juices run clear, for a total of 25 to 30 minutes. Transfer the bird to a serving platter, let it rest for 5 to 10 minutes, season with the remaining teaspoon of salt, garnish with lemon wedges, and serve immediately.

variation

Add a tablespoon of minced fresh ginger and a teaspoon of crushed red pepper to the olive oil before drizzling it over the chicken.

serves 4

roasted
chicken

Roasted chicken, served with rice or potatoes and a green salad, is a simple yet utterly satisfying meal, one I often prepare for myself when I'm alone (the leftover chicken is ideal for dishes such as the Avocado, Grapefruit, and Chicken Salad on page 156). Virtually every food writer these days recommends that a chicken be brined before roasting, but their reasons vary. Madeleine Kamman suggests that brining improves the texture of the skin, while Pamela Anderson of Cook's Illustrated *says that the process adds flavor to the bland birds so common today. I agree with both comments; only the very freshest chickens—those killed on your own farm and served shortly thereafter—don't benefit from brining. You will need to adjust the amount of water depending on the size of your container. The chicken must be completely submerged in the brine; be sure to increase the salt proportionally. Black Pepper Dressing (page 171) is a delicious accompaniment, but if you are using high-quality chicken, it doesn't really need anything but a little salt and pepper to be satisfying.*

$\frac{1}{3}$ cup kosher salt or $\frac{1}{4}$ cup fine sea salt
plus more for seasoning

1 whole, preferably free-range, roasting chicken

Black pepper in a mill

1 large sprig of fresh sage or fresh rosemary

Black Pepper Dressing (page 171), made with lemon instead of lime juice, optional

In a large container such as a stockpot, dissolve the salt in 3 quarts of water. Rinse the chicken under cool running water, shake off excess water, and submerge it in the brine. Cover the pot with a tea towel and let the chicken sit for 45 minutes. Remove the chicken from the brine and dry it with tea towels.

Preheat the oven to 400°F. Season the chicken inside and out with a light sprinkling of kosher salt and several turns of black pepper. Place the sage or rosemary inside the cavity of the chicken. Truss the chicken, set it on a roasting rack set over a sheet pan, and cook for 15 minutes. Reduce the heat to 375°F and continue to cook until the juices of the thigh run clear when pricked by a fork, about 40 to 60 minutes more, depending on the size of the chicken.

Let the chicken rest for 10 to 15 minutes before carving. Serve it with the Black Pepper Dressing, if using, alongside.

serves 3 to 4

malaysian
chicken rice
nasi ayam

*When I visited peppercorn farms in
Malaysia, I discovered the ubiquitous
Chicken Rice, one of the most popular
dishes sold throughout the country by hawkers. The secret is, I believe, the absolute freshness of the chickens, which may be either
poached or roasted. Both produce excellent
results. As we made the long drive from Sibu
to Kuching, my guides, Ramlee and Talib,
and I stopped for lunch in Sarikei, at
Restoran Malaysia Chicken Rice, which
specializes in its namesake dish. The chicken
there was by far the best I have ever tasted
anywhere. For an authentic meal, begin with
a bowl of clear chicken broth seasoned with a
little ginger and lemongrass.*

malaysian marinade

6 garlic cloves

2 or 3 shallots

One 2-inch piece fresh ginger, peeled and
grated

2 tablespoons black soy sauce

2 tablespoons light soy sauce

2 tablespoons oyster sauce

1 tablespoon bottled Thai chili sauce

2 teaspoons kosher salt

1 teaspoon chili powder

1 teaspoon ground white pepper

1 whole chicken breast, cut in half

2 chicken leg-and-thigh pieces

One 3-inch piece of fresh ginger, peeled and
grated

2 tablespoons mild olive oil (see note)

1/4 cup black soy sauce

1 tablespoon brown sugar

3 garlic cloves, minced

1 small shallot, minced

1 teaspoon crushed red pepper flakes

1 tablespoon fresh cilantro leaves

4 cups cooked long-grain white rice, hot
(see variation)

1 cucumber, peeled and sliced thin

Thai chili sauce in a small serving bowl

To make the marinade, use a mortar and pestle or a *suribachi* and pound the garlic and the shallots until both are reduced nearly to a pulp. Add the ginger and pound together. Transfer the mixture to a medium bowl, stir in the soy sauces, oyster sauce, chili sauce, salt, chili powder, and pepper. Set aside.

Rinse the chicken under cool water and dry it with a tea towel. Prick the skin of the chicken with a fork or the tip of a very sharp knife. Using your hands, rub the marinade into the chicken, set the chicken in a single layer in a glass baking dish, cover, and refrigerate for at least 4 hours or overnight.

Preheat the oven to 450°F. Place the chicken pieces on a roasting rack set on a baking sheet and roast for 20 to 25 minutes, until the chicken is cooked through.

Meanwhile, mix together the grated ginger and olive oil in a small bowl and set it aside. In a small saucepan, combine the soy sauce, brown sugar, garlic, shallot, and red pepper flakes. Cook over low heat, stirring constantly, until the sugar is dissolved. Transfer to a small bowl, add the cilantro leaves, and set aside.

Remove the chicken from the oven, let it rest for 5 minutes, and use a cleaver to hack it through the bone into pieces about 2-inches wide. Place the cooked rice on a large serving platter, add the chicken to the platter, and garnish around the edges with cucumber. Serve the chicken immediately, along with the grated ginger and soy sauce and the Thai chili sauce. Guests dip pieces of chicken into the condiments.

note

In Malaysia, as in much of Southeast Asia, coconut palm oil is the most commonly used fat. It has a very mild taste; you can substitute a mild olive oil if you like, but you want to avoid the additional flavor that would come from a fruity olive oil.

variation

Before cooking the rice, add a teaspoon of pounded fresh ginger, a teaspoon of pounded garlic, 3 teaspoons butter, and 2 strips of pandan (screwpine) leaves to the cooking water. Top the rice with 1/4 cup fried shallots.

serves 3 to 4

seasoned game hens
roasted in salt

These succulent little hens are so incredibly delicious you can serve them with nothing more than wedges of lime, corn tortillas, and rice, or you can serve a more complex condiment to complement them. Grilled Corn with Pepper Butter (page 137) is perfect alongside, and Pineapple with Black Pepper (page 57) makes a refreshing starter.

4 Cornish game hens

1 tablespoon olive oil

1 tablespoon chipotle powder

1 teaspoon freshly ground black pepper

2 teaspoons kosher salt

1 package dried corn husks, soaked in
   hot water for 2 or 3 hours and drained

5 to 6 pounds rock salt or kosher salt

2 egg whites

Preheat the oven to 375°F. Rinse the game hens under cool water and dry on tea towels. In a small bowl, mix together the olive oil, chipotle powder, black pepper, and the 2 teaspoons of salt and rub the mixture into the skin of each hen. Set several corn husks on your work surface, overlapping them. Set a game hen in the center and fold the husks over the hen, tying each end tightly either with thin strips of husk or with string. Wrap all of the hens and set them aside.

In a large bowl, combine the rock salt, egg whites, and 1/2 cup water until it forms a sticky mixture. Spread about a third of the mixture on the bottom of a pan large enough to hold the game hens with about 2 inches of space between them. Use the remaining salt to completely cover the hens.

Bake for approximately 30 to 40 minutes, until the internal temperature of the hens reaches about 160°F (poke through the salt crust directly into one of the hens). Remove the pan from the oven and let it rest for at least 10 minutes, during which time the hens will continue to cook, before breaking the salt crust and extracting the hens. Cut the ties and serve the hens immediately on the opened corn husks.

serves 4

The breast from the plump Muscovy duck used in the United States to make foie gras is as thick and tasty as a good steak and lends itself to similar preparation. In this version, ginger and garlic contribute spicy, aromatic elements. I like to serve a chutney, too, and either creamy polenta or mashed potatoes. A green vegetable, such as braised broccoli rabe or wilted spinach, provides a refreshing contrast to the rich and spicy flavors.

1 whole Muscovy duck breast

One 1-inch piece fresh ginger, peeled and chopped

2 garlic cloves

1 teaspoon kosher salt

2 teaspoons freshly crushed black peppercorns

1 teaspoon freshly crushed white peppercorns

1 teaspoon freshly crushed dried green peppercorns

1 teaspoon Sichuan peppercorns, toasted, crushed, and sifted (see note, page 66)

1/2 teaspoon allspice, crushed

Olive oil

1/2 cup dry Marsala

Cut the duck breast in half down the center, separating the two halves. Using small sharp knife, remove the fat, which will come off easily in most places. Reserve the fat for another purpose and set the breasts on your work surface.

Using a *molcajete* or *suribachi,* grind the ginger, garlic, and salt into a fine paste. Stir in the peppercorns and allspice, and use your fingers to rub the paste into the entire surface of each duck breast. Cover and let sit for at least 1 hour or, refrigerated, overnight.

Brush a ridged cast-iron skillet very lightly with olive oil and set it over medium-heat heat. When the pan is very hot, add the duck breast and cook, rotating once to mark the breasts, for about 6 minutes for 1-inch-thick breasts (less for thinner meat). Turn, mark on the ridges, rotate, and add the Marsala, pouring it over the duck. Cook for 3 to 4 minutes more for rare meat, 7 to 8 minutes for medium rare. Let the duck rest for 5 minutes before cutting on a slant into 1/4-inch slices.

Arrange on individual plates and serve immediately.

serves 4 to 6

a salt & pepper cookbook

k a l u a
p o r k

*True Kalua pork is the centerpiece of the
Hawaiian luau today staged in resort hotels
on several of Hawaii's islands. It's a big production in which a whole pig is rubbed heavily with salt and baked in an underground
pit (called an* imu*) lined with rocks that
hold the heat of the fire. The cooked pig is
carried on a platform with bamboo handles
by Hawaiians in native dress; its arrival sig-
nals the beginning of the meal. You can find
Kalua pork in many casual restaurants in
Hawaii, including take-out restaurants, and
it is almost always delicious. It is seasoned
heavily with salt, which draws out the natural flavors of the buttery, melt-in-your-
mouth meat. The traditional accompaniment
is* poi, *a sticky, purplish gray purée of taro
root that seems very unusual to those who
encounter it for the first time. Hawaiian red
salt—the real thing, dark reddish brown
with bits of dirt and sand in it, not the pale
commercial variety available in our markets—is the traditional condiment with poi.
I recommend serving this version of Kalua
pork with hot corn tortillas, cilantro, Pineapple with Black Pepper (page 57), and
steamed rice, unless, of course, you have some*

*taro root, in which case you probably already
know how to boil it and pound it into poi.*

3¹/₂ pounds boneless pork shoulder or butt
Liquid smoke
3 tablespoons kosher salt
Ti leaves, optional

If you have a clay roaster, soak it according
to the manufacturer's instructions; otherwise
preheat the oven to 300°F.

Using a pastry brush, brush the pork all
over with a thin coating of liquid smoke. Rub
all of the salt into the pork. Wrap the pork in
ti leaves, if using, tie with cotton twine, and
place the pork in a clay roaster or heavy roasting pan with a tight-fitting lid. (If you don't have
ti leaves, you can use parchment paper or
leave the pork unwrapped.) Add about 1 cup
water (enough to come ¹/₄ inch up the side of
the pork), cover, and bake for 3 to 4 hours, until
the pork falls apart when touched.

Let the meat rest for 10 minutes before
serving. Use two forks to pull the pork apart
into big chunks, set on a platter, and serve
immediately.

serves 4 to 6

spicy pork chops
with sarawak sambal

As I gathered, developed, and tested recipes for this book, I invited friends over to taste the results at the end of the day. I served this simple dish, along with about a dozen other, more complex dishes, so that it would not go to waste. I had decided not to include it, but was overruled when it proved to be the hit of the evening.

4 to 6 pork loin chops, about 6 ounces each

1 tablespoon freshly cracked black pepper

1 teaspoon dried green peppercorns,
    cracked

¼ cup white vinegar (see note)

Kosher salt

4 tablespoons Sarawak Sambal (page 180)

Set the loin chops on a plate or in a shallow dish that holds them in a single layer. Mix the peppers together and sprinkle over the chops, covering them lightly but entirely. Drizzle the vinegar over the chops, cover the dish with plastic wrap, and let it sit for at least 1 hour or up to 6 hours in the refrigerator.

Warm the chops to room temperature 30 minutes before cooking them. Heat a stove-top grill or ridged cast-iron pan and when it is hot, cook the pork chops, rotating once to mark them, for 7 to 8 minutes, until they are lightly browned. Turn them and cook, again rotating once, until just done, an additional 5 to 7 minutes depending on the thickness of the meat.

Set the chops on a work surface, cut the meat on the diagonal into thin slices, arrange on individual plates, and add a spoonful of sambal to each serving.

note

Use Vinaigre de Banyuls, sherry vinegar, or a champagne vinegar. In a pinch, any white vinegar will do, though keep in mind that distilled vinegar has a sharp taste that can dominate a dish.

serves 4

pork roast with dried plums and black pepper

The inspiration for this dish came from the farmers' market near my home, where a local farmer was selling dried red plums. For the longest time, I did nothing more than eat them. After experimenting with seasoning the scarlet plums with pepper and bay, I tried cooking them slowly with pork. It's a wonderful combination of flavors that lends itself to the slow, moist cooking of a clay pot. Although not absolutely essential, the pork will taste best when it has been marinated overnight.

2 teaspoons crushed black peppercorns

1 teaspoon Sichuan peppercorns, toasted,
    crushed, and sifted (see note, page 66)

2 tablespoons fresh, minced orange zest

One 3-pound pork shoulder or butt, boned

3 red onions, peeled and cut into 1/4-inch
    rounds

12 dried plums (see note), cut in half

1 to 2 dried chipotles, optional

1 bay leaf

Zest of 1 orange, cut into strips

2 teaspoons whole black peppercorns

2 teaspoons kosher salt plus more to taste

Juice of 1 orange

1/2 cup hot water

1 orange, cut into wedges

3 tablespoons cilantro leaves, optional

1 dozen flour tortillas, hot

The night before cooking, combine the Sichuan peppercorns, the crushed black pep-

percorns, and minced orange zest in a small bowl and rub the mixture over the surface of the pork. Set the meat on a baking sheet, cover with plastic wrap, and refrigerate. Remove from the refrigerator 30 minutes before cooking.

If you are using one, prepare the clay pot according to the manufacturer's instructions; otherwise, select a roasting pan with a tight-fitting lid. Spread the onions over the bottom of the pot, top them with the dried plums; add the chipotles, if using, bay leaf, orange zest strips, whole peppercorns, and 2 teaspoons salt. Set the pork loin on top and pour the orange juice over it. Cover, place in a cold oven, and set the thermostat at 300°F. Bake until the pork is fork tender, about 2½ to 3 hours. Remove the pot from the oven and let it rest for 10 to 30 minutes. Chop the pork into large chunks, set it on a platter, and keep warm. Add the hot water to the onions and pan drippings, stir, taste, and season with salt; remove and discard the bay leaf. Spoon the onion mixture around the pork, garnish with orange wedges and the optional cilantro, and serve immediately, with the hot tortillas alongside.

note

If you have them, use the Peppered Dried Plums (page 69), together with the candied orange peel, but only one one of the bay leaves; also, omit the bay leaf called for in this recipe.

serves 4 to 6

a salt & pepper cookbook

brine-cured
pork tenderloin

*Meats cured in a brine of salt and sugar are
called* demi-sec; *they are very easy to make
successfully at home. Saltpeter, available at
pharmacies, preserves the color of the meat;
without it, the flesh would turn gray. Pork
tenderloin is one of the easiest meats to prepare in this way because it is only about
1½ to 2 inches in diameter; it takes about
a week to be fully cured. Larger cuts of pork,
beef, or lamb require longer curing because it
takes more time for the brine to penetrate
them completely. Once the pork is cured, you
can use it in a variety of recipes. It is excellent baked with a mustard, maple syrup, and
black pepper glaze. Bean ragouts and potato
gratins are good accompaniments. One tenderloin provides a generous serving for three
people.*

8 ounces kosher salt

8 ounces sugar

1 tablespoon saltpeter

½ cup whole black peppercorns

2 tablespoons allspice berries

4 pork tenderloins, about 1¼ to 1½ pounds
   each

In a large pot, combine 8 cups spring water
with the salt, sugar, and saltpeter, and set over
high heat. Bring to a boil and stir until the sugar
and salt are dissolved. Remove from the heat,
add the peppercorns and allspice, and cool to
room temperature.

Rinse the pork in cool running water and dry
on a tea towel. Place the loins in a nonreactive
container and pour the cooled brine over them.
Use a clean plate or a small, clean cutting
board to weight the tenderloins; they must be
completely submerged in the brine. Cover
tightly and place in the refrigerator or in a very
cool pantry for 1 week. Discard the brine, wrap
the pork, and use it within 10 days.

makes 5 to 6 pounds cured meat

lamb loin baked
in a salt crust

Lamb is often described as "spring lamb," a designation that has nothing to do with the time of year. Rather, it describes the age of the lamb at harvest. Spring lamb is from animals that are between four and six months old; because lambs were traditionally born in December and January, they received the seasonal designation. Today, the breeding of flocks is controlled and spring lamb is available nearly year round. As delicate and flavorful as spring lamb is, there's a prejudice against the meat that lingers from decades past when most lamb came from yearlings, older animals with a strong, gamy smell that many people find offensive. If they've smelled it once, mention the word "lamb" and they'll smell it again, although the odor is totally absent from spring lamb. Usually it takes little more than a surreptitious taste— a slender morsel tucked into a sandwich, for example—to win instant converts. Loins from spring lamb can be fairly small; you may need to place two side by side to make this dish. Although New Zealand lamb is often less expensive than domestic meat is, the lamb raised in this country is usually better, both more tender and more delicate.

1½ cups kosher salt

½ cup minced fresh herbs (rosemary, oregano, and flat-leaf parsley)

2 tablespoons freshly ground black pepper

2½ cups all-purpose flour

2 egg whites

2 tablespoons olive oil

1 lamb loin, boned, about 1¼ pounds

Celtic gray sea salt

Black pepper in a mill

Fresh herb sprigs, for garnish

Place the kosher salt, ¼ cup of the minced herbs, the black pepper, and flour in the bowl of a heavy-duty mixer fitted with a paddle. Mix briefly. In a small bowl, whisk together the egg whites and ½ cup plus 2 tablespoons water until slightly foamy. With the mixer operating at low speed, slowly pour the egg and water into the salt mixture. When the water is fully incorporated, increase the speed to high and knead until a firm but moist dough is formed, about 3 or 4 minutes. Turn out onto a very lightly floured surface, form into a ball, and cover with plastic wrap. Let the dough rest at room temperature for at least 4 hours and up to 24 hours.

Preheat the oven to 400°F. Heat the olive oil in a heavy skillet over medium heat and sear the lamb loin. Transfer to a plate and set aside. Roll out the salt dough on a lightly floured surface to form a rectangle approximately 8 by 11 inches (adjust the size according to the lamb). Set the loin in the center of the dough, sprinkle the remaining ¼ cup of herbs over the it, turning it to spread the herbs evenly over the surface of the meat, and wrap the dough tightly around the loin, sealing the edges by pinching the dough together. Set on an ungreased baking sheet and bake for 20 minutes for rare lamb, 25 for medium rare.

Remove from the oven and let the lamb rest for at least 20 minutes and up to 1 hour before removing the salt crust (keep in mind that the meat will continue to cook in its crust of salt). Slice off one end of the crust, pull the lamb out, and cut it into thick slices. Arrange on a platter, season lightly with Celtic gray sea salt and several turns of black pepper, garnish with fresh herb sprigs, and serve immediately.

serves 3 to 4

lamb shanks tagine with olives and preserved lemons

When I was developing this lemony stew, based on the traditional stews, or tagines, of Morocco, I served it with riced potatoes, a combination I loved. Potatoes are often included in a tagine, but I liked the way the riced potatoes soaked up the juices better than I liked chunks of potatoes in the stew itself. I have also served this savory stew with quinoa, which has a bit more texture than couscous, the classic accompaniment to Morrocan stews.

4 garlic cloves

1 teaspoon kosher salt

$^1/_4$ teaspoon saffron threads, soaked in
     1 tablespoon hot water

1 teaspoon ground ginger

2 teaspoons paprika

2 teaspoons ground cumin

1 tablespoon crushed black peppercorns

$^1/_4$ cup plus 2 tablespoons olive oil

4 lamb shanks, fell and outer fat removed

2 yellow onions, minced

2 garlic cloves, crushed and minced

1 tablespoon crushed coriander seed

$^3/_4$ cup green olives, pitted and sliced

8 preserved lemon wedges

Several hours or the night before serving, crush the garlic with the kosher salt in a *suribachi* or mortar and pestle until it is nearly liquid. Add the saffron (and its liquid), ginger, paprika, cumin, black peppercorns, and the 2 tablespoons of olive oil. Using your hands, rub some of the spice mixture into each lamb shank, place the shanks in a large container, cover, and let them sit for several hours or overnight.

Preheat the oven to 300°F. In a large, ovenproof pot, heat the remaining olive oil, add the onions, and sauté over medium-low heat until soft and fragrant, about 7 to 8 minutes; add the minced garlic and cook for 1 more minute. Add the lamb shanks and brown them evenly all around. Add 1$^1/_2$ cups water, cover the pan with its lid or aluminum foil, and bake until the lamb falls off the bone, about 2$^1/_2$ to 3 hours, depending on the size of the shanks. Check occasionally and add more water if it seems to be dry. Remove the cover for the last 20 minutes of cooking.

Cut 4 of the preserved lemon wedges into thin slivers. Place the lamb shanks on a serving plate and place the pot on a medium-low burner. If there is a lot of liquid in the pan, reduce it until there is about $^1/_2$ cup. Scrape to loosen any particles that might stick. Fold the sliced olives and slivered lemons into the liquid, pour the sauce over the shanks, garnish with the wedges of preserved lemons, and serve immediately.

serves 4

steak au
poivre blanc

"It was my favorite seduction dinner when I was single," a friend told me when I mentioned steak au poivre, "and it always worked." Whether you are courting Aphrodite or merely fixing dinner, the many variations of steak au poivre will rarely if ever let you down. In this version, white peppercorns, whose flavors blossom with high heat, are the key ingredient. The result is a sultry dish with a great depth of flavor. If seduction is your goal, don't skimp on the red wine and don't overeat (or overfeed your guest); you want a little hunger to linger after the meal is over.

4 tablespoons white peppercorns

1 tablespoon black peppercorns

1 tablespoon kosher salt

4 thick steaks (New York, rib-eye, or market steaks), about 8 to 10 ounces each

Olive oil

1/2 cup dry Marsala

1/2 cup heavy cream

1/3 cup half-and-half

Using a mortar and pestle (or a tea towel and rolling pin) crush the peppercorns to medium coarseness. Combine the crushed peppercorns and the salt in a small bowl. Using a pastry brush, brush each steak on both sides with a little olive oil. Using your fingers, cover both sides of each steak with the peppercorn mixture, pressing the pepper into the steak. Set the steaks in a single layer on a plate or tray, cover with plastic wrap, and refrigerate for at least 1 hour or up to 4 hours.

Preheat the oven to 200°F. Remove the steaks from the refrigerator and heat a large, very heavy skillet over high heat. When the skillet just begins to smoke, add the steaks. Cook on one side for between 4 and 5 minutes, turn, and cook for 3 to 4 minutes more for rare steaks (6 to 7 minutes for medium rare). Turn off the oven. Set the steaks on a warm platter and place them in the warm oven. Reduce the heat under the pan to medium, add the Marsala to the hot skillet, and deglaze the pan, using a whisk or wooden spoon to loosen pan drippings. When the Marsala has reduced to about 2 tablespoons, add the heavy cream, bring to a boil, and reduce by one-third. If the sauce seems too thick, thin with half-and-half until you reach the desired consistency. Set each steak on an individual plate, top with some of the sauce, and serve immediately.

variation

You can use duck breast, from the Muscovy duck, instead of the steak. Remove the skin of the duck and continue as directed in the main recipe. Before serving, cut the duck in 1/4-inch slices, cutting at a slight slant. Spoon sauce onto individual serving plates and top with several slices of duck. A single duck breast will serve 2 to 3.

serves 4

a salt & pepper cookbook

steak au
poivre rouge

Black peppercorns are more aromatic than white peppercorns are, and perfect in concert with the red wine of the sauce. Serve with a simple green salad and roasted new potatoes.

4 tablespoons whole black peppercorns

1 tablespoon whole white peppercorns

1 tablespoon kosher salt

4 thick steaks (New York, rib-eye, or market steaks), about 8 to 10 ounces each

Olive oil

1½ cups hearty red wine

2 tablespoons butter, cut into 4 pieces and chilled

1 tablespoon snipped chives

Using a mortar and pestle (or a tea towel and rolling pin) crush the peppercorns to medium coarseness. Combine the crushed peppercorns and the salt in a small bowl. Using a pastry brush, brush each steak on both sides with a little olive oil. Using your fingers, cover both sides of each steak with the peppercorn mixture, pressing the pepper into the steak. Set the steaks in a single layer on a plate or tray, cover with plastic wrap, and refrigerate for at least 1 hour or up to 4 hours.

Preheat the oven to 200°F. Remove the steaks from the refrigerator and heat a large, very heavy skillet over high heat. When the skillet just begins to smoke, add the steaks. Cook on one side for between 4 and 5 minutes, turn, and cook for 3 to 4 minutes more for rare steaks (6 to 7 minutes for medium rare). Turn off the oven. Set the steaks on a warm platter and place in the warm oven. Reduce the heat under the pan to medium, add the red wine to the hot skillet, and deglaze the pan, using a whisk or wooden spoon to loosen the pan drippings. Simmer until the wine is reduced by half. Quickly whisk in the butter, one piece at a time. Remove from the heat immediately after whisking in the last piece of butter. Set each steak on an individual plate, top with some of the sauce, scatter chives over each steak, add accompaniments, and serve immediately.

serves 4

nana's
pot roast

I didn't know my grandmother very well and she died while I was a young girl. I remember her cooking as well as I remember her, and I regret that I didn't know her well enough to ask her questions in the kitchen. The dish I remember most clearly was her pot roast; the gravy had a wonderfully tangy flavor, the meat melted in my mouth, and the chunks of potatoes with their perfectly browned sides were the best I'd had back then. While I was experimenting with slow-cooked beef, inspired by a recipe in Laurie Colwin's More Home Cooking, *I came up with something that tasted surprisingly like my grandma's pot roast. It's hard to imagine that those complex flavors came from just five ingredients, and I'm sure there were other elements in hers, but this is the closest I've come. The meat cries out for potatoes, so be sure to serve some alongside. Do not cook them in the pot with the meat, though; they'll soak up all the juices and both meat and potatoes will be dry.*

One 3 1/2- to 4-pound chuck roast

2 teaspoons kosher salt

Black pepper in a mill

1 1/2 cups red wine or 1 1/2 cups beef stock

1 tablespoon kneaded butter (see note)

Preheat the oven to 200°F. Season the meat all over with salt and a generous quantity of black pepper, place it in an ovenproof pot with a lid, cover, and bake for between 4 1/2 and 5 hours, until the meat is fork tender. Remove the pot from the oven, transfer the meat to a serving dish, cover, and keep hot. Set the pot over a medium-high burner, add the wine or stock, stir with a whisk to loosen any bits of meat stuck to the pan, and simmer until the liquid is reduced by half. Lower the heat, whisk in the kneaded butter a teaspoon at a time, and remove from the heat as soon as the last addition is incorporated into the sauce. Pour the gravy over the meat and serve immediately.

note
To make kneaded butter, combine 1 tablespoon cool (not cold, but not too warm) butter with 1 tablespoon all-purpose flour. Use a fork to mix the ingredients together until smooth. Cover and refrigerate until ready to use.

serves 4 to 6

beef tenderloin
in a salt crust

Kosher salt, flour, and egg whites form a seamless crust that keeps this beef tenderloin tender and juicy. The salt dough can be made with or without the herbs, which contribute a subtle flavor to the meat as it cooks. Once removed from the oven, the meat continues to cook inside its crusty shell and will remain hot for as long as an hour. If it is to sit for a time before you serve it, be sure to remove it from the oven before it reaches the desired temperature, or the meat will be overcooked by the time you put it on the table.

1 1/2 cups kosher salt

1/2 cup minced fresh herbs (rosemary, oregano, thyme, and flat-leaf parsley)

2 tablespoons freshly ground black pepper

2 1/2 cups all-purpose flour

2 egg whites

2 tablespoons olive oil

1 1/2 pounds beef tenderloin, trimmed

Fleur de sel or other finishing salt

Fresh herb sprigs, for garnish

Place the kosher salt, 1/4 cup of the herbs, the black pepper, and flour in the bowl of a heavy-duty mixer fitted with a paddle. Mix briefly. In a small bowl, whisk together the egg whites and 1/2 cup plus 2 tablespoons water until slightly foamy. With the mixer operating at low speed, slowly pour the egg and water into the salt mixture. When the water is fully incorporated, increase the speed to high and knead until a firm but moist dough is formed, about 3 or 4 minutes. Turn out onto a very lightly floured surface, form into a ball, and cover with plastic wrap. Let the dough rest at room temperature for at least 4 hours and up to 24 hours.

Preheat the oven to 400°F. Heat the olive oil in a heavy skillet over medium heat and sear the tenderloin on all sides. Transfer it to a plate and set it aside. Roll out the salt dough on a lightly floured surface to form a rectangle approximately 8 by 11 inches (adjust the size according to the size of the beef). Set the beef in the center of the dough, sprinkle the remaining 1/4 cup of herbs over the beef, turning it to spread the herbs evenly over the surface of the meat, and wrap the dough tightly around the tenderloin, sealing the edges by pinching the dough together. Set on an ungreased baking sheet and bake for 20 minutes for rare beef, 25 for medium rare.

Remove it from the oven and let the beef rest for at least 30 minutes and up to 1 hour before removing the salt crust. Slice off one end of the crust, pull the beef out, and cut it into thick slices. Arrange on a platter, sprinkle lightly with *fleur de sel,* garnish with fresh herb sprigs, and serve immediately.

variation

To cook a whole chicken in a salt crust, add 1 tablespoon minced lemon zest to the dough and let the dough rest overnight. Rinse a 3- to 4-pound chicken under cool running water and dry on a tea towel. Fill the cavity with half a yellow onion, cut into wedges, half a lemon cut into wedges, and several sprigs of flat-leaf parsley. Season the outside of the chicken with olive oil and freshly ground black pepper. Roll the dough out so that it is large enough to fit loosely around the chicken. Set the chicken, breast-side up, in the center. Fold the dough up and over the chicken and seal it—it should be loose, and not fit the chicken too tightly. Set the bird on a rack in a roasting pan and bake until the chicken reaches an internal temperature of between 155 and 160°F. Remove the chicken from the oven and let it rest for between 15 minutes and 1 hour, during which time the chicken will continue to cook. Remove the crust and serve immediately.

serves 3 to 4

poached meatloaf
with peppercorns

The peppercorns in this meatloaf contribute both flavor and texture. Poaching keeps everything moist, and the mustard—both in the loaf itself and alongside—adds a tangy element.

1/3 pound pancetta, diced

2 tablespoons olive oil

1 yellow onion, diced

6 garlic cloves, minced

1 1/2 pounds ground beef

3/4 pound ground pork

3 tablespoons Dijon mustard

1 egg, beaten

3/4 cup dried (not toasted) bread crumbs

1/4 cup minced fresh flat-leaf parsley

1 to 2 tablespoons whole dried green
    peppercorns

1 tablespoon crushed dried green
    peppercorns

1 tablespoon crushed black peppercorns

1 tablespoon kosher salt, or more to taste

1 teaspoon crushed white peppercorns

6 to 8 cups beef or veal stock, hot

Green Peppercorn Mustard (page 170)

Fry the pancetta over medium heat until it is almost but not quite crisp. Add the olive oil and, when it is hot, add the onions, and sauté until they are limp and fragrant, about 8 minutes. Add the garlic, sauté for 2 minutes more, and remove from the heat. Let cool slightly.

In a large bowl, combine the onion mixture,

beef, pork, mustard, egg, bread crumbs, parsley, whole and crushed peppercorns, and salt. (To check the seasoning, shape a small quantity of the mixture into a patty and sauté it on both sides, taste, and adjust the seasonings in the mixture.) On a work surface form the mixture into a roll about 4 inches in diameter. Wrap it tightly in a double layer of good cheesecloth and tie the ends. Heat the stock in a fish poacher or other pan than will hold the meatloaf submerged in the stock and lower the loaf carefully into the liquid. Bring to a boil over medium heat, reduce the heat to low, and poach gently for 40 minutes. Turn off the heat and let the loaf cool in the stock for 1 hour. It should be quite warm, but not hot. Remove the loaf, let it drain for 10 minutes on a rack set over a plate, and add the liquid back to the stock. Reserve the stock for another purpose (such as making soup). Cut the meatloaf into thick slices and serve with Green Peppercorn Mustard alongside.

variation

This meatloaf also cooks up nicely in the oven. Pack the mixture into a 2-pound bread pan, and bake it in an oven preheated to 350°F until cooked through, about 50 minutes. Remove from the oven and it let rest, covered, for 10 minutes before slicing and serving with the mustard.

serves 4 to 6

a salt & pepper cookbook

bratwurst with
sauerkraut and apples

Bratwurst is one of the sausages that rely on white pepper for their flavor; in fact, a great deal of ground white pepper is sold to sausage makers both in the United States and western Europe. Alberger salt, too, plays an important role; because its crystals are hollow, it readily absorbs moisture and helps hold the ground meat and spices in emulsion so that the sausage has a uniform texture. Slow cooking is crucial in this dish; undercooked, the ingredients fight with one another. Given enough time, the flavors mingle together, everything turns a sort of pale golden brown, and the dish becomes truly sensational. The ideal accompaniment would be crisp potato latkes and a hearty ale.

2 firm ripe apples, such as Granny Smith or
    Rome Beauty, peeled and cored

Half a lemon

2 pounds bratwurst (about 4 or 5 sausages)

3 cups fruity white wine (Viognier, Reisling,
    or Gewürztraminer)

2 ounces diced pancetta or bacon, optional

2 tablespoons butter

2 red onions, sliced

1 teaspoon freshly ground white pepper

1/2 teaspoon caraway seed

3 cups sauerkraut (homemade, page 183,
    or commercial)

Cut the apples in lengthwise slices, cut the slices in half crosswise, and put them in a bowl of water. Squeeze the lemon into the water and set aside.

Place the bratwurst in a medium sauté pan, add 1 cup of the wine and 1 cup of water, set over medium-high heat, bring to a boil, cover, reduce the heat, and simmer for 10 minutes. Uncover, increase the heat to medium, and simmer until the liquid is nearly completely evaporated. Transfer the sausages to a plate and set it aside.

Add the pancetta or bacon to the pan and sauté for 7 or 8 minutes, until it is almost crisp. Use a slotted spoon to transfer to the plate with the sausage. Add the butter to the pan and, when it is melted, add the onions. Cook over low heat until the onions are very limp, fragrant, and sweet, about 20 minutes. Drain the sliced apples, add them to the onions, and sauté, stirring now and then, until they begin to brown, about 7 or 8 minutes.

Meanwhile, slice the sausages into 1/4-inch rounds; slice the rounds in half. Add the pepper and caraway seed to the onion mixture. Stir in the sauerkraut, add the sausages and pancetta, and stir in the remaining 2 cups wine. Bring to a boil over medium heat, reduce to a simmer, cover, and cook for 45 minutes, until the juices have thickened and the flavors have mingled. Transfer to a serving dish and serve immediately.

serves 4 to 6

Side dishes demonstrate the simple yet profound power of salt and pepper. Excellent vegetables, that is to say, produce that has been grown for taste, harvested in its own season, and sold reasonably close to its source so that it does not deteriorate during long storage and transport, need nothing more than a skillful sprinkling of good salt and a few turns from a pepper grinder filled with good-quality peppercorns. Fresh corn, cooked just after being picked, needs just a tiny bit of salt. Asparagus is never better than when fat stalks are tossed with just enough olive oil to coat them very lightly, seasoned with salt, and roasted in a very hot oven until tender, about twelve minutes. All it needs then is a generous grinding of pepper to be a succulent accompaniment to any spring meal. When vegetables, such as artichokes and potatoes, are boiled, the water should be lightly salted both to lift flavor and, in the case of green vegetables, to help preserve color.

With more elaborate preparations, scalloped or mashed potatoes, a garlicky ratatouille, or a mushroom strudel, keep in mind that salt builds flavor, so add salt in stages for the best results. If you want the full range of heat and flavor from pepper to infuse a dish, use white pepper during cooking and finish the dish with freshly ground black pepper.

Certain vegetables lend themselves to slow cooking in or on salt. This technique, suitable with root vegetables (consider potatoes boiled in brine or garlic roasted on salt), intensifies both flavor and aroma.

grilled corn with
pepper butter

Hawker centers and night markets in Malaysia often include a few stalls offering fresh boiled or grilled corn seasoned with salt and white pepper. It is so sweet and tender that it needs nothing else; I ate three ears as I made my way through the crowd in Kuala Lumpur's Saturday night market, where mostly locals gather (tourists are across town, at the Central Market). Malaysian music blasts from tinny speakers, flocks of crows squawk in accompaniment, and the enticing aromas of dozens of food stalls mix with the languid, saturated air of the tropics. The scene is about as far as you can get from a typical backyard barbecue, where Americans frequently enjoy corn on the cob, but it has never tasted more delicious than it did in this exotic environment. Corn on the cob hardly requires a recipe; you simply boil or grill the freshest corn you can find until it is just done, and then season it with a bit of salt and pepper. In this version butter and Sichuan peppercorns make for a more voluptuous, and indulgent, dish.

½ cup (1 stick) unsalted butter

2 teaspoons Sichuan peppercorns, toasted, crushed, and sifted (see note, page 66)

1 teaspoon crushed black peppercorns

1 teaspoon kosher salt

6 fresh ears of corn, shucked

Melt the butter in a small saucepan over medium heat. When it is melted, remove it from the heat and stir in the peppers and salt. Set aside and keep warm.

Grill the corn over a charcoal fire or on a stove-top grill. When it is done, transfer to a serving platter. Using a pastry brush, brush each ear of corn generously with the pepper butter. Serve immediately, with the remaining butter alongside.

serves 4 to 6

curried cactus and corn

Ever since the introduction of peppercorns to western Europe, the Indian subcontinent has been a source for spices and the exotic flavors they contribute to food. Many Indian spices and flavors are increasingly familiar, but some ingredients remain both mysterious and hard to find. We're comfortable with cumin, turmeric, coriander, and even fenugreek, all building blocks of Indian curries, but ingredients such as kokum *(a dried flower with a tart flavor),* anardana *(dried wild green pomegranate seeds), and* amchur *(dried mango powder, with a distinct tart taste) leave us puzzled. After searching unsuccessfully for* amchur, *I experimented with our own* nopales, *cactus paddles, which have a lemony tartness, as an ingredient that would seem to lend itself to the Indian palette of flavors. The result was a sort of New World curry that is quite refreshing. Nopales are available at farmers' markets and Hispanic markets from late spring through fall and are often sold cleaned and diced. If you have an entire paddle, trim the edges, remove the tough bottom stem, and use a small knife to cut away any spines (even the tiny, almost invisible ones). Cut them into thin strips or small dice and roast them in a dry pan before using them in this, or any other, recipe.*

3 fresh ears of corn, shucked

1 pound diced nopales (cactus paddles)

2 tablespoons butter

1 teaspoon curry powder

1 teaspoon freshly cracked black peppercorns

³/₄ teaspoon kosher salt

1 small red bell pepper, stemmed, seeded, and diced

2 cups cooked jasmine rice (see page 74) or other white rice

3 tablespoons minced fresh cilantro leaves

Using a sharp knife, cut the corn from the cob and set it aside. Place the diced cactus in a large, dry sauté pan, set over medium heat, and cook, stirring occasionally, until the cactus releases its water. Continue to cook and stir until all of the liquid has evaporated, about 12 minutes.

Add the butter, curry powder, peppercorns, and salt to the cactus. When the butter is melted, stir in the bell pepper, and sauté until limp, about 5 or 6 minutes. Add the corn and ¹/₂ cup water, cover the pan, and simmer for 2 to 3 minutes. Stir in the rice, heat through, taste, and correct the seasoning with additional salt and pepper. Remove from the heat, stir in the cilantro, and serve immediately.

serves 4 to 6

glazed carrots
with peppercorns

Pepper highlights virtually all sweet flavors; it goes beautifully with carrots. Here, additional elements are contributed by green peppercorns, with their fresh, mildly sour notes, and the aromatic toastiness of Sichuan peppercorns.

1 1/2 pounds carrots, trimmed and peeled
   or scrubbed

4 tablespoons butter

3 tablespoons brown sugar

2 tablespoons apple cider vinegar

1/2 teaspoon coarsely ground black pepper

1/2 teaspoon crushed green peppercorns

1/2 teaspoon Sichuan peppercorns, toasted,
   crushed, and sifted (see note, page 66)

1 teaspoon kosher salt

Cut the carrots into thin diagonal slices; if the carrots are large, cut the slices in half. Blanch the carrots, drain, refresh in cool water, and drain again, thoroughly. In a medium saucepan, melt the butter over medium heat, add the sugar, stir until it is dissolved, add the carrots, and toss to coat them thoroughly. Add the vinegar, reduce the heat, cover, and simmer over very low heat until the carrots are completely tender, about 10 to 13 minutes. Stir in the peppercorns and salt, taste, adjust the seasoning, and serve immediately.

serves 4 to 6

green beans
with salt pork

When I was growing up, canned and frozen vegetables were part of nearly every dinner. My mother favored canned and my favorite was French-cut green beans, to which she always added garlic and onion powder. Occasionally, my mother would add some bacon, too, cut into little pieces, and then I was in heaven. I'd pick out and devour the fatty little nuggets, eat all my beans, and then drink the salty-smoky cooking liquid directly from the pan when she turned her back. For a dish that more closely resembles that one, add ¾ cup of water and 2 teaspoons kosher salt to the beans, cover, and simmer until quite tender.

2 ounces salt pork, diced

1 small shallot, minced

1 small red bell pepper, cut into small julienne

1 pound Blue Lake green beans, cut into
 julienne

Black pepper in a mill, set on fine grind

Kosher salt

In medium skillet, fry the salt pork over medium heat until it is almost crisp. Add the shallot, sauté until fragrant, about 5 minutes, add the bell pepper, and sauté until limp. Add the green beans, toss thoroughly, and sauté, stirring and tossing continuously, until they are just tender, about 6 or 7 minutes. Season with 4 or 5 turns of black pepper and a light sprinkling of kosher salt, and serve.

serves 4

collard greens with ham hocks and maple syrup

Steve Garner, the host of "The Good Food Hour" on KSRO-AM in northern California, is a modest yet sensational cook. Like all the best cooks, Steve loves to eat and it is his robust passion that underscores his signature dishes, such as these classic southern collard greens-with-a-twist. His credentials for greens are intact (he's from Louisville, Kentucky), so when he says that the smoky flavor of the ham hocks adds an element lacking with traditional salt pork, you can trust him. The inspired ingredient, though, is the maple syrup, which is absolutely irresistible with the tangy, salty, peppery flavors in this homey dish.

2 pounds collard greens

2 tablespoons olive oil

2 tablespoons peanut oil plus more
   as necessary

3 or 4 ounces smoked ham-hock meat,
   minced

Kosher salt

³/₄ cup unsalted chicken broth or stock

3 tablespoons apple cider vinegar

Black pepper in a mill

¹/₂ teaspoon crushed red pepper or several
   shakes of Tabasco Sauce

1 tablespoon maple syrup

Wash the collard greens and shake them to remove some but not all of the water that clings to their leaves. Cut away the stems, stack the leaves, and roll them up (like a big cigar). Slice them into ¹/₄-inch strips.

In a large saucepan, heat the olive oil and peanut oil, add the minced ham-hock meat, and sauté over medium heat for 2 or 3 minutes. Add a handful of greens, use a wooden spoon to push them down into the pot, and sauté until they wilt; repeat, adding a handful of greens at a time and cooking until they wilt before making the next addition. Stir the greens, and if there isn't a slight glisten from the oil, add another tablespoon. Season with a generous pinch of coarse salt, add the stock, and when it begins to boil, reduce the heat as low as possible. Cover and simmer until the greens are tender but not mushy, about 15 minutes. Check now and then to be certain the liquid has not evaporated; if the pan gets dry before the greens are tender, add a little more broth or stock. When the greens are done, remove the lid, increase the heat, and evaporate any remaining liquid. Add the vinegar, several turns of black pepper, and the pepper flakes or Tabasco. Stir the mixture and pour the maple syrup over the greens. Stir again, quickly, remove from the heat, place the greens in a bowl, and serve immediately.

serves 4 to 6

new potatoes
roasted in salt

The technique of roasting foods—seafood, poultry, fruit, and potatoes—in a nest of salt has grown very popular in restaurants in recent years. I prefer roasting potatoes on top of the salt, rather than buried in it. It can be cumbersome to get all of the salt off the potato skins, but I include this version because of its popularity. Some recipes call for Celtic gray sea salt, but because of its high price it's impractical. Save expensive salts for finishing a dish, and use the relatively inexpensive rock salt for techniques that call for an abundance of salt.

3 to 4 pounds rock salt

2 pounds small creamer potatoes,
   washed but not peeled

¼ cup extra virgin olive oil

1 tablespoon black pepper

1 tablespoon minced fresh flat-leaf parsley

1 teaspoon kosher salt

Fill a medium ovenproof dish with 1 inch of salt; place the remaining salt in a separate ovenproof container. Heat both containers in a 375°F. oven for 30 minutes and then remove them from the oven. Arrange the potatoes over the surface of the 1-inch-deep container of salt and add hot salt from the other container to cover them completely. Bake for 30 minutes. Meanwhile, mix together the olive oil, black pepper, parsley, and kosher salt. Using a spoon, remove the potatoes from the salt, brush off excess salt, and set them in a serving bowl. Drizzle with a little of the sauce and serve immediately with the remaining sauce on the side.

serves 4 to 6

clay pot
garlic potatoes

Slow cooking in an unglazed clay pot is an old and popular technique, especially around the Mediterranean. If you are lucky, your Provençal grandmama will have left you her ancient clay cooker, but you can find reasonable substitutes made by two companies, SchlemmerTopf, which makes a clay baking dish with a very lightly glazed interior, and Rompertof, which makes unglazed dishes. Remember that all clay pots must be soaked in water before being used, and that they need to be started in a cold, not a preheated, oven. I make this version in midsummer, just after the local garlic harvest when the garlic is both plentiful and juicy. At other times, I omit the garlic. Serve these little nuggets with Black Pepper Dressing (page 171), Green Peppercorn Mayonnaise (page 170), or with wedges of lemon and good olive oil.

2 tablespoons coarse sea salt, such as
    Celtic gray or Korean
3 pounds small new potatoes, such as
    Yellow Finn, Yukon Gold, or new red
8 ounces garlic cloves, peeled
2 small bay leaves
1 teaspoon whole black peppercorns

Sprinkle the bottom of the clay pot with about half the salt. Add the potatoes to the pot and top with the garlic cloves. Tuck the bay leaves in the middle of it all. Sprinkle the remaining salt and the pepper over the potatoes and garlic and place the lid on the pot.

Put the clay pot in a cold oven and heat it according to the manufacturer's instructions. Bake at 300°F until the potatoes are tender when pierced with a wooden skewer, about 1 1/2 hours.

Before removing the pot from the oven, fold a tea towel and set it on top of a wooden work surface. Set the clay pot on top of the tea towel and leave the lid on until you are ready to serve the potatoes. To serve, remove the lid and set the dish on the table, with one of the recommended condiments alongside.

serves 6 to 8

sweet potatoes
with apple cider
and black pepper

Sweet potatoes, like carrots, are perfectly accented by black pepper. These tubers are not related to potatoes, but rather are members of the morning glory family and native to the American tropics. They are not, as is often assumed, yams, though they are frequently sold under that name. Yams belong to a different botanical species entirely and are native to Asia and Africa; they are huge and starchy, with a single tuber often weighing as much as a hundred pounds.

2$\frac{1}{2}$ to 3 pounds (about 2 large) sweet
    potatoes, peeled and sliced $\frac{1}{8}$ inch thick
1 cup filtered apple cider or juice
3 tablespoons apple cider vinegar
2 teaspoons freshly ground black pepper
Kosher salt

Place the sweet potatoes in a wide saucepan, add water to barely cover, bring to a boil over medium heat, reduce to low, and simmer, covered, until tender, about 10 to 15 minutes. Drain and discard the water, return the potatoes to the heat, and add the apple cider, vinegar, and black pepper. Sauté, stirring frequently and carefully, over low heat until the apple cider is reduced to a glaze. Transfer to a serving bowl, season with salt, and serve immediately.

variation
Use orange juice in place of the apple cider, reduce the pepper to 1 teaspoon, and add 1 teaspoon of toasted cumin seed. Proceed as directed, and scatter 1 tablespoon of minced cilantro leaves over the sweet potatoes before serving.

serves 4 to 6

steamed winter squash
with black pepper
and cilantro

You can use any hard-skinned winter squash for this dish, but if you can find Tahitian Melon squash, a dense-fleshed, intensely flavored winter squash, use it. These large squash can weigh ten pounds or more, and have an elongated neck extending from a plump round body. The neck is solid meat and is excellent sliced and steamed; reserve the body for pies and cookies and use the neck in this recipe. The best place to find Tahitian Melon and other uncommon winter squashes is at a farmers' market; farmers often sell portions of larger squash, but if you must purchase an entire one, you can steam it and freeze it for later use.

1¹/₂ pounds Tahitian Melon squash, or
   other firm winter squash
2 tablespoons butter
2 teaspoons freshly cracked black pepper
   plus more to taste
³/₄ teaspoon kosher salt plus more to taste
2 tablespoons fresh minced cilantro leaves

Cut the squash in half lengthwise and use a very sharp paring knife to peel it. Cut the squash into slices not quite ¹/₄ inch thick, place them in the top of a steamer, set over boiling water, cover, and steam until just tender, about 7 or 8 minutes.

Melt the butter in a large frying pan, add the black pepper, add the steamed squash, and toss gently to coat the squash evenly with butter and pepper. Season with the ³/₄ teaspoon salt and the cilantro, taste, and correct the seasoning. Remove from the heat and serve immediately.

variation

If you do not care for cilantro, use flat-leaf parsley in its place.

serves 3 to 4

a salt & pepper cookbook

145

black pepper zucchini

You can use a combination of summer squashes in this recipe—a mixture of several of the many varieties of zucchini available to the home gardener, yellow or orange crook-necked squash, whatever is fresh and available. It takes just moments to prepare, and is an excellent side dish with grilled chicken or grilled meats. Do not skimp on the quantity of black pepper, and use the best you have; it's the crucial ingredient.

3 tablespoons clarified butter

6 fresh zucchini, about 6 inches long, trimmed and sliced $1/8$ inch thick

2 tablespoons coarsely crushed black pepper

Kosher salt

Heat the clarified butter in a large heavy skillet set over medium heat. Add the zucchini and sauté, tossing frequently, until the zucchini is just barely tender, about 4 minutes. Add the black pepper, season with salt, remove from the heat, and serve immediately.

serves 4 to 6

In Italy, salad is an expression of saltiness, literally. Insalata *means* salad in Italian and comes from the phrase un'insalata, *that which is salted.* A salad is simply salted greens.

Most of us add salt after dressing our greens, but I recommend your trying the Italian method: Place fresh greens that have been rinsed and dried in a large bowl, sprinkle them with salt (I prefer kosher; if you use sea salt, it should be ground or crushed), and then toss them gently. Add a generous amount of extra virgin olive oil, toss them again, and then toss them with a miserly amount of wine vinegar. I like to add several turns of black pepper, too, though it is not, strictly speaking, traditional. This type of salad should be made immediately before serving it, as should all salads made with leafy greens.

Today we use the word "salad" to mean all sorts of combinations of fresh and cooked foods. Usually, there is something acidic involved, such as vinegar or lemon juice, and there is almost always a fresh fruit or vegetable in there, too. Salt and pepper, in one form or another, are essential for successful salads, regardless of their simplicity or complexity. Salt brings the flavors together, and often provides a pleasantly crunchy texture between the teeth, especially in salads of fresh tomatoes. Pepper contributes a sultry quality to fruit salads that without it might be more suitable as dessert.

peppery green salad
with roquefort and pears

Certain greens have a natural flavor that resembles black pepper. Some, such as nasturtium leaves, are fairly mild; others, such as peppercress, a relative of watercress, are bold and assertive. Arugula, too, depending on the variety and the season, can be full of peppery heat. The strongest should be used sparingly, in a mix with other, milder greens. Nasturtium flowers are both sweet and peppery. Many of the spicy greens, such as arugula, are best in cooler weather, when they are mild enough to be used on their own. Nasturtiums are abundant from late spring through the fall. Farmers' markets are generally much better sources than supermarkets are for specialty greens. If you have access to miner's lettuce, which is found almost exclusively in the wild, use it; it is delicately flavored and delicious.

1/2 teaspoon kosher salt plus more to taste

1 tablespoon pear vinegar, lemon juice, or white wine vinegar

2 cups (1 or 2 handfuls, about 1 bunch) peppery greens

4 cups (3 to 4 handfuls, about 1/8 pound) mixed young lettuces

1 tablespoon walnut oil

2 to 3 tablespoons mild extra virgin olive oil

Half a ripe pear, peeled, cored, and thinly sliced

2 ounces Roquefort cheese, crumbled

Black pepper in a mill

In a large salad bowl, dissolve the salt in the vinegar or lemon juice. Add all of the greens and use your hands to turn them gently in the lemon juice. Drizzle the oils over the greens and continue to turn with your hands until they are evenly coated. Scatter the pears and cheese over the top, toss lightly, taste, season with salt and several turns of black pepper, and serve immediately.

variation

Instead of including the pears and cheese in the salad, spread the cheese over toasted baguette slices, top with a slice or two of pear and little black pepper, and serve alongside the salad.

serves 4 to 6

summer jewel
salad

Make this salad only when you have excellent, in-season tomatoes. If you don't have currant tomatoes, use the smallest, sweetest cherry tomatoes available; it they are very big, cut them in quarters. Use a mix of colors. This recipe showcases the specialty salt coming from the Atlantic coast of France—although there may be little difference between salts once they are dissolved into food, textures of various salts vary widely. Here, part of the pleasure of the dish is the crunchy texture of the salt. Hence, it is crucial to add the salt just before serving so that it doesn't dissolve.

1 cup yellow currant tomatoes, halved

1 cup small golden cherry tomatoes (such as Sungold), halved

2 cups red currant tomatoes, halved

2 tablespoons extra virgin olive oil

2 tablespoons snipped chives

Black pepper in a mill

1¹/₂ teaspoons *fleur de sel* or Celtic gray sea salt

In a medium bowl, combine the tomatoes, olive oil, and chives, add 3 or 4 turns of black pepper (about ¹/₂ teaspoon total), and toss together very lightly. Divide among individual serving plates and top each portion with a sprinkling of salt. Serve immediately.

serves 4 to 6

a salt & pepper cookbook

149

citrus salad
with black pepper

To peel citrus fruit, use a very sharp knife. First, cut each end flat, removing all of the rind to expose the fruit itself. Next, set the fruit on end and use the knife to cut from top to bottom, removing the peel as well as the rind beneath it in a single cut. As you peel, you will also be shaping the fruit. When each fruit is peeled, cut away any white pith you might have missed the first time around. Serve this salad on a large clear or colored glass platter so that you can see the beautiful juices of each fruit mingling.

3 grapefruit (Ruby Red or Star Ruby), peeled

2 blood oranges, peeled

3 oranges (Valencia or navel, but preferably both), peeled

1 lemon, preferably Meyer, peeled

1 lime, peeled

Kosher salt

Black pepper in a mill

Cut the grapefruit into round slices (through the equator, not the poles) about ⅛ inch thick. Arrange them in a single layer on a glass platter. Cut the oranges into rounds slightly thinner than the grapefruit. Top each grapefruit slice with a slice of orange, alternating between blood oranges and Valencia oranges to create an appealing visual effect. Slice the lemons and limes as thin as possible (but not so thin that they fall apart) and arrange them randomly on top of the oranges. Season with salt and several turns of black pepper, and set the salad aside for 30 minutes before serving.

variation

Rather than stacking the fruits, arrange them randomly in overlapping circles.

serves 4 to 6

spicy banana
raita

Raitas are Indian salads, nearly always made with yogurt, and generally served as one of many condiments with a curry to provide a contrast in temperature and texture. They are tangy and cool, a counterpoint to the dark richness of a curry. Raitas may be made with diced tomatoes, cucumber and mint, potatoes and onions (see variation), chopped spinach, and sometimes apples or cauliflower. All are mildly spicy, most often from cayenne pepper. I prefer the heat of fresh serranos and crushed black pepper, which provide a broader range of flavor than the one-dimensional cayenne does.

1 lime

1 or 2 serrano chiles

2 firm ripe bananas, peeled

1½ teaspoons freshly crushed black pepper

3 cups plain, unflavored yogurt

2 tablespoons sugar

1 teaspoon kosher salt, or ½ teaspoon each
   kosher salt and black salt (see glossary)

2 tablespoons minced fresh cilantro leaves

1 teaspoon cumin seed, roasted and coarsely
   crushed

Zest the lime and then juice it, setting aside the zest and the juice in separate containers.

Toast the serranos in a dry pan over medium-high heat until they are lightly browned and fragrant. Let them cool, remove the stem, and mince, removing the seeds first if you prefer a milder taste; set them aside. Slice the bananas ⅛ inch thick and toss with the lime juice and pepper; set them aside.

In a medium bowl, whisk together the yogurt, sugar, salt, black salt, lime zest, and minced serrano. Fold in the bananas and cilantro, taste, and correct the seasoning, scatter the cumin seed on top. Chill for 1 hour before serving.

variation

Cook 2 or 3 medium waxy potatoes until tender. When they are cool, cut them into small dice. Omit the bananas and the lime zest and juice. Add the seasonings to the yogurt and fold in the diced potatoes, half a red onion, minced, and 1 minced garlic clove.

serves 4 to 6, about 4 cups

ruby
raita

In this raita, inspired by a recipe from The Indian Spice Kitchen *by Monisha Bharadwaj, white yogurt is nearly instantly dyed red by the beets, and a colorful as well as flavorful element is added to the table. The original recipe calls for black salt, often called rock salt in India, an earthy, fragrant salt (see glossary) with a sulfurous aroma. A scant teaspoon of the salt, finely crushed in a mortar, infuses the entire salad with a subtle but distinct smell of eggs. If you can't find the salt, or if you find the aroma unpleasant, you can make a perfectly wonderful dish using kosher salt.*

3 cups plain, unflavored yogurt

2 teaspoons sugar

1 teaspoon ground black salt or 1½ teaspoons kosher salt

4 medium red beets, baked until tender, cooled, peeled, and cut into thin julienne

2 tablespoons fresh cilantro leaves, minced

1 tablespoon fresh mint leaves, very thinly sliced

Black pepper in a mill

Place the yogurt in a medium bowl and use a whisk to whip it until it is smooth and creamy. Add the sugar and salt and mix thoroughly. Fold in the beets, cilantro, and mint, add several turns of black pepper, taste, and correct the seasoning. Cover and chill for 1 hour before serving.

serves 4 to 6

a salt & pepper cookbook

salt cod
vinaigrette

*Salt cod is an important ingredient in tradi-
tional Portuguese cooking, and it is easy to
find it in eastern New England, where there
is a large Portuguese population, primarily
from the Azores. You'll find it on the menu
of the region's restaurants, too, such as Mike's
Kitchen in Cranston, known as The Post to
its loyal customers, primarily members of the
Veterans of Foreign War, which shares quarters with the restaurant. The Post has been
discovered by students at nearby Brown
University and the Rhode Island School of
Design, who enjoy the unselfconscious retro
atmosphere and low prices. Portions are
huge, waitresses seem to have stepped out of
a 1950s truck stop, and the quality of everything, from salt cod vinaigrette to creamy
polenta with sausages, is sublime.*

1 pound salt cod, soaked for 1 or 2 days
    (see page 67)

¼ cup white wine vinegar

1 tablespoon lemon juice

1 teaspoon kosher salt

1 tablespoon minced fresh flat-leaf parsley

1 teaspoon fresh oregano leaves

1 teaspoon fresh thyme leaves

⅔ cup olive oil

Black pepper in a mill

1 head butter lettuce, washed and
    leaves separated

1 lemon, cut into wedges

Remove the salt cod from its final cold-
water bath, place it in a large sauté pan, cover
with fresh cold water, and set over medium
heat. When the water boils, remove the pan
from the fire, and cover it. Let the fish sit for
15 minutes, then drain it thoroughly and allow it
to cool. Break the fish into small pieces and
pick out any pieces of bone and set aside.

To make the vinaigrette, whisk together the
vinegar, lemon juice, and salt. Add the parsley,
oregano, and thyme, and whisk in the olive oil.
Season with black pepper.

Arrange the lettuce on individual serving
plates. Toss the salt cod with the dressing and
spoon some of it on top of each serving of lettuce. Garnish with lemon wedges and serve
immediately.

serves 4 to 6

salt cod, potato, and artichoke salad

In this elaborate version of Salt Cod Vinaigrette, artichokes add an earthy note while radishes add a refreshing heat and olives a counterpoint tanginess. Do not skimp on the black pepper; it helps bring the various elements together.

$^3/_4$ pound salt cod, soaked in cold water
    for 1 or 2 days (see page 67)

4 large or 6 medium artichokes, trimmed

4 teaspoons kosher salt

1 tablespoon olive oil

8 Yukon Gold potatoes (or other waxy-
    fleshed variety), each about 3 inches long,
    peeled

$^1/_4$ cup sherry vinegar

2 to 3 tablespoons lemon juice

3 garlic cloves, minced

Black pepper in a mill

2 tablespoons minced fresh flat-leaf parsley

1 teaspoon fresh tarragon leaves, minced

1 teaspoon fresh chervil leaves, minced

$^2/_3$ cup extra virgin olive oil

5 large eggs, hard-cooked and peeled

1 bunch (about 10) radishes, trimmed and
    thinly sliced

$^3/_4$ cup cracked green olives, pitted and
    sliced lengthwise

2 tablespoons capers, drained

Remove the salt cod from its final cold-water bath, place it in a large sauté pan, cover with fresh cold water, and set over medium heat. When the water boils, remove the pan from the fire, and cover it. Let the fish sit for 15 minutes, then drain it thoroughly and allow it to cool. Break the fish into small pieces and pick out any pieces of bone. Set aside or cover and refrigerate.

Place the artichokes in a large pot of water, add 3 teaspoons of the kosher salt, and drizzle a little of the olive oil on top of each artichoke. Bring to a boil, cover, and cook until tender, from 20 to 40 minutes depending on the size and type of artichoke. Using tongs or a slotted spoon, transfer the artichokes to a strainer or colander to cool. Keep the cooking liquid in the pot.

Cut the potatoes in half lengthwise and then cut each half into slices about $3/8$ inch wide; do not make them too narrow. Put the potatoes into the artichoke cooking water, bring to a boil, reduce to a simmer, and cook until the potatoes are tender, about 20 minutes. Drain thoroughly and set aside to cool.

Meanwhile, make the dressing. In a small bowl, whisk together the vinegar, lemon juice, garlic, the remaining teaspoon of kosher salt, and several turns of black pepper. Add the parsley, tarragon, and chervil, and whisk in the olive oil. Taste the dressing, correct the seasoning, and set aside.

When the artichokes are cool enough to handle, separate the leaves from the hearts and scoop out and discard the thistlelike choke in the center. Cut the meat from the base of each artichoke into thin julienne (on the outer leaves you will get just one strip; the inner leaves will be tender enough for you to make 3 or 4 strips). Cut the hearts crosswise into $1/4$-inch slices.

Cut 4 of the eggs into quarters. To assemble the salad, place the potatoes, artichokes, radishes, salt cod, sliced eggs, and olives in a large bowl. Add half the dressing and toss together gently. Transfer the salad to a serving platter and spoon the remaining dressing over it. Using an egg slicer, cut the remaining egg into round slices and set them on top of the salad. Scatter the capers and grind some pepper over the salad, and serve immediately.

serves 4 to 6

avocado, grapefruit, and chicken salad with black pepper dressing

Make this salad when you have roasted chicken left over from a recent meal. You can also use smoked chicken, available at many specialty stores and through mail order.

Black Pepper Dressing (page 171)

4 cups mixed peppery greens (watercress, peppercress, arugula, nasturtium leaves)

1 or 2 Hass avocados, peeled and sliced lengthwise

1 pink grapefruit, peeled and sectioned

10 ounces roasted chicken meat

1 lime, cut into wedges

Make the Black Pepper Dressing and set it aside. Divide the greens among 4 plates, placing them in a mound in the center of the plate. Arrange a circle of avocado around each mound of greens and add sections of grapefruit next to some of the avocado slices. Divide the chicken among the salads, placing it on top of the greens. Spoon dressing over each salad, drizzling some on the chicken and more on the avocado slices and grapefruit sections. Serve immediately.

serves 4

mâche salad
with soppressata

Soppressata, an Italian cured meat that looks like a large salami, is one of countless preserved meats that rely on salt for their flavor. These meats developed as a way of preserving food and were used in small quantities to flavor less expensive ingredients such as beans, pasta, and polenta. Today, we relish them for their wonderful taste. To my palate, soppressata is one of the best. Here, it is paired with mâche (corn salad), a green that grows well in cool, rainy weather.

1/3 pound soppressata, thinly sliced

4 handfuls of mâche (about 6 cups), thoroughly cleaned and dried

2 or 3 tablespoons extra virgin olive oil

1 tablespoon (or more to taste) white wine vinegar, such as Vinaigre de Banyuls (see resources, page 216)

Kosher or sea salt

Black pepper in a mill

Divide the soppressata in half. Cut one half of it into thin (1/4-inch-wide) strips and set them aside. Divide the other half among 4 salad plates, covering the surface of the plate with the meat. Place the mâche in a large bowl, drizzle with olive oil and vinegar, season with salt and pepper, and toss gently. Set some of the mâche on top of each serving of soppressata, scatter the strips of soppressata on top, grind some pepper over each portion, and serve immediately.

serves 4

broccoli, cauliflower, and bacon salad

While I was working on Salt & Pepper, *a friend invited me to dinner. Her husband made a velvety venison chili; she served this sweet and tangy salad alongside and told the story of a friend bringing the salad to dinner one night. When a guest asked for the recipe, she opened her bag and brought out several copies, saying that everyone who tasted the salad asked how she made it. The secret here is, I believe, the secret of salt, or more specifically, salty bacon, which infuses every bite. For a real treat, use a true farm bacon (see resources, page 216). The cauliflower is my touch; feel free to omit it, or to omit the broccoli; it's the combination of salty, sweet, and tangy flavors that is crucial.*

Fry the bacon over medium heat until it is just crisp. Using a slotted spoon, transfer the bacon to a brown paper bag to drain. In a large bowl, toss together the broccoli, cauliflower, and dried cranberries. Pour the bacon drippings over, toss well, and set aside.

In a small bowl, mix together the mayonnaise, sugar, vinegars, and scallions. Season with salt and several turns of black pepper. Add two thirds of the pecans and two thirds of the bacon to the broccoli and cauliflower mixture, pour the dressing over, and toss thoroughly. Scatter the remaining pecans and bacon over the salad, add several turns of black pepper, and serve immediately.

serves 4 to 6

8 ounces bacon, diced

3 cups broccoli florets, blanched and
    refreshed in cold water

3 cups cauliflower florets, blanched and
    refreshed in cold water

4 ounces (1 cup) dried cranberries or raisins

1 cup mayonnaise

1/3 cup sugar

2 tablespoons red wine vinegar

2 tablespoons balsamic vinegar

2 bunches scallions, trimmed and cut into
    thin rounds

Kosher salt

Black pepper in a mill

4 ounces (1 cup) pecan pieces

One hot afternoon in Kuching, Sarawak, I walked beyond the water-
front and its familiar food stalls and tourist shops to a string of local
markets selling meat, poultry, and mounds of familiar and unfamiliar
fruits and vegetables. I was hoping to stumble across a few out-of-
season mangosteens—the Queen of Fruit it is called, and rightly so:
It is exquisite. What I found instead was a spice merchant. Certainly,
I had seen vendors selling spices in markets around the world, but
none sold them in quite this form. Instead of huge sacks of dried
whole or ground spices, this merchant was selling spices that had been
mixed into very thick pastes. Bright red chiles, coppery cumin, creamy
cardamom, and orange turmeric had each been mixed with water
and salt. Customers told the merchant what they wanted to cook—
a chicken or fish curry, perhaps, or Sarawak laksa—and he sliced off
just enough for the dish, wrapping the colorful slabs on top of one
another in a single pandan leaf. He allowed me to taste some; each
spice, its flavors lifted by salt, blossomed full and warm in my mouth.

   This is, I believe, a unique moment in American cooking. Over the
past two decades, we have grown comfortable with ingredients that
previously were familiar only to relatively few dedicated individuals.
In the process, the quality of our ingredients has improved immensely.
We are no longer satisfied with spices and dried herbs that sit on

grocers' shelves (or in our own pantries) for months, or even years. We know their flavors and we want them, full and bold, as they should be.

Hundreds of traditional spice mixtures and condiments are used in cuisines around the world—everything from spice rubs for grilled meats and fish to complex curry powders with dozens of ingredients. This chapter includes a few of those I discovered and a handful of those I developed on my own as I combined some of my favorite flavors during endless hours of playing in the kitchen.

Salt and spices have traditionally been used to preserve food, and I have included a few of the most classic uses, homemade sauerkraut, for instance, and preserved lemons. But don't stop here. The next time you make a marmalade, toss in a handful of flavorful black peppercorns (I did, and loved the result), or purée some fresh figs and season them with salt, black pepper, and cayenne pepper for a scrumptious fresh chutney.

mixed
peppercorns

Some cooks keep several pepper grinders at the ready at all times: one for black peppercorns, one for white, one for mixed peppercorns, and one with peppercorns mixed with allspice berries or coriander. I confess to having four myself, even though I'm as likely to crush my peppercorns by hand in a suribachi *or* molcajete *as I am to use a grinder. A grinder is handy at the table, though, and for a final sprinkling over a finished dish. Keep in mind that if you use a large peppercorn such as Tellicherry, some will inevitably get stuck in the grinding mechanism. I find it happens frequently, even with my best mills. The problem is almost always solved by whacking the grinder against a hard surface; occasionally I empty out the grinder and start over with a new batch of peppercorns. This mixture offers a full spectrum of flavor. Use it as you would plain black or white pepper, when you want an additional burst of flavor and aroma.*

¹/₄ cup (¹/₂ ounce) Sichuan peppercorns, toasted, crushed, and sifted

¹/₄ cup (1 ounce) white peppercorns

¹/₂ cup (2 ounces) black peppercorns

¹/₄ cup (¹/₂ ounce) dried green peppercorns

1 tablespoon (¹/₈ ounce) whole coriander

1 tablespoon allspice berries, coarsely cracked

Mix all of the spices together in a bowl, tossing gently to distribute them evenly. Fill a pepper grinder with the mixture and store any leftover mixture in a glass jar in a dark pantry and use to refill the grinder.

makes about 1 cup

flavored salts

One morning I awoke to find a small package on my front porch. Dropped off by my friend Robert Kourik, a gardener and the author of lovely gardening books, the package was filled with small pouches of flavored sea salt from South Africa (the salt actually is made by a tribe in Namibia). The pouches were attached to one another, a daisy chain of salty flavors: salt with Indian spices, with Asian spices, with celery salt, with crushed chiles, with *herbs de Provence,* and, of course, sea salt with crushed black pepper. Another day, I received a tiny round glass jar filled with beautiful transparent salt crystals layered with green, black, and pink peppercorns, carried home from Italy by my friend Jerry Hertz. (The whole peppercorns and coarse salt don't exchange flavors, but the visual effect is striking.) The most unusual salt to come my way was a smoked salt from the north coast of Denmark, which arrived in a tightly sealed package a few days after a local newspaper ran my photograph with a story about salt. The translucent brown crystals of smoky tasting salt are stunningly fragrant. The smell of the salt is thoroughly overpowering, a quality that may limit its appeal; its scent permeated everything and seeped through at least two layers of sealed plastic. It's quite tasty—excellent on eggs, grilled fish, and delicate cheese soufflés—but its scent is so aggressive that it might be annoying to keep in the pantry all of the time.

Salt seasoned with dried herbs, ground spices, crushed chiles, lemon or lime juice, or a host of other ingredients is a simple way to add flavor to a finished dish. In making flavored salts, seeds should be toasted and ground, herbs should be dried and crumbled, and chiles should be ground before being combined with the salt. For the best flavor, make the salts in amounts you would use within a week.

caraway-flavored salt

In her book, The Cooking of the Eastern Mediterranean, *Paula Wolfert tells readers about discovering a flavored salt from the Svaneti region of Georgia, explaining that it is served as a condiment with salads, vegetable dishes, potatoes, and meats. I used her recipe to develop my own, which I sometimes rub into potatoes (coated with olive oil first) before baking or roasting them on or in salt. I add a little more, along with some butter, after the potatoes are cooked. The salt is exuberantly flavorful, and is excellent on nearly all potato dishes, as well as on grilled and roasted poultry, salmon, and a variety of other dishes.*

2 teaspoons whole caraway seeds

1½ teaspoons whole coriander seeds

½ teaspoon fenugreek seeds

1 teaspoon whole black peppercorns

3 garlic cloves

3 tablespoons kosher salt, Celtic gray
   sea salt, or other coarse salt

Pinch of cayenne pepper

Grind the seeds and peppercorns in a *suribachi* or other hand grinder; add the garlic, crushing the cloves, and grind the ingredients together until the mixture forms a fairly smooth paste. Add the salt and cayenne, and mix thoroughly. Use within a day or two.

makes about ¹/₄ cup

a salt & pepper cookbook

163

chipotle salt

If you cannot find chipotle powder, grind chipotle flakes, now readily available at natural food stores and most markets, or minced dried chipotle peppers in a spice grinder until reduced to a powder. Measure the chipotles after grinding them. Use chipotle salt on the rims of Margarita glasses, on roasted poultry and grilled meats, and to finish bean dishes.

1/2 cup kosher salt
3/4 teaspoon chipotle powder

Place the salt and chipotle powder in a small container with a lid, seal the container, and shake vigorously for several seconds until the chipotle powder is evenly distributed in the salt. You should not see large specks of red. Chipotle salt will keep indefinitely.

makes 1/2 cup

roasted pepper salt

Although this aromatic salt has many more traditional uses—with chicken livers and pâtés, for example—I find it delicious on popcorn.

1 1/2 teaspoons Sichuan peppercorns, coarsely crushed and sifted to remove husks (see note, page 66)
3 tablespoons kosher salt or sea salt

Place the peppercorns in a small heavy skillet set over medium heat and toast them, agitating the skillet slightly, until they become fragrant, 3 or 4 minutes. Reduce the heat to low, add the salt, and continue to roast, shaking the pan gently and stirring frequently with a wooden spoon, until the salt just begins to take on a little color, about 8 minutes. Remove from the heat and let cool. Crush the mixture using a mortar and pestle, *suribachi,* or electric spice mill. Store in an airtight jar.

makes about 3 tablespoons

Whole foods markets sell several commercial versions of this classic Japanese seasoning, some with seaweed, some without. The variation, adapted from a recipe from one of my favorite authors, Deborah Madison, includes a bit of heat in the form of hot pepper flakes. Sprinkle gomashio over rice dishes, eggs, steamed spinach, sautéed chard, grilled eggplant, and in miso soups. Because sesame seeds have a high oil content, they will turn rancid; it is best to make gomashio in small batches that you will use within a week or so. Raw sesame seeds should be stored in the refrigerator.

¹/₂ cup white sesame seeds

1 tablespoon kosher salt or 2 teaspoons Japanese sea salt (roasted, if available)

Toast the sesame seeds in a heavy frying pan, stirring them carefully so that they do not burn, until they are golden brown. (Be careful; sesame seeds have a tendency to jump out of the pan as they heat up.) Transfer the seeds to a *suribachi* or a mortar, put the salt in the frying pan, set over medium heat, and stir until the salt begins to take on a little color. Grind the seeds, but do not reduce them to a powder; add the salt and grind together briefly. Store in a glass jar and use within a week or two.

variation

Toast 2 sheets of nori over an open flame until it is crisp. Break it into pieces and grind it with the sesame seeds and ¹/₂ teaspoon chipotle flakes or red pepper flakes.

makes ¹/₂ cup

about curry spices and other spice mixtures

Fragrant, spicy, floral, sour, and sweet—these are the elements that shape not only a good Indian curry powder but also similar spice mixtures used the world around. Specific ingredients vary among countries, regions, recipes, and cooks, but there are several ingredients that nearly always play a role, including black and white peppercorns, and often, salt.

Turmeric, coriander, cumin, fenugreek, ginger, cloves, cinnamon, black peppercorns, and varying amounts of cayenne pepper are found in most Indian curry mixtures. Depending on the type—sweet or hot, from Madras or Goa, for vegetable stews or roasted meats—amounts of these and other ingredients will vary a great deal. White or brown mustard seed, nutmeg, fennel, paprika, and cardamom might appear. If you are new to curry powders, you will not want to make your own—it's not difficult, but it can be time consuming to locate high-quality spices and prepare them properly. You must also use them fairly quickly, or they will lose their aroma and potency. To become acquainted with curry powder, purchase commercial mixtures from small companies (see resources, page 216) that insure freshness.

Thai curries come in the form of pastes, with crushed fresh garlic, shallots, chiles, and fresh herbs. They, too, can be purchased, though if you fancy Thai cooking, you should take the time to make your own; they are superior to purchased types.

Classic African spice mixtures resemble, but are not identical to, Indian curries. One of the most classic European mixtures is *quatre épices*, made with white pepper, nutmeg, cloves, and ginger.

In the United States, too, there are several spice mixtures that shape our regional cuisines. The classic Cajun spice mixture (see page 93) used in gumbos, jambalayas, beans, and rice dishes relies on onion powder, garlic powder, paprika, finely ground black and white pepper, ground cumin, mustard flour, dried thyme, oregano, basil, cayenne, and salt. There are countless variations of this mixture, many of them rubs for barbecue and the typical New Orleans dish, blackened redfish.

Crab boil, with black pepper, mustard seed, dill seed, coriander, cloves, allspice, ginger, and bay leaf, is common from Maryland south to Louisiana. In the South, a mixture of black pepper, nutmeg, coriander, cumin seed, cloves, cinnamon, green cardamom seeds, paprika, and ground chiles is used as a rub for meats and vegetables to be grilled.

The most important element in all of these mixtures is freshness. The flavors of spices can lose their intensity fairly quickly once they are ground, so it is crucial to buy from a reliable source, store the spices properly in a cool, dark cupboard, and use them or replace them within about six months.

black peppercorn and
red onion vinegar

A clean wine bottle is the perfect container for storing this (or any) vinegar. Use it in vinaigrettes, in sauces, or spooned over raw oysters on the half shell.

3 red onions, thinly sliced

2 tablespoons whole black peppercorns

1 tablespoon kosher salt

1 tablespoon granulated sugar

3 1/2 cups champagne or white wine vinegar, medium (6 to 6 1/2 percent) acidity

Combine the onions, peppercorns, salt, and sugar in a medium, nonreactive bowl, cover, and set aside for 1 hour. Pour the vinegar over the onions, cover, and place in a cool, dark pantry or cupboard for 10 days. Strain, discard the onions and peppercorns, and strain the liquid again, using a coffee filter. Pour into a bottle, close with a cork, and use within 3 months.

makes about 3 cups

salted anchovies

If you happen upon some very fresh anchovies—an unlikely occurrence in the United States except in certain ethnic and specialty seafood markets—you can preserve them in salt. First, remove the heads, gut them, rinse them in cool water, and set them on a tea towel to drain. Place a layer of kosher salt 1/4-inch deep in the bottom of a nonporous, nonreactive container (a large, wide-mouthed canning jar works well), followed by a single layer of anchovies. Sprinkle generously with salt; repeat until you've layered all of the fish; end with a final quarter-inch layer of salt. Store in a cool, dark pantry. The anchovies will be ready to use in ten to fourteen days and will keep for several months.

mignonette

The word "mignonette" refers to coarsely cracked white peppercorns. It also is the name of the classic condiment served with raw oysters on the half shell, and that name likely refers to the pepper in the sauce. There are many versions of mignonette, made with sherry vinegar, balsamic vinegar, raspberry vinegar, or rice vinegar seasoned with ginger. If the vinegar is of good quality, the sauce will be good, though those with too aggressive a taste (sherry and balsamic vinegars, in my opinion) overpower the delicate sea flavors of an oyster, which seems to concentrate the ocean's salty aromas better than any other creature does. This recipe makes enough sauce for about four dozen small to medium oysters; each one needs just a scant half teaspoon of mignonette, enough for a tiny burst of peppery tartness to mingle with its natural saltiness.

½ teaspoon kosher salt or ¾ teaspoon Celtic gray sea salt
½ cup Vinaigre de Banyuls (see resources, page 216)
1 finely minced shallot (about 2 tablespoons)
½ teaspoon crushed white peppercorns
1 teaspoon crushed black peppercorns
2 tablespoons fresh lemon juice

Stir the salt into the vinegar and when it is dissolved, add the shallot, peppercorns, and lemon juice. Chill for 30 minutes before serving. Mignonette may be stored in the refrigerator for a week.

makes about ½ cup

peppercorn
oil

The volatile oils of the peppercorns infuse olive oil with a lusty heat and aroma; use this oil to make dressings and as a condiment where you want the flavor but not the texture of pepper. A buttery Ligurian olive oil is ideal for this recipe.

¹/₄ cup (¹/₄ ounce) Sichuan peppercorns

¹/₄ cup (1 ounce) white peppercorns

¹/₂ cup (2 ounces) black peppercorns

¹/₄ cup (¹/₂ ounce) dried green peppercorns

¹/₈ cup (¹/₄ ounce) whole coriander

3 cups mildly fruity olive oil

Toast the Sichuan peppercorns in a small dry sauté pan set over medium-low heat until they are fragrant, about 3 to 4 minutes. Remove them from the heat and let them cool. Put all the peppercorns and the coriander in a glass quart jar, pour the olive oil over the peppercorns, seal the jar with its lid, and place in a cool, dark cupboard for 2 to 3 weeks. Strain, store in a clean glass jar or bottle, and use within 3 months. Use the peppercorns to make a second batch of oil, letting it sit for 3 to 4 weeks before straining. Discard the peppercorns after making the second batch of oil.

makes 3 cups

green peppercorn mustard

I always use PIC Dijon (see resources, page 216) when I make flavored mustards. It's a perfectly balanced mustard, and fairly inexpensive. In its place, you can use Grey Poupon, although you might want to add 1 tablespoon mustard flour (such as Colman's) mixed with 2 teaspoons cold water to give it a little extra heat. This mustard, if refrigerated, will maintain peak flavor for about two weeks. Use it on sandwiches, with meatloaf, and with pâtés and meat terrines.

6 tablespoons Dijon mustard

2 teaspoons crushed dried green
 peppercorns

1 tablespoon whole dried green peppercorns

Combine the ingredients in a small bowl or glass jar, cover, and refrigerate overnight before using.

variation

Combine the mustard with ¼ cup best-quality mayonnaise; use as a condiment with salt-baked fish, cured sardines, and crudités.

makes about ⅓ cup

green peppercorn mayonnaise

This mayonnaise is excellent with gravlax (pages 65 and 66), with radishes, and on many sandwiches, from roasted eggplant and salami to BLTs and grilled salmon on focaccia.

½ cup mayonnaise, preferably homemade

1½ to 2 teaspoons crushed dried green
 peppercorns

1 teaspoon fresh minced lemon zest

In a small bowl, combine the mayonnaise with the peppercorns and lemon zest. Cover, refrigerate, and let rest for 30 minutes before serving.

variation

In place of the dried ones, use 2 teaspoons green peppercorns in brine, strained and crushed. Omit the lemon zest and add ¼ teaspoon each ground white pepper and ground black pepper.

makes ½ cup

black pepper dressing

Mary Sue Milliken and Susan Feniger have a version of this intensely flavored dressing in their book Mesa Mexicana; *they recommend spooning it over avocados, which is indeed quite wonderful. I use it as a dip for steamed artichokes, shrimp, and crudités, as a sauce for steamed or grilled fish, and as a dressing for certain salads, such as the Avocado, Grapefruit, and Chicken Salad on page 156.*

2 limes

2 teaspoons kosher salt

3 tablespoons black peppercorns,
   coarsely crushed

2/3 cup extra virgin olive oil

Peel the zest off one of the limes, mince it, and set it aside. Juice the two limes and combine the lime juice (about 3 tablespoons) and salt in a small bowl, stirring until the salt is dissolved. Add the peppercorns, lime zest, and olive oil, and set the dressing aside, covered, until ready to use.

variation

Use lemon juice and lemon zest in place of the lime.

makes about 2/3 cup

green peppercorn vinaigrette

Vinaigre de Banyuls, an aged white wine vinegar made in the south of France, is the best vinegar I have tasted. It is beautifully balanced, smooth, and full of complex flavors, an ideal vinegar to use in a dressing where it will play an important role.

2 tablespoons white wine vinegar, such as
   Vinaigre de Banyuls (see resources, page
   216) or Black Peppercorn and Red Onion
   Vinegar (page 167)

1 tablespoon minced chives or 1 small
   shallot, minced

2 teaspoons crushed dried green
   peppercorns

1/2 teaspoon crushed black peppercorns

1 to 2 teaspoons kosher salt

1 egg yolk, optional

1/3 to 1/2 cup extra virgin olive oil

In a small bowl, combine the vinegar, chives, peppercorns, and salt. Let the mixture sit for 15 minutes. Whisk in the egg yolk, if using; slowly whisk in the olive oil. Taste and correct the seasoning. Use immediately, or refrigerate, covered, until ready to use. Use within 3 or 4 days.

makes about 2/3 cup

creamy feta dressing

When this vinaigrette rests before serving, the flavors of the green peppercorns mingle with the creamy saltiness of the feta cheese. Although too thick to dress a leafy green salad, this is excellent served with crudités or as a dip for chilled artichokes.

3^1/$_2$ ounces feta cheese (Greek, Bulgarian, or French)

1 tablespoon red wine vinegar or sherry vinegar

1 tablespoon lemon juice

3 garlic cloves, crushed

2 teaspoons green peppercorns in brine, drained

1 teaspoon dried Greek oregano

1 teaspoon fresh snipped chives

^{3}/$_4$ teaspoon freshly cracked black pepper

^{1}/$_4$ cup sour cream

^{1}/$_3$ cup mayonnaise

^{1}/$_2$ teaspoon kosher salt

Put the feta in a small bowl and use a fork to break it up. Add the vinegar, lemon juice, green peppercorns, oregano, garlic, and black pepper and mix together until smooth. (Alternatively, place the ingredients in the work bowl of a food processor, pulse until smooth, and transfer to a small bowl.) Add the olive oil, mix thoroughly, and add the salt. Let the dressing rest for at least 30 minutes before serving. Store, covered, in the refrigerator for 2 or 3 days.

makes about ^{2}/$_3$ cup

sorrel butter

We have grown accustomed to salted butter because, for decades, salting was the primary method of extending the life of butter, which goes rancid fairly quickly at room temperature. With modern refrigeration, it is no longer essential to salt butter, but we are used to its taste and so most commercial butter is salted. If you live in dairy country, as I do, you don't have to worry about the butter in local markets being old, but if you live where the butter you buy may have been shipped a distance, you are insured of a fresher product if you buy unsalted butter.

1/2 cup (1 stick) unsalted butter, at room
    temperature
2 teaspoons minced shallot
3/4 cup finely shredded sorrel
1 tablespoon flat-leaf parsley leaves
1 teaspoon lemon zest
1/2 teaspoon popcorn salt (see glossary,
    page 221) or 3/4 teaspoon kosher salt
Black pepper

Heat 1 tablespoon of the butter in a small sauté pan, add the shallot, and sauté over medium-low heat until limp and fragrant, about 5 minutes. Add the sorrel and sauté, stirring continuously, until it is limp. Remove from the heat and let cool to room temperature. Place the cooled sorrel mixture, parsley, lemon zest, and remaining butter in a food processor, and pulse until the mixture is smooth and evenly mixed. Add the salt, several turns of black pepper, taste, and correct the seasoning if necessary.

Transfer to a large sheet of plastic wrap, mold into a log about 1 inch in diameter, and wrap tightly. Chill thoroughly before using. To serve, slice off thin coins of the butter, which will keep in the refrigerator for 4 to 5 days, or up to a month in the freezer.

makes about 1/2 cup

olive and artichoke
tapenade

Tapenade is one of the classic salty condiments of southern Europe, made in one version or another virtually everywhere olives are grown. It might be a smooth purée, it might be chunky, but it almost always includes brine-cured olives, garlic, and anchovies. In this version two other ingredients common to Provence and northern Italy, artichokes and walnuts, are added and combined with green peppercorns for a chunky sauce that is excellent on crostini or tossed with hot pasta.

1 tablespoon kosher salt

3 large artichokes

1 tablespoon olive oil

3 garlic cloves

2 or 3 anchovy fillets, drained

2 teaspoons green peppercorns in brine, drained

1 teaspoon minced lemon zest

1 tablespoon fresh lemon juice

$^1/_2$ cup extra virgin olive oil

1 cup (6 ounces) cracked green olives, pitted and minced

$^1/_4$ cup (2 ounces) walnut pieces, toasted and minced

1 tablespoon flat-leaf parsley, minced

Black pepper in a mill

Fill a large pot two-thirds full with water, add the salt, and bring to a boil over high heat. Using kitchen shears, snip off the tips of the outer leaves of the artichokes. Drizzle a little of the olive oil in the center of each artichoke and place them in the boiling water. Return to a boil, cover, reduce the heat, and simmer until the artichokes are tender, from 20 to 40 minutes, depending on their size and age.

Meanwhile, use a *suribachi* or mortar and pestle to grind the garlic and anchovies together until they form a smooth paste. Fold in the green peppercorns, lemon zest and juice, and olive oil, scraping the sides of the bowl as you mix. Set aside.

Transfer the artichokes to a colander or strainer, rinse them under cool water, drain thoroughly, and let them cool. When they are cool enough to handle, remove all of the leaves, reserving them for another use. Use a teaspoon or a small, sharp paring knife to cut away the choke in the center of each artichoke heart. Discard the chokes and cut the hearts into $^1/_4$-inch dice.

In a medium bowl, combine the diced artichoke hearts, olives, walnuts, and olive oil mixture. Add the parsley and several turns of black pepper. Taste and season with salt. Let the tapenade rest 30 minutes before serving.

makes about 2$^1/_4$ cups

jalapeño
pickles

This recipe came to me from Mexico, by way of my friend (and former restaurant coworker) Patrick Bouquet, who got it from his wife's aunt. She is used to the slightly moist sea salt from Baja California, which is difficult to find here. The crucial factor is that she is familiar with the size and feel of the salt and measures only with her fingers. "Three generous pinches" is how Patrick described it as he watched her make the spicy pickles. Korean sea salt, which is very moist and with about the same size crystals as Celtic gray sea salt, is a good alternative. It's easy to find in Asian markets and sells for about a dollar for two pounds. Serve them as a condiment with a Mexican meal or, on a hot night, as one of several Mexican appetizers, with a pitcher of Margaritas or plenty of cold beer.

18 medium jalapeño chiles, or 30 serrano
  chiles

3 tablespoons mild olive oil

4 to 5 large garlic cloves

2 teaspoons coarse, moist sea salt,
  such as Celtic gray or Korean

1 cup apple cider vinegar

2 tablespoons dried oregano

1 tablespoon dried thyme

2 tablespoons dried marjoram

3 to 4 bay leaves

3 to 4 carrots, peeled and sliced on bias

1 sliced yellow onion

Using a sharp paring knife, make two lengthwise slits from end to end in each jalapeño. (If using serranos, pierce each pepper in several places with a fork.) Heat the oil in a large heavy frying pan set over medium-low heat. Add the peppers and garlic, and sweat them, turning frequently, until the peppers begin to soften slightly and release their aroma, about 15 minutes. (Do not let the garlic burn.) Add the salt and vinegar. Agitate the pan and, when the salt is dissolved, add 1 cup of water, the oregano, thyme, marjoram, and bay leaves, and bring to a boil. Reduce the heat and simmer the jalapeños until they turn greenish yellow. Add the carrots and onion, remove the pan from the heat, and allow the mixture to cool to room temperature. Pack into a glass quart jar, pour all of the liquid over the vegetables, and seal the jar. These pickles will keep, refrigerated, for several months.

makes about 1 quart

bread and butter
pickles

Taste in pickles is remarkably personal. Who knows why you prefer crunchy sweet pickles seasoned with garlic while I crave salty kosher dills? As a kid, one of my favorite snacks was the big dill pickles I could buy for fifteen cents from the butcher counter at the little market around the corner. It wasn't until I was an adult that I developed a taste for these salty-sweet bread and butter pickles, which are one of the easier pickles to make at home. True dill and kosher pickles require lengthy brining in steady temperatures that are often difficult to maintain at home.

1 gallon (about 5 pounds) pickling
    cucumbers, sliced ¼ inch thick

4 cups (about 4) yellow onions, peeled
    and cut into ⅜-inch lengthwise slices

1½ cups kosher salt

1 quart apple cider vinegar

3 thin slices fresh ginger

3 cups granulated sugar

1 tablespoon black peppercorns

1 tablespoon celery seeds

1 tablespoon white mustard seeds

1 tablespoon ground turmeric

Place the cucumbers and onions in a large bowl. Sprinkle 1 cup of the salt over them, cover with plastic, and add a weight, such as a heavy ceramic plate. Refrigerate overnight. Drain, rinse in cool water, and drain again, letting the vegetables sit in a strainer or colander until no more liquid leaches out.

In a large pot, combine the remaining ½ cup salt, vinegar, ginger, sugar, peppercorns, celery seed, mustard seed, and turmeric, set over medium heat, and stir continuously until the salt and sugar are dissolved. Reduce the heat to low, add the cucumbers and onions a large handful at a time, stir very gently and quickly, heat through, and remove from the heat. Cool slightly and pack into sterilized pint glass jars. Cover with the cooking liquid, seal the jars, and process in a boiling-water bath for 15 minutes (see note). Remove the jars from the bath, let them cool, and check the seals. Let the pickles mature in a cool, dark pantry for a couple of weeks before using. If the seal is not secure, if the lid bulges, or if the pickles have an off smell, discard the pickles.

note

For canning be sure that the canning jars are sterilized in boiling water immediately before they are used. Fill them to within half an inch of the top of the jar. Use new seals and rings to close the jars. To process canned foods in a water bath, the water should come two inches above the jars. It is best to use a canning pot fitted with a rack; if jars come in contact with the bottom of the pot, they can crack. A rack will also keep the jars upright. Use tongs to remove jars from the pot, and set them on a wooden cutting board or a tea towel to cool. After they are cooled, check the seals by tapping on the top; if it sounds dull, the jar probably needs to be re-processed or else stored in the refrigerator and used within a few days. Never taste canned foods with bulging lids; discard them immediately.

makes 6 to 8 pints

asian
salt eggs

Salt eggs, made with duck or chicken eggs, are found throughout China and Southeast Asia. In Malaysia, I found baskets of what looked like black golf balls; they were salted chicken eggs with a thick coat of black ash to preserve them further. Most of the ash is easily brushed off, and then the eggs can be soaked in cool water for a few minutes; wipe the wet eggs clean with a tea towel. The eggs are then hard-cooked, shelled, and served as an accompaniment to a variety of dishes. They may also be topped with a dressing of garlic, shallots, serranos, and lime juice, and served as a simple salad. They can also be fried. Although we no longer need this technique to preserve eggs, it produces a pleasantly intense flavor that is not duplicated by merely adding salt to fresh eggs.

1¼ cups kosher salt or 1 cup pickling salt
(see glossary, page 221)
4 quarts water
12 eggs

Combine the salt and water in a large pot, bring to a boil, remove from the heat, and let cool completely. Place the eggs in a large earthenware or glass jar, pour the brine over the eggs, cover the jar with a tight-fitting lid, and store in a cool, dark cupboard or pantry for at least 4 weeks and up to 3 months.

To use the eggs, boil them in tap water for about 12 minutes, until hard-cooked. Remove from the water, briefly rinse under cool water, and peel. Cut the eggs in quarters and use as a garnish, or use in specific recipes.

makes 1 dozen

spicy salt
egg sauce

This sauce, Thai in origin, is so good, one of those enticing combinations of flavors that calls out to you from the refrigerator at odd hours. Be careful, or you won't have any actually to serve. Although the sauce is most intense when made with salted eggs, you can make a good version with fresh eggs; just add more salt. I use salt egg sauce on baked and grilled fish; it is also an excellent condiment with simple steamed rice, Salted Mustard Greens (page 184), and sliced summer tomatoes.

4 Salt Eggs (page 178) or 4 fresh eggs, hard-
 cooked and cooled

3 cilantro (coriander) roots, washed and
 trimmed

4 garlic cloves

2 serrano chiles, chopped

2 shallots, chopped

1 teaspoon dried shrimp paste

2 teaspoons sugar

2 tablespoons fish sauce

Juice of 2 limes

2 scallions, white and green part, trimmed
 and minced

Shell the eggs, separate the whites from the yolks, and set the whites aside for another use. Press the yolks through a sieve, grate them on the small blade of a grater, or mash them with a fork.

Using a mortar and pestle or a *suribachi,* grind the cilantro roots and garlic until they form a paste. Add the serranos and shallots and continue to grind to incorporate them into an almost smooth paste. Add the shrimp paste and sugar, mix thoroughly, and then use a rubber spatula to fold in the egg yolks. Stir in the fish sauce and lime juice, transfer to a small serving bowl, and fold in the scallions. Cover the sauce and let it rest at room temperature for 30 minutes before serving.

makes about ¹/₂ cup

sarawak
sambal

I first tasted this condiment in the test kitchen of the Pepper Marketing Board in Kuching, the capital of Sarawak, Malaysia. Moments before, I had been handed a jar of Creamy White Pepper, which fell out of my hands as I removed the lid to smell the pepper. Glass shattered, peppercorns darted all over the floor of the immaculate laboratory, I was mortified, and my charming host quickly shifted our attention to a selection of condiments that Shazat Khan, the PMB's chef, had developed. This was my favorite.

Dried anchovies are common throughout Asia and they are very different from the canned anchovies we are used to in the West. Look for them in Asian markets, as you will not get the proper flavor if you used canned or even salted ones.

1 cup (1¹/₂ ounces) dried anchovies

4 large shallots

2 teaspoons kosher salt

5 garlic cloves

¹/₄ cup (1¹/₂ ounces) green peppercorns in brine, drained

¹/₃ cup mild olive oil, or other mild vegetable oil

1 teaspoon sugar

1 tablespoon rice vinegar

Soak the anchovies in cool water for at least 30 minutes, drain, and set them aside on a tea towel to dry. Using a *suribachi* or mortar and pestle, crush the shallots and 1 teaspoon of the salt together, add the garlic and peppercorns, and grind to a paste. Heat the oil in a medium sauté pan and fry the anchovies until they are almost crisp; remove them from the pan with a slotted spoon and set them aside. Sauté the shallot mixture in the same oil, stirring continuously, until it is very fragrant and beginning to brown; do not allow it to burn. Stir in the remaining teaspoon of salt, the sugar, and the vinegar, remove from the heat, and add the anchovies. Serve immediately, or refrigerate, covered, for up to 5 days.

makes about ²/₃ cup

raisin, onion, and green peppercorn chutney

A chutney is an ideal dish to highlight the tangy flavor of green peppercorns preserved in brine; their flavor merges perfectly with the vinegar in the chutney and the peppercorns themselves provide spicy bursts of flavor in this hot-sweet condiment. Serve this chutney as you would any traditional cooked chutney, with curries, biryani, and tandoori meats. It is also excellent with American-style grilled and roasted meats and poultry.

1 pound raisins

1 1/2 cups (12 ounces) sugar

2 1/2 cups apple cider vinegar

2 medium yellow onions, halved and
thinly sliced

8 large garlic cloves, minced

One 2-inch piece of ginger (about 1 inch
in diameter) peeled and cut into very
small julienne

2 tablespoons green peppercorns in brine

1 teaspoon red pepper flakes

1 teaspoon kosher salt

One 3-inch piece of cinnamon

3 whole cardamom pods

3 whole cloves

In a large nonreactive pot, combine the raisins, sugar, vinegar, onion, and garlic, and set over medium heat. Bring to a boil and stir continuously until the sugar is dissolved. Add the ginger, peppercorns, red pepper, salt, cinnamon, cardamom, and cloves, reduce the heat to low, cover, and simmer until the raisins are tender and the chutney very thick, about 2 hours. Ladle into hot clean jars and store in the refrigerator for up to 3 months, or ladle into sterilized jars and process in a hot-water bath (see note about canning, page 177). Cool, check seals, and store in a cool dark cupboard. Refrigerate after opening.

makes about 4 cups

preserved lemons

Salty, tangy lemons, preserved in salt, vinegar, oil, or their own juice, have been a traditional element in North African cooking for centuries. They might be served alongside a savory tagine or minced and folded into the stew itself. They might be part of a platter of appetizers, to be enjoyed for their own distinctive flavor.

I've experimented with every technique I've come across and this recipe, a combination of two methods, produces lemons I like very much. Try to find organic lemons and if you can't, wash and rinse the skins of your lemons thoroughly to remove any chemical residue. It is also important to realize from the start that the process takes a minimum of a week, so you can't begin in the morning and have preserved lemons for dinner, though if you're desperate, you can mince a clean, whole lemon, mix it with a tablespoon of kosher salt, set it aside, covered, for the day, and use it as you would preserved lemons in a recipe. Brining the fruit for several days before preserving them softens their skin, leaches out some of the pectin, and results in a slightly milder preserved lemon.

12 to 16 lemons, depending on their size

1 cup kosher salt

3 tablespoons sugar

1 teaspoon whole black peppercorns

2 bay leaves, optional

Thoroughly wash between 8 and 12 of the lemons (the number will depend on their size; as many whole lemons as will, when cut into wedges, fill a quart jar), and place them in a large crock or glass bowl. (The remaining lemons will be used for their juice.) Dissolve 1 tablespoon of the salt in a quart of water and pour it over the lemons. If it does not cover the lemons, mix more brine (using the same ratio of salt to water) and pour it over until they are covered. Cover the crock and set it aside for 1 day. (You can make the preserved lemons at this point, or you can cover them with new brine daily for up to 7 days.)

Rinse and dry the brined lemons. Cut each lemon lengthwise into 6 to 8 wedges. Place them in a large bowl and top with ¾ cup of the remaining salt, the sugar, and the peppercorns. Toss thoroughly and pack into a sterilized quart glass jar, tucking in the bay leaves about halfway through filling the jar. Juice the reserved lemons and pour the juice over the lemon wedges. If necessary, add fresh water until the lemons are covered completely. Cover the jar with heavy-duty plastic wrap and then seal with its lid.

Set the jar of lemons in a cool, dark cupboard for a week, giving it a good shaking once or twice a day. At the end of a week, move the jar to the refrigerator and use the preserved lemons within two or three months.

makes 1 quart

For decades, Imwalle Gardens, a farm and fruit stand founded in Sonoma County, California, in 1886, made its own sauerkraut using huge cabbages—weighing up to twenty pounds each—shredded and then fermented in large oak barrels. Customers came from all over to purchase the sauerkraut, which was scooped out to order. Although there had never been a problem with contamination, revised health department regulations required that the Imwalles switch to expensive stainless-steel containers; instead of changing, they quit making their sauerkraut and eventually the specific recipe was lost.

Today, commercial cabbage weighs a fraction of what it did then, when making sauerkraut was a common practice. You can still do it, though, and in small quantities if you like. The cabbage must be completely submerged in the brine; if there is not enough liquid initially, add brine (1 1/2 tablespoons salt to 1 quart water). To keep the cabbage submerged, put one plastic bag inside another, fill the inner bag with water, close it tightly, and set it on top of a clean plate set directly over the cabbage; this will both seal and weight the cabbage. A friend adds caraway seeds, and occasionally grated carrots, to the cabbage when he makes sauerkraut; I generally add seasonings and other ingredients just before serving.

1 large white cabbage, about 3 pounds
1 ounce kosher salt and more as needed

Remove any bruised outer leaves of the cabbage, core it, and slice it into very thin strips. In a large bowl, toss together the shredded cabbage and salt and let sit for 30 minutes. Pack the cabbage and its juices into a glass or porcelain container (a soufflé dish works perfectly); press down so that the juices completely cover the cabbage. Weight with a clean plate and a double plastic bag of water and set in a dark, moderately warm place. The cabbage will begin to ferment at between 68 and 70°F; it will take between 5 and 6 weeks for the fermentation to be complete. When done, use immediately or pack into jars and process in a water bath (see note about canning, page 177). Before serving the sauerkraut, simmer it for 10 minutes.

makes about 1 quart

salted mustard
greens

In the outdoor markets of Asia, there are often plastic tubs of greens preserved in brine—bok choy, cabbage, and sometimes greens it is hard for a Westerner to recognize. I came across a variation of this recipe, made with tangy mustard greens and the starchy liquid drained from cooked rice, in the delightful book Filipino Cuisine *by Gerry Gelle. You can serve these greens as a side dish, add them to soup, or chop them and stir them into rice, as on page 97.*

2 pounds mustard greens, washed and dried

1/2 cup kosher salt

1/4 cup white rice

Combine the mustard greens and the salt in a large bowl, tossing them together well. Let the greens sit for an hour and then squeeze out all the liquid.

Rinse the white rice in running water until the water runs clear. Place the rice in a medium saucepan, add 4 cups of water, set over medium heat, and bring to a boil. Lower the heat, cover, and simmer for about 30 minutes. Strain the rice, saving the cooking liquid. Reserve the rice for another use and set the rice water aside to cool.

Pack the greens into a sterile pint glass jar. Pour the cooled rice water over the greens, cover with plastic wrap, and seal the jar. Age in a cool cupboard for 3 weeks.

Place in the refrigerator and use within six weeks.

makes about 1 pint

yogurt
cheese

Making cheese from yogurt is extremely easy, and produces very good results very quickly, especially if you enjoy tangy flavors. You will need clean cheesecloth to make this cheese, and you will need a place to suspend the bag while the whey drips out. I close the cheesecloth with a length of twine and then tie the twine to one of my kitchen cupboard doorknobs, which works fine as long as I don't absentmindedly pull the door open. (Even then, the cheese is soft enough that it doesn't leave a bruise.) Use yogurt cheese as you would cream cheese; I find it especially good on toast.

Shortly before Salt & Pepper *went to the printer, I received an e-mail from Gordon and Doris Weir of Santa Rosa, California, telling me of their visit to Katmandu and of their search for authentic Nepalese food among the pizzerias and burger joints that line the major thoroughfare of Durbar Marg. They found what they were looking for, and after enjoying a particularly good dessert made with yogurt cheese, sugar, black pepper, and other spices, they were asked if they would like the recipe. They said yes, of course, and when it was brought to the table it came with a bill for 100 rupiah (about 60 cents). The dessert, called* sikarni, *is included here in the variation at the end of this recipe.*

1 tablespoon kosher salt or fine sea salt

2 pounds plain, unflavored lowfat (not nonfat) yogurt

Stir the salt into the yogurt. Line a large strainer or colander with 4 layers of cheesecloth and pour the yogurt into it. Gather up with edges of the cheesecloth and tie it with twine close to the yogurt. Suspend the bag over a bowl or other container to catch the whey; it should be away from direct sunlight or heat. Let the cheesecloth hang for between 24 and 36 hours, until no more whey drips from the cheese. Remove the cheese from its cheesecloth bag and store, covered, in the refrigerator. The cheese will keep for at least 10 days.

variation

To make sikarni, mix together 1¼ cups yogurt cheese, 1 cup sugar, 2 tablespoons raisins, 1 tablespoon grated coconut, 1 tablespoon chopped dried dates, 2 teaspoons cracked black peppercorns, ½ teaspoon ground cinnamon, ¼ teaspoon ground cardamom, and ⅛ teaspoon saffron that has been dissolved in a teaspoon of water. Chill and serve.

makes about 1¼ cups

When I was a child I often saw friends reach for a salt shaker whenever we ate watermelon or cantaloupe. The salt made it sweeter, they always said, and although I don't agree, I do like a few grains on a pippin apple. A friend from the Midwest tells me that her father taught her to sprinkle pepper over slices of cantaloupe, or muskmelon; she still swears by the combination, which works equally well on pears, papaya, and mango.

Using salt and pepper to accent the flavors of fruit (and other sweets) has a long history. Salt is used to boost the flavors of countless desserts; a few sweets, saltwater taffy, for example, rely on saltiness in addition to sweetness for their characteristic taste.

Adding white or black pepper to desserts was commonplace in Roman and medieval times; from simple fruit syrups to puddings, cakes, and cookies, pepper contributed a sultry, lusty dimension to sweets. Although the practice had all but disappeared in the early twentieth century, it began to reemerge as jalapeños, serranos, and other hot chiles began making their way into desserts. Increasingly, professional chefs and bakers began to discover the suave, subtle characteristics of the peppercorn, which enhances rather than dominates a sweet dish.

roasted strawberries
with black pepper

Serve these strawberries with vanilla bean
ice cream, black pepper ice cream, or a spoon-
ful of mascarpone, and with cookies such as
biscotti or spicy sugar cookies alongside.

2 pint baskets strawberries, stems removed

3 tablespoons sugar

1 tablespoon freshly ground black pepper

2 tablespoons balsamic vinegar

Rinse the strawberries in cool water, place in a strainer or colander, and shake off most of the water. Slice the strawberries about $1/8$ inch thick, place them in a large bowl, and sprinkle them with the sugar. Cover and refrigerate for at least 1 hour and up to 4 hours.

Preheat the oven to 375°F. Toss the strawberries with the black pepper, add the balsamic vinegar, and put the strawberries and all of their juices into a large sauté pan or a large oven-proof dish. Roast for 8 to 10 minutes, until the juices are bubbling and the strawberries are hot but not mushy. Divide among individual dishes and serve immediately.

serves 4

a salt & pepper cookbook

chilled
pear soup

Fruit soups are particularly refreshing as dessert following a rich, spicy meal. The peppercorns in this soup are not overpowering, but rather add a sultry, sexy dimension to the delicate pears. This dessert might not delight those who crave a rich, gooey, chocolatey indulgence to conclude a meal, but anyone else will be pleased by its lightness. For a slightly more elaborate dessert, serve some Roquefort cheese, at room temperature, alongside. Because tastes are pure and pristine in a fruit soup, use spring water if your tap water has off-flavors.

4 ripe Bartlett pears, peeled, cored, and
    sliced
2 slices fresh ginger
2 teaspoons whole black peppercorns
$1/2$ teaspoon whole white peppercorns
2 cardamom seeds (not pods)
Tiny pinch of salt
1 cup fruity (not sweet) white wine, chilled
2 tablespoons fresh mint leaves, cut into
    thin strips

Place the pears, ginger, peppercorns, and cardamom seeds in a saucepan, and add $2^{1}/2$ cups water. Bring to a boil over medium heat, reduce the heat to low, and simmer until the pears are tender, about 15 minutes. Remove from the heat and cool the pears in the liquid.

Remove and discard the ginger slices. Use a slotted spoon to remove the pears from the cooking liquid; pass them through a fine sieve or food mill fitted with the smallest blade. Strain the cooking water, discard the peppers and seeds, and stir it into the pear purée. Chill the mixture for at least 3 hours or overnight.

Stir the wine into the pear purée. Ladle into soup plates, garnish with mint leaves, and serve immediately.

serves 4

fruit roasted in salt with black pepper ice cream

Both Madeleine Kamman and her famous protégé, the chef Jimmy Schmidt, have written recipes for salt-roasted fruit; Madeleine credits Jimmy with being the first to apply to fruit this ancient technique for cooking meats. I first tried the method using pears, with the salt preheated in the oven. The pears quickly became so soft they were impossible to extract from their cozy salt bed. One summer when I had an abundance of excellent white peaches, I wrapped the fruit first in French lavender stems (which are more pliable than those of English lavender) and used room-temperature rather than hot salt. Thirty minutes later I had the most succulent peaches with just a subtle hint of lavender aroma and flavor. If you have excellent fruit, you won't need to add a thing to them; if your peaches, nectarines, or pears aren't as sweet as they could be, sprinkle them with a little bit of sugar after slicing them. You can also use grape leaves to wrap the fruit.

4 ripe white or yellow peaches, white or yellow nectarines, or ripe pears

8 to 12 thin branches, each about 10 inches long, of French lavender

6 pounds (2 boxes) kosher salt or sea salt

1 pint Black Pepper Ice Cream (page 192) or commercial French vanilla ice cream

Preheat the oven to 375°F. Wash the fruit and dry it thoroughly. Wrap each piece of fruit in 2 or 3 branches of lavender, covering as much of the surface of the fruit as possible. Pour 1 inch of salt into a deep pot; place the fruit on top of the salt, leaving at least an inch of space between each piece. Carefully cover the fruit with salt until it is completely buried. Bake the fruit in the oven for 20 minutes for peaches, nectarines, or Bosc pears, 25 to 30 minutes for firm Comice pears.

Remove the pot from the oven and set it aside for 10 minutes. Carefully extract the fruit by pushing away the salt from the top and then tugging on the branches of lavender to pull out the fruit. Remove the lavender and use a pastry brush to brush off any salt. Let the fruit cool until it is easy to handle and then peel it carefully. Slice the fruit, divide it among 4 dessert dishes, and top with 2 scoops of black pepper ice cream. Serve immediately.

serves 4

pineapple granita
with black pepper

The inspiration for this dish comes from my visit to Sarawak, one of the thirteen states of Malaysia. Looking through the cookbook Sarawak Pepper, *published by the Pepper Marketing Board of Malaysia, I saw a photograph of pineapple studded with black pepper and knew instantly how wonderfully the flavors would fit together. That night, I scattered some crushed black pepper over sliced pineapple and my suspicions were confirmed. My recipe is adapted from one in the book.*

1 medium (about 3½ pounds) ripe pineapple,
    peeled and cored
Black pepper in a mill
1 cup Simple Syrup with Pepper
    (recipe follows)
Juice of 2 lemons
Sprigs of fresh mint

Set aside about 8 ounces of the pineapple. Cut the remaining pineapple into ¼-inch slices, arrange them on a plate, grind pepper over the slices, cover the plate tightly with plastic wrap, and refrigerate.

Coarsely chop the reserved pineapple and purée it in a food processor or food mill. Place it in a bowl, stir in the simple syrup and lemon juice, place in a shallow pan, and put it in the freezer until it is nearly frozen. Remove from the freezer, mix with a fork to break it up, and return to the freezer until it is completely frozen.

To serve, place several slices of chilled pineapple on individual serving plates and top with a generous spoonful of the granita. Garnish with a mint leaf and serve immediately.

simple syrup with pepper

2 cups sugar
1 teaspoon crushed white peppercorns
1 teaspoon whole black peppercorns

Combine the sugar, white peppercorns, and 1 cup water in a small heavy saucepan set over high heat; do not stir. Bring to a boil, reduce the heat, and simmer for 4 to 5 minutes, until the sugar is completely dissolved and the syrup transparent. Remove from the heat, add the black peppercorns, cover, and cool to room temperature. Strain into a glass jar, cover, refrigerate, and use as needed.

serves 6 to 8

Dulce de leche *is common throughout Mexico and South America, where it is served in small portions as a pudding or as a sauce for fruit. It is almost sinfully delicious, something that is extremely difficult to stop eating. One of the best versions I've had was made by the Bodega Goat Cheese Company with nothing more than sugar and goat's milk. When I make it, I use goat's milk when I can get it very fresh, I use salt to heighten the flavors, and add some black pepper for a little aromatic pungency.* Dulce de leche *will keep for several weeks in the refrigerator.*

2 quarts fresh goat's milk or whole cow's milk

2$\frac{1}{2}$ cups sugar

$\frac{3}{4}$ teaspoon kosher salt

1 vanilla bean

1 tablespoon whole black peppercorns, tied in a spice bag

Combine all of the ingredients in a large, heavy saucepan, set over medium heat, and stir until the sugar is completely dissolved and the mixture begins to thicken, about 30 minutes. Remove the spice bag and the vanilla bean (which can be rinsed, dried, and used again), and reduce the heat to low. Cook, stirring frequently, until the mixture is very, very thick and turns a golden, caramelized color, about 2 $\frac{1}{2}$ hours. Remove from the heat and stir as the mixture cools. Chill, covered, before serving in small, espresso-size cups.

serves 10 to 12

a salt & pepper cookbook

black pepper
ice cream

Ice cream spiked with black pepper has become very popular in restaurants in the 1990s, yet it has ancient roots. Two thousand years ago, pepper, along with many other spices, was a common ingredient in custards and other desserts.

4 cups half-and-half

1 tablespoon black peppercorns,
   coarsely cracked

Half a vanilla bean, split open

³/₄ cup sugar

4 egg yolks

2 teaspoons freshly ground black pepper

¹/₂ teaspoon kosher salt

Scald the half-and-half in a medium saucepan over medium-high heat. Remove from the heat, add the cracked peppercorns and vanilla bean, cover, and let the mixture steep for 30 minutes. Strain into a clean saucepan, discard the peppercorns, and set aside the vanilla bean (it may be rinsed, dried, and used again).

In a medium bowl, whisk together the sugar and egg yolks, whipping vigorously until the mixture is pale yellow and forms a ribbon when dropped from a spoon. Stir in the ground pepper and salt, and whisk the mixture into the half-and-half. Set the saucepan over medium-low heat and stir constantly until the custard thickens.

Remove from the heat immediately and whisk until the mixture cools slightly. Cover tightly with plastic wrap and refrigerate until thoroughly chilled.

Freeze in an ice cream maker according to the manufacturer's instructions. Store, tightly covered, in the freezer until ready to serve.

makes about 1¹/₂ quarts

red hot
cookies

These cookies are too spicy for most children's palates, but adults love the bright, sharp kick provided by a blend of salt, pepper, and spices.

1 ½ cups butter, at room temperature

1 cup sugar

2 whole large eggs or 4 egg yolks, beaten

1 teaspoon vanilla extract

2 teaspoons grated fresh ginger

3 ¾ cups all-purpose flour

1 tablespoon kosher salt

1 teaspoon finely ground white pepper

1 teaspoon finely ground black pepper

2 teaspoons hot mustard flour (such as
   Colman's)

1 teaspoon ground ginger

½ teaspoon cayenne pepper

1 egg white

Red Hot Sugar (see note)

Using a heavy-duty whisk or an electric mixer, cream together the butter and sugar. Add the eggs, vanilla, and fresh ginger, and mix thoroughly. In a separate bowl, combine the flour, salt, pepper, mustard, ground ginger, and cayenne. Add the flour mixture, one half at a time, to the butter mixture, and mix together thoroughly. Press the dough into a ball, wrap it in plastic, and chill for at least 2 hours.

To make the cookies, remove the dough from the refrigerator 30 minutes before rolling it out. Preheat the oven to 350° F. Cut the dough into 3 equal pieces. Use the palms of your hands to roll out the dough on a lightly floured surface until it forms a rope about 1 ¼ inches in diameter. Using a very sharp knife, slice the dough into ¼-inch-thick rounds and set them about 1 inch apart on an ungreased baking sheet. Mix the egg white with 2 tablespoons of water and brush the surface of each cookie lightly with the mixture; sprinkle with Red Hot Sugar. Bake for 7 to 9 minutes, until the cookies just barely begin to color. Remove from the oven and cool on a rack. Serve immediately or store in an airtight container.

note

To make 1 cup Red Hot Sugar, combine 1 cup granulated sugar and ¼ teaspoon (or more to taste) cayenne and place in a container with a lid. Add several drops of red food coloring, close the container, and shake it until the sugar is evenly colored. Repeat until the sugar is intensely colored. Colored sugar will keep indefinitely in a tightly sealed container.

makes about 7 dozen cookies

a salt & pepper cookbook

193

walnut
pfeffernüsse

*Nearly everyone I know remembers a grand-
mother or aunt making a version of these
classic holiday cookies. Pepper is a traditional
ingredient, though I've added a little extra
to the powdered sugar that coats the cookies
after they've been made.*

2 cups all-purpose flour

3/4 teaspoon ground cardamom

1/2 teaspoon ground cinnamon

1/2 teaspoon kosher salt

1/2 teaspoon freshly ground black pepper

1/4 teaspoon freshly ground white pepper

1/4 teaspoon freshly ground nutmeg

1/8 teaspoon ground cloves

3/4 teaspoon baking powder

1/8 teaspoon baking soda

4 ounces (1/2 cup) unsalted butter

1/3 cup sugar

1 egg

2 teaspoons freshly minced lemon zest

1/4 teaspoon vanilla extract

1/2 cup walnut halves, minced

1/2 cup light molasses

1/4 cup brandy

1 tablespoon lemon juice

1 cup powdered sugar

1 teaspoon finely ground white pepper

In a large bowl, sift together the flour, cardamom, cinnamon, salt, peppers, nutmeg,
cloves, baking powder, and baking soda. Set
aside.

Using a heavy-duty whisk or an electric
mixer, combine the butter and sugar until light
and fluffy. Add the egg, lemon zest, and vanilla,
and mix thoroughly. Fold in the walnuts. In a
separate bowl, combine the molasses, brandy,
and lemon juice.

Add one third of the flour mixture to the butter mixture, mix thoroughly, and add one third
of the molasses mixture. Continue, alternating
additions, until all the ingredients have been
combined. Cover tightly with plastic wrap and
refrigerate the dough for several hours or
overnight.

Sift together the powdered sugar and finely
ground pepper. Set aside. Preheat the oven to
350°F; lightly butter a baking sheet. Using a
teaspoon or a melon-ball cutter, make 1 1/4-inch
balls and set them 1 inch apart on the buttered
baking sheet. Bake for 12 minutes, until the
cookies just begin to take on color. Remove the
pan from the oven, let the cookies cool slightly,
and roll them in the powdered sugar mixture.
Let the cookies cool completely; store in a
sealed container until ready to serve.

makes about 12 dozen cookies

During 1998 several of my friends visited Tibet. Each time one returned, I asked: "How was the tea?" Usually, they would mumble something about being tired of yak butter and change the topic to the spectacular landscape or vanishing culture. It was hard to get a direct answer.

"You certainly drink gallons of it," Forrest Tancer, the winemaker at Iron Horse Vineyards, commented shortly after his return from a long trek, "and you're really happy to have it after hiking."

The tea in question is a mild black tea flavored with butter and salt. I've had it in the United States, and I must confess that I found little to recommend it, though I suspect this is because of context. Traditional beverages exist not only because certain ingredients are available in a specific location, but also because those ingredients fill certain needs, in Tibet, for instance, the need for energy and warmth, the need for sufficient fat, the need for salt. Tibetan-style tea, with butter made from cow's milk rather than from yak's milk, is available in restaurants in this country, but it may take a visit to Tibet to understand exactly why the beverage is so widely consumed.

It took just one sip of limeade in Malaysia for me to understand its appeal. In tropical countries, it is crucial to replenish your body's supply of salt, which is constantly being depleted through sweat. A pinch of salt in a cool drink is an efficient way to do this, and the beverage itself is a yummy combination of sweet, sour, and salty flavors. I make it at home all the time, especially in hot weather.

Tea-drinking habits in India were influenced by decades of the British Raj. Black tea sweetened with sugar and smoothed with milk is ubiquitous in both Great Britain and India, but the Indians went a step beyond the English style. They added spices, including black pepper, to create chai, a sweet, milky black tea that has an enticing richness and depth. Although several commercial brands of chai are now sold in the United States, it is very easy (and much less expensive) to make your own.

asian
limeade

In a tropical climate, people sweat a lot and need to replenish the salt constantly lost. One way they do it is to add a big pinch of salt to cooling drinks such as limeade and lemonade, a combination I find remarkably good (much better than Gatorade, our closest equivalent, which athletes use to replace salt lost through vigorous exertion). Neither the limes nor the lemons are quite as sour as ours are, nor is as much sugar added as we add. Thus, the icy drink is subtle, mildly sweet, mildly sour, and mildly salty, perfect in the afternoon when you're feeling limp from heat and humidity. The first time I tried the real thing was in Kuching on the island of Borneo, while sitting in a little kiosk café near the Heroes' Memorial and Botanical Gardens. Geckos, the same pale green color as my limeade, scurried across the walls; I don't think I've ever felt so far from home. Trying to capture the exact flavors I remember, I've experimented with different combinations; this easy, casual version comes closest. For complete authenticity, do not remove the seeds. In India, you'll find a lemonade spiked with coarsely ground aromatic black salt (kala namak).

1 lemon or lime

2 teaspoons Simple Syrup (page 190, omitting the pepper, or from any basic recipe)

1/8 to 1/4 teaspoon kosher salt

Ice cubes

Fill a large drinking glass three-quarters full with water. Cut the lemon or lime in half and squeeze the juice into the water. Add the Simple Syrup and salt, stir, and fill the glass to the top with ice cubes.

serves 1

a salt & pepper cookbook

spiced
lassi

Lassi is one of several drinks common in areas of the world where yogurt is eaten daily. In the United States, we see lassi most often in Indian restaurants (kefir, also made of yogurt, is more common in markets), but it is very easy to make at home. There are numerous sweet versions, but the savory one always includes a little salt, a little cumin, and frequently cayenne. Indian black salt contributes an aroma and flavor of sulfur; if you find it unpleasant, use kosher salt in its place.

1 cup plain, unflavored yogurt (see note)
1 teaspoon minced fresh mint leaves
1 teaspoon minced fresh cilantro leaves
$1/2$ teaspoon ground black salt or kosher salt
$1/4$ teaspoon cumin seed, toasted and
   crushed
Pinch of cayenne pepper
Ice

Whisk together the yogurt, herbs, salt, and $3/4$ cup water; stir in an additional $1/4$ cup water for a thinner drink. Stir in the cumin seed and pinch of cayenne. Fill glasses with ice cubes and pour the lassi over the ice. Sprinkle with the mint or cilantro leaves, and serve immediately.

note
Much of the yogurt sold in supermarkets in the United States has agar, gelatin, or dry milk solids added to make it thicker. The best yogurts (sometimes described as natural yogurts) are made of nothing more than milk and yogurt culture, so be sure to read the ingredients list on the label.

serves 1 or 2

Chai has become remarkably popular in the 1990s and it is sold everywhere, already made and packaged in little boxes. To me, it makes about as much sense to buy commercial chai as it does to buy tea that's been steeped and packaged. Why would you? There are many versions of the sweet and spicy drink, and I've been enjoying this one since I became used to drinking it every day during a two-month stay in India in the 1970s. In this simple version, India's black peppercorns play a primary role. Although all traditional chai includes black pepper, contemporary recipes sometimes omit it and add other ingredients such as ginger, mint, and nutmeg. Commercial versions are often loaded with cloves, which should be used sparingly, if at all.

2 cups water

1 cup milk

2 teaspoons loose black tea leaves, such as Assam

6 black peppercorns (Tellicherry), coarsely crushed

One 1-inch piece of cinnamon

2 whole cardamom pods

2 tablespoons sugar

Combine all of the ingredients in a small saucepan, set over medium heat, bring to a boil, remove from the heat, cover, and let steep for 10 minutes. Strain and serve.

serves 2

spicy mulled cider

From late fall through the coldest part of winter, hot apple juice, spiced or not, is a wonderful, warming beverage, excellent in the afternoon in place of tea or at night by a hot fire.

6 cups apple cider or apple juice

2 strips lemon zest

2 strips orange zest

Juice of 1 lemon

Juice of 1 orange

One 2-inch piece of vanilla bean

1 stick cinnamon

6 or 7 whole cloves

Generous pinch of toasted, crushed, and sifted Sichuan peppercorns (see note, page 66)

Black pepper in a mill, set on coarse-grind

Kosher salt

In a large saucepan, combine the apple cider, lemon and orange zests, lemon juice, orange juice, vanilla bean, cinnamon, cloves, and Sichuan peppercorns. Add 6 or 7 turns of black pepper and a small pinch of salt. Set over medium heat and when the apple juice begins to simmer, remove from the heat and cover. Let steep 30 minutes. Return to the heat and when it is hot, strain it into a teapot or into individual tea cups and serve immediately.

serves 4

black pepper vodka

Flavored vodkas have recently become extremely popular in the United States, but they have been made for decades in Russia and by people of Russian heritage. Black pepper is one of the most common flavorings; it adds an earthy aroma and a spicy richness to the sharp, hot taste of vodka.

In Poland, black pepper is added to vodka, the country's most popular alcoholic beverage, and drunk to relieve a stomachache. In Russia, the combination is used as a cure for the common cold.

1 tablespoon black peppercorns or 2 tablespoons mixed peppercorns

16 ounces vodka

Combine the peppercorns and vodka in a glass jar or bottle. Store in a cool, dark cupboard for 2 to 3 weeks. Decant into a clean jar and store in the freezer.

makes 1 pint

salty dog

Although it is not traditional to do so, you can moisten the rim of the glass with a wedge of grapefruit and dip it into a saucer of kosher salt before pouring the cocktail.

3 to 4 ounces vodka

16 ounces grapefruit juice

1/2 teaspoon kosher salt

Ice cubes

Combine the vodka, grapefruit juice, and salt, and mix with a cocktail spoon or stirrer until the salt is dissolved. Pour over a glass of crushed ice and serve.

serves 2

salt lick

3 lemon wedges

Kosher salt in a saucer

Ice cubes

3 ounces vodka

4 ounces bitter lemon soda

4 ounces grapefruit juice

Run one of the lemon wedges around the rim of each glass and invert the glass onto the saucer of salt. Fill the glasses with ice, add half the vodka to each glass, followed by the bitter lemon soda and the grapefruit juice. Stir carefully with a cocktail spoon, add a wedge of lemon to each glass, and serve immediately.

serves 2

salty rim

Several beverages, most notably, of course, the margarita, depend on a ring of salt around the rim of the glass for an important flourish of flavor. Even simpler is tequila neat, sipped with a squeeze of lime and a lick of salt. In certain bars, it has been fashionably flirtatious to lick the neck of your object of affection for that bit of salt before sucking on the wedge of lime. Whatever its source, salt is often paired with tequila, as well as with vodka and, less frequently, whiskey. The names of the cocktails often acknowledge the pairing.

salty john

1 or 2 lemon or grapefruit wedges
Kosher salt in a saucer
Ice cubes
3 ounces whiskey
16 ounces grapefruit juice

Run one of the lemon wedges around the rim of each glass and invert the glass onto the saucer of salt. Fill the glasses with ice, add half the whiskey to each glass, fill it with grapefruit juice, and serve.

serves 2

salty josé

3 lime wedges
Chipotle Salt (page 164) in a saucer
3 ounces chipotle tequila (see the headnote on page 204)
16 ounces grapefruit juice

Run one of the lime wedges around the rim of each glass and invert the glass onto the saucer of chipotle salt. Fill the glasses with ice, add half the tequila to each glass, fill it with grapefruit juice, add a squeeze of lime juice, and serve.

serves 2

malaysian
martini

The lounge revival of the mid-1990s saw the return of such retro pleasures as Martin Denny's music, the black cocktail dress, and the martini. College students hosted cocktail parties rather than beer bashes, and martini bars were set up everywhere from art openings to corporate galas. Bars specializing in martinis opened in several cities, and some of their concoctions stretched the imagination of even the trendiest imbiber. This version is closer to the original classic martini and is not as trendy as you might think. Vodka has been flavored with peppercorns for decades (or, more likely, centuries) in Russia. It might be more fitting to include the traditional gin, particularly because gin was often the drink of choice among colonists in Malaysia, where today peppercorns are farmed, but I prefer the flavor of vodka and pepper to that of gin and pepper. If I were making this on the island of Borneo, near one of the thousands of peppercorn farms that cover the island, I would pinch off a cluster of fresh peppercorns as a garnish for each drink.

Cracked ice cubes

3 ounces Black Pepper Vodka (page 200)

$\frac{1}{2}$ ounce sweet Italian vermouth

2 dashes orange bitters

Fill a cocktail shaker with cracked ice, add the vodka, vermouth, and bitters, and shake for several seconds, until the shaker is frosty. Strain into a chilled stemmed glass and serve immediately.

serves 1

spicy margaritas

Dried chipotles add another dimension to the already smoky flavor of tequila. Put two chipotles in a bottle with eight ounces or so of tequila and let the mixture steep for a few weeks. The result is a rusty gold liquid with a heady tequila aroma mingled with the irresistible scent of smoked chiles. It is delicious—strong, spicy, and bold. Be advised, these margaritas are not for the timid!

3 lime wedges

Chipotle Salt (page 164) in a saucer

Cracked ice cubes

2½ ounces chipotle tequila, or other tequila of choice

⅓ cup fresh lime juice

1 ounce Cointreau

Rub the rim of each of two glasses with one of the lime wedges and then dip the rim of each glass into the saucer of Chipotle Salt. Fill the glasses with cracked ice cubes, add half the tequila to each glass, followed by half the lime juice and half the Cointreau. Stir with a cocktail spoon, garnish with a lime wedge, and serve immediately.

serves 2

When my assistant, Lesa Tanner, was a young teenager, her first job was babysitting for a group of kids while their parents played volleyball. Responsible even at that age, Lesa asked a friend's mother, who was a schoolteacher, how she could best entertain the children.

"Make playdough," the teacher responded, "and they will love you forever."

Now, with three children of her own, Lesa still swears by playdough, calling it one of the all-time greatest (and one of the cheapest, if you make it at home) entertainments for children. Her boys roll it into snakes, coil it into structures, make tiny beads with it, and hone their skills with tools. It lasts "forever," Lesa says, if you keep it wrapped in plastic in the refrigerator between uses. And if you tint it with bright colors, it never looks dirty.

Salt dough, too, provides excellent entertainment for kids, though it is not as resilient as playdough. Once baked, however, it lasts a long time, and even longer when it is sprayed with a plastic sealant.

playdough, uncooked

Lesa Tanner, who has been my invaluable assistant for several years, exerts a remarkable calm over my day, surprising in light of the fact that she has three energetic young boys. In addition to working for me, she works in her boys' schools and keeps them and their friends entertained on weekends and during the summer. This recipe is from her. The dough will keep for several months if stored in a sealed bag between uses. (Look for alum in your local pharmacy.)

5 cups all-purpose flour

1½ cups salt

6 tablespoons vegetable oil

3 cups boiling water, with food coloring added

6 tablespoons alum

Combine the flour and salt in a large mixing bowl. Add the boiling colored water, the oil, and the alum. Mix together, turn out onto a floured board, and knead until the dough is no longer sticky. Once the dough is cooled, store in a heavy-duty plastic bag.

makes two 6- to 8-inch balls

playdough, cooked

To color dough with natural ingredients, use water in which you have boiled yellow onion skins or red or golden beets.

2 cups all-purpose flour

1 cup table salt

4 teaspoons cream of tartar

2 cups water

4 tablespoons vegetable oil

10 to 15 drops of food coloring (or more, as desired)

Combine all the ingredients in a large, heavy pot set over medium heat. Cook, stirring constantly, until the dough comes together in a ball. Turn out onto a smooth work surface (unfloured) and let cool. Knead the cool dough several times, then place it in a heavy-duty plastic bag. The dough will keep for several months if stored in a sealed bag between uses.

makes one 6- to 8-inch ball

salt dough
decorations

No Christmas tree is complete without a few salt dough decorations, though certainly the dough's decorative possibilities are not limited to the winter Christian holidays. If you're the crafty sort, you can shape place card holders out of salt dough. If you regularly entertain the same guests, you can paint in their names before glazing them.

4 cups all-purpose flour

1 cup table salt (or 1 1/4 cups kosher salt)

1 3/4 cups water

1 egg white

2 tablespoons water

Place the flour and salt in the bowl of a mixer fitted with the dough hook and mix briefly. Continue to operate while slowly adding the water. Knead for 5 minutes (15 minutes by hand), turn out onto a floured work surface, and roll out until the dough is 1/4 inch thick. Use cookie cutters to create shapes. For ornaments, use an ice pick (a meat thermometer also works) to poke a hole in the top of each ornament before baking it. Combine the egg white with the water; using a pastry brush, brush the surface of each shape with water. For wreaths, set the shapes in an overlapping circle on a greased baking sheet and press down lightly to seal. Bake the decorations in a 300°F oven until hard and lightly browned, about 1 hour. Let cool and either decorate or leave natural. Coat with a clear sealant such as craft glaze.

makes about 2 dozen 2 1/2-inch decorations

Anandan Abdullah, the general manager of the Pepper Marketing Board of Sarawak, Malaysia, told me one afternoon that you can make paper using the plant material left after the peppercorns have been stripped off. "If you add some crushed peppercorns," he said, "it will remain fragrant for a long time."

Making homemade paper is a wonderful activity for children, especially during holidays and vacations. It is, of course, important that each child end up with his or her own finished product; this recipe can be doubled or tripled as necessary, though you should process each sheet individually. You will need one or more small portable window screens (9 by 12 inches is the ideal size), a large roasting pan and a baking sheet for each screen, new sponges, and plenty of cheesecloth on hand before you begin. (If you don't have a roasting pan of the proper size, you can let the paper drain over the sink.) The paper, beautiful, fragrant, and heavily textured, is decorative, being rather too thick to be used for writing.

1 tablespoon citrus zest (orange, grapefruit, lemon, or lime), cut in very thin julienne, optional

2 cups (packed) *small* pieces of paper (see note)

1 tablespoon dried flower petals (roses, herb flowers, lavender, marigolds, daisies)

2 tablespoons freshly cracked black peppercorns

Let the zest dry in the air for at least an hour.

In a medium bowl or other container, pour 4 cups water over the scraps of paper and set aside to soak for at least 1 hour. (This can be done in the processor container.) Put the mixture into the container of a food processor, add the flowers, peppercorns, and zest, if using, and pulse several times at high speed. Run the processor steadily at high speed for 1 minute; stop, stir the mixture, and operate for another minute.

Set a window screen over a roasting pan slightly larger than the screen, pour the paper mixture over the screen, and use your hand to distribute the tiny bits of paper and herbs evenly. Let the water drain into the roasting pan for 10 minutes, pressing it down occasionally to squeeze out more water.

Cut a triple-thick piece of cheesecloth to fit over the screen, set it on top of the wet mixture, and then press down to continue to remove excess water.

Set a sheet pan bottom-side down over the cheesecloth and turn the whole affair over, so that the cheesecloth and the wet paper are on top of the bottom of the sheet pan. Carefully lift off the screen so that the cheesecloth and paper remain on the sheet pan.

Use a clean, new sponge to press the paper down and absorb excess water. Make another triple-thick piece of cheesecloth and press it on top of the paper, pushing down evenly and firmly. Let sit in a cool dry place until completely dry. It will take from 1 to 5 days, depending on temperature and humidity. When it is thoroughly dry, peel off both layers of cheesecloth and use as you like.

note

Construction paper, artist's drawing paper, wrapping paper, thin paper bags (not standard brown shopping bags) are all suitable. Tear or cut the paper into small pieces, or the bits may be caught in the blade of your processor or blender. For the best results, coordinate colors too, choosing a selection of papers of similar colors.

makes one 8- by 11-inch sheet

common culinary salts

type	source & price	texture & appearance	taste*	uses
Table salt; plain salt	Mined deposit; seawater; cheap	small, identical cubes; very dry	Mild, sharp on front of palate; slow-dissolving	Limited: household cleanser; cooking emergencies
Table salt, iodized	Mined deposits and seawater, with iodine added	Small, identical cubes; very dry	Mild, sharp on the front of palate, hint of bitterness; slow-dissolving	Limited, but iodine is a preventative against goiter
Kosher, Alberger	Mined deposits; cheap	Uneven, hollow pyramids; very dry	Moderately salty, delicate; fast-dissolving	Baking, general cooking, preserving, finishing
Kosher	Mined deposits; cheap	Flattened cubes or fused cubes; very dry	Mild tasting, delicate; slow-dissolving	Preserving, salt doughs, crusts

type	source & price	texture & appearance	taste*	uses
Granulated sea salt	Seawater; cheap to moderate	Small, identical cubes; very dry	Mild, sharp on front of palate; slow-dissolving; almost identical to table salt	Limited: household cleanser; cooking emergencies
Celtic gray sea salt, coarse	Seawater; Atlantic coast of France; moderate to expensive	Uneven, moderate to large solid crystals; moist to very moist	Mild, full in mouth; briny, earthy, tangy; slow-dissolving	Baking, roasting, finishing; in salt mills
Celtic gray sea salt, ground	Seawater; Atlantic coast of France; moderate to expensive	Small, fairly even grains; fairly moist	Tangy	General cooking
Maldon Crystal Salt (brand name)	Seawater; coastal England; moderate	Hollow, pyramid-shaped crystals; dry	Delicate, briny; fast-dissolving	Finishing
Trapani	Seawater; northwestern coast of Sicily; moderate	Sharp square and rectangular crystals; very dry	Briny	In salt mills; in water for pasta and vegetables
Ō-shima Island	Seawater, Japan; moderate	Light, tiny crystals; fluffy	Mild, slightly tangy; some say sweet	Finishing; in water for vegetables, pasta

type	source & price	texture & appearance	taste*	uses
Lima Sea Salt (brand name)	Seawater; Atlantic coast of France; moderate	Small granules tinged with purple	Very salty, sharp, acidic; almost hot	In water for vegetables and pasta; general cooking
Korean sea salt	Seawater; coastal Korea; cheap	Uneven moderate crystals; hard, moist	Mild, earthy, full	Baking, roasting, finishing; in salt mills
Sea Stars (brand name)	Seawater; Guérande, France; expensive	Uneven large crystals; hard, moist	Salty, briny, earthy, minerally	Baking, roasting, finishing; in salt mills
Fleur de sel	Seawater, Atlantic coast of France; expensive	Small, hard, off-white crystals; moist	Delicate; full in mouth	Finishing
Indian black salt	Mined deposits; moderate	Large, hard rocks; purple to black; very dry	Mildly salty, earthy, sulfuric	Seasoning traditional Indian dishes
Hawaiian alae salt	Seawater, often with red clay added; Hawaii; cheap	Moderate crystals, pale orange; dry	Delicate, silky	Finishing
Smoked salt	Seawater; Denmark	Moderate crystals, translucent; dry	Smoky, moderately salty	Finishing, especially fish, eggs, cheese

*To assess and compare their characteristics, the salts were tasted blind. Equal quantities by weight were dissolved in equal quantities of water, coded, and then tasted without reference to the code.

appendix

213

commonly available peppercorns

Although peppercorns are produced in more countries than are listed here, most pepper sold in the United States comes from the countries mentioned. The source of pepper is not always included on a retail label; when it is, then it is usually because there is a perception of superior quality associated with the location.

name	source	description
Lampong	Indonesia	Black; medium berries, average quality
Malabar★	India	Black; medium to large berries; average to superior quality
Naturally Clean Black Pepper★ (brand name)	Malaysia	Black; medium berries; superior quality
Sarawak★	Malaysia	Black or white, generic; average to superior quality
Tellicherry★	India	Black, frequently with reddish cast; very large berries; superior quality
Brazilian	Brazil	Black, white, or green; medium berries; average quality
Muntock★	Indonesia	White; medium berries; average quality

appendix

214

name	source	description
Creamy White Pepper★ (brand name)	Malaysia	White, consistently sized medium-large berries; creamy color; superior quality
Ponape★ (brand name)	Micronesia	Black; medium berries; average to superior quality; very limited production
Green, freeze-dried	Various	Small, light (weight) berries; very fragile, fair quality
Green, air-dried	Various	Medium berries, average to superior quality
Green, in brine	Various	Soft, medium to large berries; average to superior quality
Green, in vinegar	Various	Soft, medium to large berries; average to superior quality

★Sources most likely to be identified.

appendix

Information

**American Spice Trade Association
(ASTA)**
P. O. Box 1267
Englewood Cliffs, NJ 07632
Tel: (201) 568-2163
Fax: (201) 568-7318
Website: www.astaspice.com
*Consumer and industry information about
spices, including black, white, and green
peppercorns*

Aquasel
10 rue des Marouettes
85330 Noirmoutier
France
Tel: 33.2.51.39.08.30
Fax: 33.2.51.39.74.08
*Bernard Chamley, Director
Cooperative of regional salts*

British Salt Limited
Cledford Lane
Middlewich
Cheshire CW 10 0JP
England
44 0 1606 832 881
*Information on the history and production of
mined salt in England*

International Pepper Community
4th Floor, Lina Building
JL. H.R. Rasuna said Kav. B7
Jakarta, Indonesia
Tel: 021-522-4902
Fax: 021-522-4905
*Dr. IR. S. N. Darwis, Executive Director
Organization of pepper producing counties*

**La Coopérative des Sauniers de l'Île de
Ré**
Ars-en-Ré
France
Tel: 33.05.46.09.23.09
Salt on the Île de Ré

Maldon Crystal Salt Company Limited
The Downs,
Maldon, Essex
CMp 5 HR
England
Fax: 44 (0) 1621 858191
Website: www.maldonsalt.com
*Consumer information on the history and
production of sea salt in England*

Pepper Marketing Board
P. O. Box 1653
93916 Kuching, Sarawak
Malaysia
e-mail: pmb@pepper.po.my
Website: www.sarawakpepper.gov.my/
sarawakpepper
Anandan Adnan Abdullah, General
Manager

Polish National Tourist Office
275 Madison Avenue, Suite 1711
New York, NY 10016
Tel: (212) 338-9412
Fax: (212) 338-9283
e-mail: pntonyc@polandtour.org

Salt Institute
700 North Fairfax Street
Fairfax Plaza, Suite 600
Alexandria, VA 22314-2040
Tel: (703) 549-4648
Website: www.saltinstitute.org
Andrew Briscoe III, Director of Public Policy
Consumer information about salt and
related health issues

Tourism Malaysia
818 West 7th Street, Suite 804
Los Angeles, CA 90017
Tel: (213) 689-9702
Fax: (213) 689-1530

Tourism Malaysia
2nd Floor, Bangunan Rugayah
Jalan Song Thian Cheok
93100 Kuching, Sarawak
Malaysia
Tel: (60) 082-246-575
Fax: (60) 082-246-442

Museums and Galleries

The Cat Museum
Kuching North City Hall
Bukit Siol, Jalan Semariang, Petra Jaya
93050 Kuching, Sarawak
Malaysia
Tel: (60) 082-446-688
The world's only cat museum, in one of the
world's major pepper producing regions

The Clay Studio
139 N. 2nd St.
Philadelphia, Pennsylvania
(215) 925-3453

German Salt Museum
Industrial Monument Saltworks of
Lüneburg
Sülfmeisterstraße 1
D-21335 Lüneburg
Germany
49.413145065

Reno County Museum
100 S. Walnut
P. O. Box 664
Hutchinson, KS 67501
Tel: (316) 662-1184
Information on the salt industry that was
founded in Hutchinson in 1875

Royal Wieliczka Salt Mine
Kopalnia Soli Wieliczka
ul. Danilowicza 10
32-020 Wieliczka, Poland
Tel: (4812) 278-73-02
Fax: (4812) 278-73-33
Wieliczka salt mine; the Muzeum Zup
Krakowskich Wieliczka (a salt museum) is
located at the mines with a separate entrance
(and additional entry fee)

Tobacco and Salt Museum
1-16-8, Jinnan, Shibuya-ku
Toyko, Japan
Tel: 81-3-3476-2041

The Salt Museum
P. O. Box 146
Liverpool, NY 13088
Tel: (315) 453-6767
Artifacts, photographs, and replicas of
production facilities in exhibits exploring the
history of salt making in Onondaga County

Trapani Provincial Tourist Office
Via S. Francesco d'Assisi
n 27 Trapani, Sicily
39 9 923 545 511
Information about the salt museum in
Nubia, Sicily

Newsletters

"The Art of Eating"
Box 242
Peacham, VT 05862
Tel: (800) 495-3944
Fax: (800) 592-3400
Website: www. artofeating.com
Edward Behr's quarterly newsletter; selected
back issues available

See also, under Supplies:
    The Grain & Salt Society
    Kermit Lynch Wine Merchant
    La Cuisine—The Cook's Resource

Supplies

Corti Brothers
P. O. Box 191358
Sacramento, CA 95819
Tel: (916) 736-3800
Japanese sea salt, Trapani salt, other specialty
salts as well as olive oils, vinegars, etc.;
newsletter

De Medici Imports
315 West 57th Street
New York, NY 10019
Tel: (212) 974-8101
Fax: (212) 581-1939
Importers of fleur de sel *from Île de Ré; call*
for retail locations

R. M. Felts Packing Company
Box 199
Ivor, VA 23866
Tel: (757) 859-6131
Fax: (757) 859-6381
Purveyors of authentic smoked bacon, hog jowls, and country ham

Gazelle Glass Inc.
31364 Peterson Road
Philomath, OR 97370
Tel: (541) 929-6464
Fax: (541) 929-4364
Producers of elaborate blown-glass salt and pepper shakers

The Grain & Salt Society
273 Fairway Drive
Asheville, NC 28805
Tel: (800) 867-7258
French sea salts, wooden salt boxes; seasonal newsletter for members

KL Imports
6114 La Salle #608
Oakland, CA 94611
Tel: (510) 482-0855
Kitty Keller, owner
Wholesale source for fleur de sel, *Celtic gray sea salt,* vinaigre de Banyuls, *and other products*

Kermit Lynch Wine Merchant
1605 San Pablo Avenue
Berkeley, CA 94702-1317
Tel: (510) 524-1524
PIC mustard from France, superior anchovies, rare olive oils, olives, and outstanding French and Italian wines; mail order, newsletter

La Maison des Paludiers et Le Groupement des Producteurs de Sel de La Presqu'île Guérandaise
18, Rue des Prés Garnier
44350 Guérande
France
Tel: 33.2.40.62.21.96
Fax: 33.2.40.15.03.46
Location source for regional salt

Island Traders
Box 704
Federated States of Micronesia, 96941
Exporters of Ponape black pepper; retail

Kalustyan
123 Lexington Avenue
New York, NY 10016
Tel: (212) 685-3888
Fax: (212) 683-8458
Quality spices

La Cuisine—The Cook's Resource
323 Cameron Street
Alexandria, VA 22314-3219
Tel: (800) 521-1176
Fax: (703) 836-8925
e-mail: lacuisine@worldnet.att.net
French, English, and Spanish sea salts; peppercorns; grinders, including the electronic grinder, A Touch of Pepper; newsletter, mail order

Oakville Grocery Mail Order Company
101 South Coombs, Suite Y-3
Napa, CA 94559
Tel: (800) 455-2305
Portuguese salt, fleur de sel, *Hawaiian alae salt, O Olive Oil, Vinaigre de Banyuls; catalogue*

resources

Penzeys, Ltd.
P. O. Box 933
Muskego, WI 53150
Tel: (414) 679-7207
Mail-order spice company; excellent peppercorns, including some from Malaysia; Zassenhaus pepper mills and nutmeg grinders; catalogue

San Francisco Herb Co.
250 14th Street
San Francisco, CA 94103
Tel: (800) 227-4530 and (415) 861-7174
Fax: (415) 861-4440
Spices, teas, botanicals, and essentials wholesale to the public; store and mail-order; catalogue

Tabasco Country Store
McIlhenny Company
Avery Island, LA 70513
Tel: (800) 634-9599
The famous Louisiana hot sauce company shares Avery Island with one of the country's oldest salt mining companies; catalogue

Tierra Vegetables
13684 Chalk Hill Road
Healdsburg, CA 95448
Tel: (707) 837-8366
Fax: (707) 433-5666
E-mail: evie@tierravegetables.com
Quality dried and smoked chiles, including chipotles and chipotle powder; catalogue; mail order

Williams-Sonoma
P. O. Box 7356
San Francisco, CA 94120-7456
Tel: (800) 541-2233
Maldon salt, grinders, and other speciality foods and cookware; catalogue

Zingerman's
422 Detroit Street
Ann Arbor, MI 48104
Tel: (888) 636-8162
Mail-order source for specialty salts, cheese, vinegars, etc.; catalogue

Restaurants

Malaysian Chicken Rice
14 Jalan Central
Sarikei, Sarawak
Malaysia
Small coffee-shop style restaurant specializing in Malaysian chicken rice

Mandalay Restaurant
4344 California Street
San Francisco, CA 94118
Tel: (415) 386-3895
A traditional Burmese restaurant, with an excellent Black Pepper Soup

Alberger salt • A method of producing hollow, pyramid-shaped crystals of pure salt developed by J. L. Alberger and patented in 1889. Alberger salt has replaced grainer salt; the largest crystal is sold as Diamond Crystal kosher salt; four other sizes are sold under various names, and primarily to the food service industry.

Alae salt • *See* Hawaiian sea salt.

Bittern • The bitter liquid that remains after salt has been made from seawater or from dissolved rock salt. In some countries, but not in the United States, where the practice is prohibited, bittern is drained into the sea. Here it is sold for various industrial uses, including dust control on state and national park roads.

Black peppercorns • The berries of the *Piper nigrum* vine, picked while green and dried either in the sun or in forced-air dryers.

Black pepper oil • Volatile oils responsible for the aroma of black pepper; used in small quantities in therapeutic massage (to relieve muscle stiffness) and in aromatherapy as a stimulant and an aphrodisiac.

Black salt (*kala namak*) • Sometimes called rock salt (but not what is called rock salt in the United States), black salt ranges in color from pale violet to purple black; it has a strong sulfuric aroma and is used almost exclusively in regional Indian cooking.

Black soy sauce • *See* Soy sauce.

Brine • A solution of salt dissolved in water; a saturated brine is 26.4 percent salt by weight; at higher percentages, salt will not remain in solution and begins to precipitate out, forming fragile crystals on top of the liquid that quickly collapse from their own weight and sink.

Celtic Gray sea salt • From the Atlantic coast of France, Celtic gray salt is harvested as medium-sized crystals. Moderate to expensive in price, some is sold as is, some is crushed before it is sold. In the resurgence of interest in salt during the 1990s, it has been the most popular of the specialty salts.

Condiment salt • A contemporary name for salts that should be sprinkled onto food immediately before serving rather than used during cooking.

Creamy White Pepper • A high grade of white pepper, with all the dark-colored and lightweight berries sorted out; produced by the Pepper Marketing Board of Sarawak, Malaysia.

Cubeb • A small berry (*Piper cubeba*), native to Southeast Asia, related to *P. nigrum* but more closely resembling allspice or nutmeg than pepper; gathered in the wild, cultivated in limited areas, and little used outside Asia.

Danish salt • *See* Smoked salt.

Dark soy sauce • *See* Soy sauce.

Dendridic salt • Small hollow salt crystals (the size of table salt), made by introducing yellow prussiate of soda into a saturated brine; drawbacks include the small size (larger crystals break apart) and limited uses in the food industry because it forms a blue compound in the presence of iron.

Fagara • *See* Sichuan peppercorns.

Finishing salt • *See* Condiment salt.

Fish sauce • A clear, brown liquid made by fermenting anchovies with sea salt and water. The most important seasoning in Thai cuisine (*nam pla*) and Vietnamese cuisine (*nuoc mam*).

Flavor salt • Monosodium glutamate, used as a flavor enhancer in many Asian cuisines, and in Asian countries often labeled as "flavor salt" or "salt with flavor."

Fleur de sel (flower of the sea) • The queen of the sea salts, produced along the French Atlantic coast; the top crust of salt in the salt pans in Brittany. Once discarded as unprofitable, it is now the world's highest-priced salt and the favorite of many chefs. It is delicately flavored, but it's main contribution to a dish is its texture. Too expensive for an all-purpose salt; use to finish a dish.

Flower pepper • *See* Sichuan peppercorns.

Fresh green peppercorns • The freshly picked clusters of green peppercorns before they are dried or further processed; used in a few classic dishes, such as a Thai green curry; almost impossible to find except locally where pepper is grown.

Gomashio • A Japanese condiment of toasted sesame seeds crushed with salt and, sometimes, dried seaweed.

Grainer salt • Evaporated salt produced using heat-stimulated evaporation (originally, from direct heat under the pans; later, from steam pipes directly in the brine). Although the process created a desirable crystal form (a hollow pyramid), grainer salt is no longer produced commercially because of the cost of the heating fuel.

Grains of Paradise • Seeds of a perennial reed, cultivated in west Africa; a relative of cardamom, it is milder, with a pungent and peppery flavor; sometimes called Guinea pepper.

Granulated salt • *See* Table salt.

Green peppercorns • Pickled, freeze-dried, or air-dried peppercorns picked several weeks before white and black peppercorn berries are harvested. Fresh-tasting, mildly sour, and peppery in flavor; widely available.

Hawaiian alae salt • A pale orange salt made with Hawaiian red clay; the commercial equivalent of traditional Hawaiian red salt, which includes significant quantities of soil and other ingredients and is not approved by the Food and Drug Administration for human consumption.

Indian salt • *See* Black salt.

Industrial salt • A general term that refers to all non-food-grade salt and which makes up over 90 percent of the salt used in the United States each year.

Iodized salt • Table salt to which potassium iodide has been added as a preventive against goiter (a thyroid condition).

Japanese pepper • *Sansho,* the ground pod of the Japanese prickly ash tree (*Zanthoxylum piperitum*), is occasionally referred to as "Japanese pepper" although it is not hot and not related to *P. nigrum.* Rather, it is tangy and the ground spice is sprinkled on food at the table as a contrast to fatty flavors, especially those of grilled poultry and seafood.

Japanese sea salt • Generic name for sea salt from Japan.

Kala namak • *See* Black salt.

Korean sea salt • Generic name for sea salt from Korea.

Kosher salt • Virtually without exception, what is known as kosher salt is a coarse crystal that is efficient at withdrawing liquid from meat, the most crucial part of koshering.

Ksosian sea salt • Generic name for salt from the Ksosian area of South Africa.

Lampong pepper • The primary black pepper from Indonesia, now shipped out of the port of Pendjang; Lampong is on the island of Sumatra; Krakatoa, formidable and steamy, looms across the bay.

Light soy sauce • *See* Soy sauce.

Lima sea salt • Brand name for a type of sea salt produced along the Atlantic coast of France.

Liquamen • A seasoning, used in Roman times, in place of salt; similar to a crude fish sauce, its simplest versions consisted of fish dried in the sun and combined with salt, water, and various seasonings; also known as *garum.*

Long pepper • *Piper longum,* from India, has a peppery taste, with spicy cinnamon notes; once more common than *P. nigrum,* it is rarely found today outside India and Indian markets.

Malabar pepper • A medium-sized, intensely-flavored variety of *P. nigrum* from India; said by many to have the best taste among black peppercorns.

Maldon salt • Coarse, uneven flakes from Essex, England, available in the United States through Williams-Sonoma. Because of its thin, flaky texture that melts quickly on the tongue, it is an excellent finishing salt.

Miso • Fermented bean paste, essential in Japanese cooking. There are several types of miso, nearly all made with a mixture of crushed boiled soybeans and grain (wheat, barley, or rice) that is inoculated and allowed to ferment. Most are salty; a few are sweet; some are sweet-sour.

Muntock pepper • White peppercorns from Indonesia.

Naturally Clean Black Pepper • Premium-grade black pepper of consistent quality produced by the Pepper Marketing Board of Malaysia; unlike most black pepper on the world market, NCBP is washed twice immediately after picking to remove bacteria and then processed in air-dryers rather than dried in the sun (where it is exposed to both salmonella and *E. coli*). It is sterilized using steam and has the lowest bacteria count of all black pepper.

Oshima Island Red Label Salt • Brand name of the top grade of salt produced on Ō-shima Island, Japan.

Paulidier • A salt farmer, the term used along the Atlantic coast of France, as is *saunier.*

Pepperberry • A spicy berry, about twice the size of a peppercorn from a shrub (*Schinus molle*) native to Tasmania; common in Australia.

Pepperleaf • Native to Australia, the dried leaf has a mildly spicy flavor reminiscent of black pepper; ground, it is used as a seasoning in Australia.

Pickling salt • Pure food-grade salt, without additives (such as anticaking agents) that will cloud liquid.

Pink peppercorns • Not a true peppercorn, these pink berries from a bushy tree (*Schinus terebinthifolius*) that grows in Florida, Brazil, and the island of Réunion, are colorful, sweet, have just a hint of mildest pepper flavor, no heat, and a lengthy bitter finish. More of a novelty item than a useful ingredient.

Piperine • The active ingredient in pepper responsible for its heat and pungency; does not dissipate when heated or over time. Can be extracted as piperine oleoresin, which is used in both the food and beverage industries.

Piper spp.
    P. grande • A variety of wild pepper, with red berries.
    P. longum • *See* Long pepper.
    P. nigrum • *See* Black peppercorns; Green peppercorns; White peppercorns.
    P. vestitum • A variety of wild pepper, with golden brown and black berries.

Popcorn salt • Very fine salt that clings readily to popped corn.

Portuguese salt • Generic name for sea salt from Portugal.

Red salt • *See* Hawaiian alae salt.

Rock salt • Chunk salt that does not meet the Food and Drug Administration's requirements for food-grade salt; generally used in ice cream freezers and for melting winter ice.

Salt beef • Salted and dried beef, popular in Caribbean and Cuban cooking; in England, salt beef is similar to corned beef.

Salt fish • Salted and dried fish; cod is the most popular and most common, but various other fish are dried in this way.

Salt with flavor • *See* Flavor salt.

Salt pork • Pork belly cured in brine; not smoked.

Salt-Sense • Brand name for medium-sized Alberger salt crystals, slightly smaller than kosher salt. Less dense than granulated salt and so, by volume, it contains less sodium chloride; advertised as an alternative to table salt.

Salt substitute • Usually potassium chloride in granular form marketed to people who want to lower their sodium intake; slightly bitter and acidic in taste.

Salumi • Salt-cured meats; Italian.

Sansho • See Japanese pepper.

Sarawak pepper • Generic name for peppercorns processed by the Pepper Market Board from peppercorns grown in the Malaysian state of Sarawak, on the island of Borneo.

Sea salt • Any salt made from evaporated sea water; much table salt is also sea salt and many sea salts are, as table salt is, completely refined.

Sel gris • Generic name for gray sea salt.

Shrimp paste • A pungent fermented paste made from salt and shrimp, essential in Southeast Asian cuisines (*kapi* in Thai, *blachan* in Malay, and *terasi* in Vietnamese). There are two types, fresh, which needs no preparation, and dried, which should be wrapped in foil and roasted in a dry skillet before being used.

Sichuan pepper • An aromatic reddish brown berry from the Chinese prickly ash tree (*Zanthoxylum simulans*), sometimes called flower pepper and more often, fagara. Used toasted in Chinese cooking (it's essential in Chinese five-spice powder) and combined with salt, as a condiment.

Sicilian salt • Generic name for sea salt from Sicily.

Smoked salt • Sea salt that is smoked over wood; made in Denmark.

Soy sauce • A salty fermented condiment with a thousand-year history that has become one of the most essential seasonings throughout Asia. Made from roasted soybeans, wheat, salt, and a culture, the best is fermented for a year or more. The least expensive, and least desirable, are synthesized from vegetable protein, hydrochloric acid, caramel coloring, and corn syrup.

Dark soy sauce • In Japanese cooking, dark soy sauce is the standard soy sauce, nearly black in color, with substantial body and less saltiness that light soy sauce. Most Chinese soy sauces, which are less common than the Japanese sauces are in this country, are thick and dark and often called black soy sauce.

Light soy sauce • Traditionally, light soy sauce is one of two types of soy sauce generally used in Japan. It is thinner and lighter in color than is dark soy sauce, but it is also saltier.

Suribachi • A Japanese mortar and pestle, consisting of a deep bowl of ridged ceramic and a long wooden pestle. It's inexpensive and highly effective for crushing salt and peppercorns, as well as for grinding garlic, chiles, and herbs into pastes quickly and efficiently.

Table salt • Small, uniform cubes, also called granulated salt, usually iodized.

Tamari • Similar to soy sauce, but made without wheat.

Tellicherry pepper • The name once referred to pepper shipped through the port of Tellicherry in southern India, but now indicates a grade of Indian black pepper: the larger, more mature peppercorns with a complex, round flavor.

Virgin pickle • A 100-percent saturated brine of evaporated sea water or dissolved rock salt; the last stage of evaporation before natural crystallization begins.

Volatile oils • The oils responsible for the aroma of pepper; they dissipate quickly when heat is applied and when pepper is crushed or ground, leaving behind piperine, which accounts for the lasting heat of pepper.

White peppercorns • Peppercorns picked shortly (a week or less) after the berries for black pepper are harvested, and soaked in water for ten to fourteen days to remove the skins before being dried; less aromatic than black pepper, but often hotter, due to a slightly higher piperine content.

glossary

Alderman, Michael H., and Bernard Lamport. "Moderate Sodium Restriction: Do the Benefits Justify the Hazards?" *American Journal of Hypertension* 3 (1990): 499–504.

Alford, Jeffrey, and Naomi Duguid. *Flatbreads and Flavors.* New York: Morrow, 1995.

Aragon, Jane Chelsea. *Salt Hands.* New York: Puffin Unicorn, 1989.

Barron, Rosemary. *Flavors of Greece.* New York: Morrow, 1991.

Behr, Edward. *The Artful Eater.* New York: The Atlantic Monthly Press, 1992.

Bharadwaj, Monisha. *The Indian Spice Kitchen.* New York: Dutton, 1997.

Bosker, Gideon. *Great Shakes: Salts and Peppers for All Tastes.* New York: Abbeville Press, 1986.

Bremness, Lesley, and Jill Norman. *The Complete Book of Herbs & Spices.* New York: Viking Studio Books, 1995.

Carey, Benedict. "Shake-Up in the Saltshaker." In *Health* (May/June 1990): 24.

Carey, Larry, and Sylvia Tompkins. *1002 Salt Shakers: Nodders, Fitz & Floyd, Parkcraft with Prices.* Atglen: Schiffer Publishing, Limited, 1995.

Chan, Dunstan, and Woon Yoke Heng, eds. *Sarawak Pepper Flavors the World.* Malaysia: Pepper Marketing Board Malaysia, 1994.

Collins, Larry, and Dominique Lapierre. *Freedom at Midnight.* New York: Simon and Schuster, 1975.

Colwin, Laurie. *More Home Cooking.* New York: HarperCollins, 1993.

David, Elizabeth. *Spices, Salt and Aromatics in the English Kitchen.* Middlesex, England: Penguin, 1970.

de Groot, Roy Andries. *Feasts for All Seasons.* New York: Knopf, 1966.

Devi, Yamuna. *The Vegetarian Table: India.* San Francisco: Chronicle Books, 1997.

"Does Salt Raise Your Blood Pressure?" *Consumer Reports on Health* (April 1994): 42–43.

Eskew, Garnett Laidlaw. *Salt: The Fifth Element.* Chicago: Ferguson, 1948.

Evans, John, and Lynette Evans. "A Pinch of Salt." *San Francisco Examiner* (February 25, 1998).

Field, Carol. *Italy in Small Bites.* New York: Morrow, 1993.

Fussell, Betty, and Michele Anna Jordan. "Savoring Salt." *Bon Appetit* (March 1998): 58.

Gelle, Gerry G. *Filipino Cuisine.* Santa Fe: Red Crane Books, 1997.

Gugino, Sam. "Worth Its Salt." *The Wine Spectator* (15 September 1998): 25–26.

Hachten, Harva. *Kitchen Safari.* New York: Atheneum, 1970.

Hamlin, Suzanne. "Salt is Regaining Favor and Savor." *New York Times* (5 June 1996): C1.

Hanneman, Richard L. "The Politics of Sodium Restriction in the United States." In *Seventh Symposium on Salt*. i vols., ii–iv 1993. 2, 231–39. Amsterdam: Elsevier Science Publishers.

Harris, Dunstan A. *Island Cooking: Recipes from the Caribbean*. Freedom, Calif.: The Crossing Press, 1988.

Hazan, Marcella. *Marcella Cucina*. New York: HarperCollins, 1997.

Hendra, Tony. "Salty Talk." *Food & Wine* (April 1998): 55–56.

Hesser, Amanda. "From the French Marshes, a Salty Treasure." *New York Times* (6 May 1998): F1.

Hutton, Wendy, ed. *The Food of Malaysia*. Singapore: Periplus Editions, 1995.

Ibrahim, M. Y., C. F. J. Bong, and I. B. Ipor. *The Pepper Industry: Problems and Prospects*. Bintulu: Universiti Pertanian Malaysia, 1993.

Jenkins, Steve. *Cheese Primer*. New York: Workman, 1996.

Jones, Evan. *The World of Cheese*. New York: Knopf, 1976.

Kamman, Madeleine. *The New Making of a Cook*. New York, Morrow, 1997.

Kaufmann, Dale W. *Sodium Chloride: The Production and Properties of Salt and Brine*. New York: Hafner, 1968.

Koch, Ulrike, director. *The Saltmen of Tibet*. Digital video, 110 min. Catpics Coproductions, Zurich, Switzerland, 1998.

Kytle, Calvin. *Ghandi, Soldier of Non-Violence*. Cabin John, Md.: Seven Locks Press, 1983.

Lang, Jenifer Harvey. *Tastings*. New York: Crown, 1986.

Lewallen, John, and Eleanor Lewallen. *Sea Vegetable Gourmet Cookbook and Wildcrafter's Guide*. Mendocino, Calif.: Mendocino Sea Vegetable Company, 1996.

Loha-unchit, Kasma. *It Rains Fishes*. San Francisco: Pomegranate Art Books, 1994.

McGee, Harold. *On Food and Cooking*. New York: Charles Scribner's Sons, 1984.

———. *The Curious Cook*. San Francisco: North Point Press, 1990.

Madison, Deborah. *Vegetarian Cooking for Everyone*. New York: Broadway Books, 1997.

"The Many Reasons to Cut Back on Salt." *University of California at Berkeley Wellness Letter* 2, no. 10 (July 1995): 1–2.

Moore, Thomas. J. "Overkill." *The Washingtonian* (August 1990): 64.

Multhauf, Robert P. *Neptune's Gift: A History of Common Salt*. Baltimore: Johns Hopkins University Press, 1978.

Niman, Skip. "Salt Is Not Just Salt—Considerable Differences Exist." *Cereal Foods World* 42, no. 10 (October 1997): 808–811.

O'Neill, Molly. "All It's Cracked Up to Be." *New York Times Magazine* (12 January 1997): 41–42.

———. "Doctor Pepper." *New York Times Magazine* (19 January 1997): 53–54.

Paniz, Neela. *The Bombay Cafe*. Berkeley: Ten Speed Press, 1998.

bibliography

Pepper Marketing Board of Malaysia. *Report of National Pepper Investment Seminar.* Kuching, Sarawak: Pepper Marketing Board, 1995.

Robinson, Marilynne. *Housekeeping.* New York: Farrar, Straus & Giroux, 1981.

Root, Waverley. *Food.* New York: Simon and Schuster, 1980.

Rosenblum, Mort. *Olives.* New York: North Point Press, 1996.

Severance, John B. *Ghandi, Great Soul.* New York: Clarion Books, 1997.

"The Shake Out on Sodium: An Interview with David A. McCarron, M.D." *Total Health* (December 1994): 46.

Sigal, Jane. *Backroad Bistros, Farmhouse Fare.* London: Pavilion Books, 1994.

Silverton, Peter. "Sneezy Spice." *The Observer Review* (London) (23 November 1997): 7.

Sim, E. S. "Pepper Industry in Sarawak." Sarawak, Malaysia: Department of Agriculture, 1990.

Steingarten, Jeffrey. *The Man Who Ate Everything.* New York: Knopf, 1997.

Stewart, Katie. *The Joy of Eating.* Owing Mills, Md.: Stemmer House, 1977.

Tisdale, Sallie. *Lot's Wife: Salt and the Human Condition.* New York: Henry Holt, 1988.

Trager, James. *The Food Chronology: A Food Lover's Compendium of Events and Anecdotes, from Prehistory to the Present.* New York: Henry Holt, 1995.

Tsuji, Shizuo. *Japanese Cooking: A Simple Art.* Tokyo: Kodansha International, 1980.

Turner, Peter, Chris Taylor, and Hugh Finlay. *Malaysia, Singapore & Brunei.* 6th ed. Hawthorne, Australia: Lonely Planet Publications, 1996.

Visser, Margaret. *Much Depends on Dinner.* New York: Grove Press, 1986.

———. *The Rituals of Dinner.* New York: Grove Weidenfeld, 1991.

Waldron, Maggie. *Cold Spaghetti at Midnight.* New York: Morrow, 1992.

Watson, Francis. *A Concise History of India.* London: Thames and Hudson, 1974.

Welsh, Willard. *Hutchinson: A Prairie City in Kansas.* Salem: Higginson Book Company, reprint, Oct. 1995.

Whyte, Karen Cross. *The Complete Yogurt Cookbook.* San Francisco: Troubador Press, 1970.

Willan, Anne. *La France Gastronomique.* New York: Arcade Publishing, 1991.

Wolfert, Paula. *The Cooking of the Eastern Mediterranean.* New York: HarperCollins, 1994.

Wolpert, Stanley. *A New History of India.* 4th ed. New York: Oxford University Press, 1993.

Young, Gordon. "Salt: The Essence of Life." *National Geographic* 152, no. 3 (September 1977): 381–401.

Zane, Eva. *Greek Cooking for the Gods.* San Francisco: 101 Productions, 1970.

bibliography

a

Abdullah, Anandan, 36, 208
Aidells, Bruce, 26
Alberger, J. L., 24
Allsop, Michael, 43
allspice, 121, 125, 161, 166
almonds, salted, **54**
American Spice Trade Association, 37
anchovies, 174
    dried, in sambal, 180
    to salt fresh, **167**
Anderson, Pamela, 117
apple cider, mulled, **200**
apples, 74
    with bratwurst and sauerkraut, **135**
aromatherapy, pepper for, 41
"Art of Eating, The," 17, 60
artichokes
    to cook, **87**
    dip for, 171, 172
    with feta and pasta, **87**
    and olive tapenade, **174**
    salt cod, and potato salad, **154**
    shallots, and potatoes, roasted on salt, **100**
arugula, 86, 148, 156
Atlas pepper mill, 44, 51-52
Avery Island (Louisiana), 14, 22
avocado, grapefruit, and chicken salad, **156**

b

bacon, 17-18, 134, 158
banana raita, **151**
Bangka (Indonesia), 32
Barron, Rosemary, 69
beans
    fava, 87, 103
    green
        with pasta, **90**
        with salt pork, **140**

beef
    chuck roast, 131
    corned, 18
    ground, for meatloaf, 134
    pot roast, **131**
    shanks, stock of, **80**
    steak
        au poivre blanc, **129**
        au poivre rouge, **130**
        stock, Malaysian, **80**
        tenderloin, in salt crust, **132**
beet raita, **152**
beet tops, 60
Behr, Edward, 17, 60
Bell, Valerie Jackson, 61
Bertolli, Paul, 48
Bharadwaj, Monisha, 152
Blanchard, Ben, 14
bonito flakes, in *dashi*, 71
Bouquet, Patrick, 175
brandade de morue, **67**
Brazil, pepper in, 30, 33, 214
bread, 19, 60
    three-peppercorn, **94**
    as pizza dough, 102
bread sticks, **95**
brining, 16, 20, **26**, 31, 125, 182
broccoli salad, with cauliflower and bacon, **158**
broth
    chicken, 73, 91, 92, 141
    vegetable, 91, 92
    see also stock
bruschetta, 59
    with sautéed greens, **60**
butter, 173
    kneaded, **131**
    sorrel, **173**

c

cabbage (sauerkraut), **183**
cactus (*nopales*)
    and corn, curried, **138**

paddles, to prepare, 138
Cajun seasoning mix, **93**, 166
canning jars, to process, **177**
capers, 154
caraway seed, 135
    salt flavored with, **163**
cardamom, 76, 166, 181, 188, 194, 199
Cargill Corp., 9-10, 22
Carnes, Jonathan, 45
carrots, 175
    glazed, with pepper, **139**
cauliflower, in salad with broccoli and bacon, 158
caviar
    golden, with black pasta, **89**
    salt in, 19, 64
celery seeds, 176
Celtic gray sea salt, 10, 11, 19, 212
    caraway-flavored, **163**
    for finishing, 115, 126, 149
    recipes using, 58, 60, 95, 168, 175
    for roasting vegetables, 100, 142, 143
Ceylon pepper, 33
chai, 196, **199**
chard, 60, 73
Charles, Prince of Wales, 42
cheese
    Asiago, 100
    chabis, 20, 59
    feta, 19, 87, 90
        dressing of, **171**
    Fontina, 102
    goat (chèvre), 20, 59
    Greek, 20, 87
    Monterey Jack, 20, 98
    Parmigiano-Reggiano, 20, 85, 98, 100
    pecorino, 85
    pepato, 20, 86, 91
    pepper in, 20

Polish, 19-20
ricotta, fresh, 88
Roquefort, 148, 188
yogurt, 59, **185**
cheesemaking, salt for, 19-20
Chef Specialties, 51, 52
Chenel, Laura, 20
chervil, 98, 154
chicken
    alla diavola, 116
    brining, 117
    drummettes, lemon pepper,
        68
    gizzards, 93
    livers, 93
    roasted, **117**, 156
    in a salt crust, **133**
    smoked, in salad, 156
    stock. *See* stock
    see also game hens
chicken rice, Malaysian, **118**
chile peppers
    jalapeño, pickled, **175**
    serrano, 76, 104, 105, 110,
        114, 151, 179
        pickled, 175
    see also chipotle
chili powder, 118
China
    pepper production in, 33
    salt production in, 21
chipotle
    dried, 124, 204
    flakes, 105, 164, 165
    powder, 82, 104, 120, 164
    salt, **164**, 202, 204
chives, 171, 172
chowder
    salt cod, **78**
    Thai salmon and mushroom,
        76
    see also soup
chutney, raisin, onion, and
        green peppercorn, 59, **181**
cider, spicy mulled, **200**
cilantro
    root, in sauce, 179
    for wrapping food, 108, 114
cinnamon, 74, 103, 166, 181,
        194, 199, 200

citrus, salad, with black pepper,
    150
clay roaster
    pork baked in, 122, 124
    potatoes baked in, 143
cloves, 166, 181, 194, 200
cocktails, **201-204**
coconut milk, 74, 76, 103
Cointreau liqueur, 204
Collins, Larry, 6
Colwin, Laurie, 131
cookies, red hot, **193**
    see also pfeffernüsse
*Cooking of the Eastern Mediter-
    ranean* (Wolfert), 163
Cooking with Spices (Heal and
    Allsop), 43
Cook's Illustrated, 51, 117
coriander seeds, 76, 128, 161,
    163, 166, 169
corn
    curried, with cactus paddles,
        138
    grilled, with pepper butter,
        120, **137**
corn husks, dried, for wrapping
    food, 120
corn salad. *See* mâche
Corti, Darrell, 13
cranberries, dried, 158
cream
    heavy, 67, 129
    sour, 82, 172
Creamy White Pepper (brand),
    36-37, 180, 215
cress, 86
crostini, with olive and arti-
    choke tapenade, **59**
crudités, dip for, **171**, **172**
cucumber, 64, 118
    bread and butter pickles of,
        176
Culpeper Ltd., 41
cumin, 74, 93, 106, 128, 144,
    151, 166, 198
*Cunningham's Encyclopedia of
    Magical Herbs,* 24
curry, potato, **103**
curry paste, Thai, 166
curry powder, 74, 103, 138, 166

d
Dante, Alighieri, 60
dashi, **71**, 72
decorations, salt dough, **207**
Deli Book, The (Harris), 18
Denmark, salt from, 55, 162, 213
Diamond Crystal salt (brand),
    22-23, 24
diet, salt and, 3-8
dip, creamy feta, **171**
dirty rice, **93**
Divine Comedy, The (Dante),
    60
dough
    pizza. *See* bread, three-
        peppercorn
    salt. *See* salt, dough
dressing, salad
    black pepper, 117, 143, 156,
        171
    creamy feta, **172**
dry-salting, 16-17, 18
duck
    breast au poivre blanc, **129**
    ginger pepper, **121**
dulce de leche, **191**
dulse, 71
Dunialiella (algae), 14

e
edamame, **56**
eggs
    Asian salt, **178**
        sauce of, **179**
    hard-cooked, 55, 154, 178
    perfect deviled, **55**
    in spaghetti carbonara, 85
    whites of
        for cookies, 193
        for salt crust, 106, 108, 114,
            120, 126, 132
    yolks of, 171, 192, 193
England, salt from, 10, 213
Esche, Otto, 18
Europe, market for pepper in,
    32, 37

f
Facts About Salt (Salt Institute),
    21, 25

fagara. See peppercorns, Sichuan

Felts, R. M., Packing Co., 17

Feniger, Susan, 171

fennel seed, 166

fenugreek seeds, 163, 166

figs

    grilled, with prosciutto and black pepper, **62**

    peppered dried, 69

Filipino Cuisine (Gelle), 184

film, 15, 17

fish

    anchovies, to salt fresh, **167**

    baking in salt, 106, 108, 111, 114

    halibut, gravlax, **66**

    rock

        baked in salt, **111**

        in soup, 73

        roe. *See* taramosalata

    salmon

        chilled, **114**

        gravlax, **65**

        grilled, with sorrel, **113**

        with sweet-and-sour peppercorn sauce, **112**

        in Thai chowder, 76

        whole, baked in a salt crust, **114**

    salt cod

        brandade de morue, **67**

        chowder, **78**

        potato, and artichoke salad, **154**

        to soak, 67

        vinaigrette, **153**

    snapper, baked in salt, **106**

    stock, 76

    swordfish, grilled, with parsley and green peppercorn sauce, **115**

    trout, baked in salt, **108**

fish sauce, Thai, 76, 179

fleur de sel, 9, 10, 11, 213

    for finishing, 68, 115, 132, 149

Food Chronology, The (Trager), 45

Food (Root), 23, 44

France

    feta cheese in, 19, 87

salt, 8, 10–12, 149

salt production in, *see also* Celtic gray sea salt; fleur de sel; sel gris

sin eaters in, 23

Freedom at Midnight (Collins and Lapierre), 6

fruit, roasted in salt, *189*

g

gabelle, the, 8

game hens, seasoned and roasted in salt, **120**

Gandhi, Mahatma, 6

garlic, roasted

    with potatoes, **143**

    whole, **100**

Garner, Steve, 141

Gelle, Gerry, 184

gemelli, in harvest pasta, 90

Georgia, Republic of, 163

gnocchi, dried, with lemon, pepper, basil, and ricotta, **88**

goiter, thyroid, 5

Goldsmith, Marty, 33–34

gomashio, 97, **165**

Good Housekeeping, 51

Graham, Sylvester, 44

Grain & Salt Society, the, 44

granita, pineapple, **190**

grapefruit, 150, 156

grapefruit juice, 201, 202

grape leaves

    to blanch fresh, **107**

    in brine, to use, 107

    for wrapping food, 106, 108, 114, 189

gravlax

    halibut, **66**

    salmon, **65**

Greece, cheese from, 19, 20, 87

Green Man Farms (California), 62

greens

    collard, with ham hocks and maple syrup, **141**

    mustard, salted, 97, **184**

    peppery

        avocado, grapefruit, and chicken salad, **156**

Roquefort and pear salad, **148**

salad, with pasta, 86

sautéed, on bruschetta, **60**

Guérande (France), 10, 11, 213

h

Hain Sea Salt (brand), 10

half-and-half, 82, 129, 192

halite, 3

ham, dry-salted smoked, 18

ham hocks, collard greens, and maple syrup, **141**

haricots verts, with pasta, **90**

Harris, John, 18

Hawaii, salt from, 14–15, 213

    recipes using, 58, 95, 112, 122

Heal, Carolyn, 43

health

    pepper and, 43

    salt and, 3–8

herbs

    for a salt crust, 126, 132

    for wrapping food, 106

Hertz, Jerry, 162

Hotel Ritz (Paris), 16

Hutchinson (Kansas), 14, 15

hypertension, salt and, 7

i

Iban, the, 40–41

ice cream, black pepper, 189, **192**

Île de Ré (France), 10, 100

Imwalle Gardens (California), 183

India

    pepper from, 30, 32, 33, 52, 214

    salt

        black (rock) (*kala namak*) from, 151, 152, 197, 198, 213

        production in, 6, 9

        spices in, 138, 166

Indian Spice Kitchen, The (Bharadwaj), 152

Indonesia, pepper from, 32, 52, 214

International Pepper Community, 33

iodine, 5
irradiation, for pepper, 34
Italy, 20, 44-45

j

Japan
  market for pepper in, 32, 37
  recipes influenced by, 56, 71, 72, 97, 165
  salt in, 7, 13-14, 27, 165, 212
Johnson, John, 9

k

kaffir lime leaves, 80
kala namak. See salt, black Indian
kale, on bruschetta, 60
Kamman, Madeleine, 117, 189
kashering, 21-22
kelp, giant. *See* konbu
Khan, Shazat, 180
Koch, Ulrike, 17
konbu (giant kelp), 71
Korea, salt from, 143, 175, 213
Kourik, Robert, 162
Kuching (Malaysia), 35, 42, 80, 159

l

La Baleine (brand), 12
lamb
  loin, baked in salt crust, **126**
  shanks, tagine, with olives and preserved lemons, **128**
Lampong (Indonesia) pepper, 32, 214
Lapierre, Dominique, 6
lassi, spiced, **198**
lavender, for wrapping food, 108, 189
leeks, 91
lemongrass, 76, 80, 114
lemons, 108, 150, 171
  preserved, 68, 87, 128, **182**
Leslie Salt Company, 9, 10
lettuce, 104, 148, 153
  Roquefort and pear salad, **148**
Lima Sea Salt (brand), 89, 213
limeade, Asian, **197**
linguine, with fresh artichokes and feta, **87**

longhouse, 40-41
Lot's Wife (Tisdale), 3

m

McCarley, Jack, 62
McCormick and Schilling Corp., 33
McGee, Harold, 15-16
mâche (corn salad) and soppres-sata salad, **157**
Madagascar, pepper in, 30, 33
Madeira, 78
Madison, Deborah, 165
Malabar (India), pepper from, 32, 52, 214
Malaysia
  pepper growing in, 32-33, 34, 35-42
  recipes from, 80, 103, 110, 118, 178, 180, 190, 197
  types of pepper from, 36-37, 39, 52, 214, 215
Maldon Crystal Salt (brand), 212
maple syrup, 141
margaritas, spicy, **204**
marinade
  for chicken, **116**, **118**
  for mushrooms, **98**
Marine, David, 5
marjoram, 175
Marsala, 104, 121, 129
martini, Malaysian, **203**
Mason Cash, 51
mayonnaise
  green peppercorn, 114, 143, **170**
  prepared, 55, 158, 170, 172
measuring
  peppercorns, 52
  salt, 25
meat
  to brine, 26, 125
  cured, 17-19, 21, **125**, 157
  kashering, 21-22
  salt to preserve, 16-18
meatloaf, poached or baked, **134**
Medeiros, Jim, 15
Mendocino Sea Vegetable Co., 71

Mesa Mexicana (Milliken and Feniger), 171
Mexico, salt from, 175
  recipe using, 175
Michigan State Medical Society, 5
Micronesia, pepper in, 30, 33, 215
mignonette, **168**
Milliken, Mary Sue, 171
miner's lettuce, 148
mint, 152, 188, 190, 198
mirin, 72, 104
miso, red, soup of, **72**
molasses, 194
Mondavi, Holly Peterson, 11
Moore, Thomas, 6
More Home Cooking (Colwin), 131
Morton Salt Co., 12, 14
Moryl, Mariusz, 2
Mueller Company, Inc., 33
Muntok (Indonesia) pepper, 32, 52, 214
mushrooms, 76
  bolete. *See* mushrooms, porcini
  chanterelles, 102
  Chinese black, 73
  crimini, 102
  morels, 76
  oyster, 76
  porcini (bolete), Fontina, and sage pizza, **102**
  portobello, grilled, with black pepper polenta, **98**
mustard, 134, 170
  green peppercorn, 65, 134, **170**
mustard flour, 93, 166, 170, 193
mustard greens, salted, **184**
  with rice, 97
mustard seed, 65, 97, 166, 176

n

Nana's pot roast, **131**
nasi ayam, **118**
nasturtiums, 86, 148, 156
Naturally Clean Black Pepper (brand), 37-38, 214

nectarines, salt-roasted, **189**
Nepal, dessert from, 185
Nevada, silver mining in, 18
Nigeria, pepper in, 30, 33
Niman, Skip, 23
Noirmoutier (France), 10
noodles, rice, 72, 80
nopales. See cactus
nori, 71, 165
    for wrapping food, 111
nutmeg, 82, 166, 194
    cream, **82**
nutmeg mill, 86

o
Oakes, Nancy, 26
oil
    coconut palm, 119
    olive
        O (brand), 88
        peppercorn-flavored, 59,
            169
        in pepper. *See* pepper, black
    walnut, 148
Olde Thompson's Manor, 51,
    52
olives, 19, 58, 64
    appetizer of mixed, **58**
    and artichoke tapenade, **174**
    green, 78, 128, 154, 174
Olives (Rosenblum), 58
onion, red
    and black peppercorn vine-
        gar, **167**
    raita, **151**
oranges, 150
    juice, 124, 144, 200
oregano, 93, 153, 166, 172, 175
Oshima Island Red Label salt
    (brand), 13-14, 212
Ō-shima (Japan), 13, 212

p
pancetta, 22, 85, 94, 134, 135
pandan (screwpine), 119
paper, pepper-scented, **208**
paprika, 93, 128, 166
parsley, 108, 145, 154, 173, 174
    and green peppercorn sauce,
        115

pasta
    black, with caviar, **89**
    to cook, 47, 84
    harvest, with tomatoes, *hari-
        cots verts*, sausage, and feta,
        90
    tapenade with, 174
    see also gnocchi, linguine,
        spaghetti
pastrami, 18-19
Patterson, Daniel, 23
Paula Wolfert's World of Food
    (Wolfert), 100
peaches, roasted in salt, **189**
pear/s
    and Roquefort salad, **148**
    salt-roasted, **189**
    soup, chilled, **188**
pecan nuts, 158
Peng-tzao-kan-mu, 21
Penzey, Bill, 35
Penzeys Ltd., 35, 98
peppercress, 148, 156
Pepper Festival (Kuching,
    Malaysia), 42
Pepper Marketing Board
    (Malaysia), 35-42, 180,
    190, 208
pepper mills, 44, 51-52
pepper/peppercorns
    adulteration of, 45
    black, 30-45, 166
        in brine, 125
        oil of, 36, 41
        oils, volatile, in, 34, 35, 48,
            169
    Brazilian, 30, 33, 214
    Brown Label (brand), 37
    Ceylon (type), 33
    in cheese, 20
    Chinese, 21
    cleanliness in, 34
    consumption of, 33
    cost of, 32, 36, 43
    to crack, 50-51
    to crush, 51
    cultivation of, 30-31, 37-38
    decorticated, 31
    dust, 38
    flavor of, 34

    on fruit, 57, 186, 187
    grades of, 32, 33-34, 37, 39
    green, 30-31, 65, 94
        in brine, 31, 215
        recipes using, 55, 88, 112,
            115, 170, 172, 174, 180,
            181
        dried, 31, 215
        recipes using, 56, 65, 76, 92,
            94, 112, 115, 121, 123,
            134, 139, 161, 169, 170,
            171
        fresh, 76
        in vinegar, 215
    to grind, 51
    history of, 42-45
    immature, in brine, 31
    Indian, 30, 32, 33, 52, 214
    Indonesian, 32, 52, 214
    irradiation of, 34
    Lampong, 32, 214
    Madagascan, 30, 33
    Malabar, 32, 52, 214
    Malaysian. *See* Malaysia
    measuring, 52
    Micronesian, 30, 33, 215
    mixed (black, green, and
        white), 90, **161**, 200
    Muntok, 32, 52, 214
    myths about, 44
    Nigerian, 30, 33
    organically produced, 34, 36
    in perfume, 35
    pink, 32
    Ponape (brand), 33, 215
    for preserving, 21
    processing, 38, 41
    rent in, 42, 43
    from Réunion, 32
    Sarawak, 52, 214
    Sichuan (*fagara*)
        to prepare, 66
        recipes using, 66, 104, 121,
            124, 137, 139, 161, 169,
            200
    Sri Lankan (Ceylon), 33, 34
    sterilization of, 34, 39
    tax on, 45
    Tellicherry, 32, 52, 199, 214
    Thai, 33

trade in, 33–34
types of, 30–33, 214–15
uses for, 43–44
Vietnamese, 33
white, 31, 32, 41, 48, 52, 166
   recipes using, 65, 80, 94, 112,
      121, 129, 130, 134, 161,
      168, 169, 188, 191, 194
   see also Creamy White Pep-
      per; Naturally Clean Black
      Pepper
perfume, pepper and, 35
Pernod, 65
Peugeot pepper mill, 51, 52
pfeffernüsse, walnut, **194**
pickles
   bread and butter, **176**
   jalapeño, **175**
pickling, 19
pineapple
   with black pepper, **57**, 120,
      122
   granita, with black pepper,
      190
Piper grande, 30
   P. longum, 43
   P. nigrum, 30, 32, 43, 74
   P. vestitum, 30
pizza, pepper-crusted, with
      porcini, Fontina, and sage,
      102
playdough, 205, **206**
plums, dried, peppered, **69**, 124
Poland
   cheese from, 19–20
   salt mining in, 2, 13
polenta
   to bake, 99
   black pepper, with grilled
      portobellos, **98**
Ponape (brand) pepper, 33, 215
Ponsford, Craig, 19
popcorn, salt for, 164
pork
   to brine, **26**
   butt, 122, 124
   ground, 93, 134
   Kalua, **122**
   loin chops, spicy, with
      Sarawak sambal, **123**

roast, with dried plums and
      black pepper, **124**
salt, 22, 140
shoulder, 122, 124
tenderloin, brine-cured, **125**
Portugal, 45
   recipes from, 78, 110, 153
   salt from, 12, 78
potato/es
   clay pot garlic, **143**
   curry, **103**
   new, **61, 100, 142**
   Onandaga salt, **61**
   and red onion raita, **151**
   to rice, 64
   roasted on salt, **142**
      with artichokes and shallots,
         100
   russet, 64, 67, 82
   salad, with salt cod and arti-
      chokes, **154**
   Yellow Finn, 78, 103, 143
   Yukon Gold, 78, 103, 143,
      154
poultry
   to brine, 26, **117**
   kashering, 22
   see also chicken, duck, game
      hens
preserving
   green peppercorns, 30–31
   salt for, 5, 211
prosciutto, 18
   with grilled figs, **62**

r
radishes, 64, 154
raisins, 158, 181
raita
   potato and red onion, **151**
   ruby, **152**
   spicy banana, **151**
Rego, Nilda, 18
rent, peppercorn, 42, 43
Réunion, pink peppercorns
      from, 32
rice
   dirty, **93**
   flavored, **119**
   Italian, 91, 92

jasmine, 74, 76, 97
   to cook, **75**
   long-grain white, 93, 118
   Malaysian chicken, **118**
   see also risotto
Rio Maior (Portugal), 12
risotto
   pepato, **91**
   zucchini, green peppercorns,
      and basil, **92**
Rome, pepper in ancient, 43
Root, Waverley, 23, 44
Rosenblum, Mort, 58
Royal Wieliczka Salt Mine
      (Poland), 2, 13

s
saffron, 128
sage, 102, 117
salad, 147
   avocado, grapefruit, and
      chicken, **156**
   broccoli, cauliflower, and ba-
      con, **158**
   citrus, with black pepper, **150**
   dressing, **171, 172**
   mâche and soppressata, **157**
   peppery green, with Roque-
      fort and pears, **148**
   salt cod, potato, and arti-
      choke, **154**
   salt cod vinaigrette, **153**
   summer jewel (tomato), **149**
salt
   alae. *See* salt, Hawaiian
   Alberger, 23–25, 135, 211
   black
      Indian (*kala namak*), 151,
         152, 197, 198, 213
      Polish, 13
   brand names of, 10, 32, 52,
      214–15
   for brining, 16, 117, 125
   caraway-flavored, **163**
   chemical composition of, 3,
      4, 14–15
   chipotle, **164**, 202, 204
   condiment (finishing), 11,
      149, 212–13
   consumption of, 5–6, 7, 27

containers for, 49, 50
cooking in/on
  chicken, 120, 133
  fish and seafood, 63, 106,
    108, 111, 114
  fruit, 189
  meat, 126, 132
  vegetables, 100, 142
as a cosmetic, 26
cost of, 10, 11, 15
crust, 96, 106, 108, 111, 114,
  120
Danish smoked, 55, 162, 213
dough
  for cooking, 96, 126, 132,
    133
  for decorations, 207
effects of, 15-16, 20, 23
fat and, 20-21
finishing. *See* salt, condiment
flavored, **162-65**
French, 8, 10-12, 149, 212,
  213
  see also Celtic gray sea salt;
    fleur de sel; sel gris
grainer, 24
granulated, 24
gray. *See* Celtic gray sea salt
Hawaiian alae, 14-15, 58, 95,
  112, 122, 213
health and, 3-8
Indian. *See* salt, black Indian
iodized, 5, 211
Japanese, 13-14, 56, 165, 212
for kashering, 21-22
Korean, 143, 175, 213
kosher, 21-25, 211
  for brine, 117, 125, 132
  cooking in/on, 106, 120,
    126, 132, 189
  in pickles, 176, 178, 182,
    183
legends about, 1-3
measuring, 25
Mexican, 175
mills, 44, 49
mines, 2, 13, 15
as a pest deterrent, 16
physiology and, 6-7
pickling, 178

plain, 211
popcorn, 173
Portuguese, 12, 78
for preserving, 5, 16-20, 211
in processed food, 8
production of, 8-15, 21, 23-
  25
properties of, 8, 14-15, 23-
  24, 49
rock, 3, 4, 14
  cooking in/on, 63, 106,
    108, 111, 114, 120, 142
  Indian. *See* salt, black Indian
sea, 61, 117, 164, 189, 212
Sicilian, 12, 212
  in silver mining, 18
  smoked, 55, 162, 213
  South African, 162
  table, 14, 23, 211
  tax on, 6, 8
  Tibetan, 17
  types of, compared, 211-12
  to use, 47, 70, 83, 147
  uses for, 24, 25
salt cod. *See* fish
Salt Institute, The, 21, 25
salt lick (cocktail), **201**
Saltmen of Tibet, The (film), 17
Salt Museum (Onanadaga
  County, New York), 61
saltpeter, 125
salt pork, 22
  with green beans, **140**
salty dog (cocktail), **201**
salty john (cocktail), **202**
salty josé (cocktail), **202**
sambal. *See* Sarawak sambal
Sandwich, John Montague, earl
  of, 10
San Francisco Bay, 8-10, 18
Sarawak (Malaysia), pepper
  from, 52, 214
Sarawak Pepper (Pepper Marketing Board), 190
Sarawak sambal, 59, 123, **180**
sauce
  dipping, for shrimp, **105**
  mignonette, **168**
  for roasted shrimp, 63
  spicy salt egg, 65, 97, 108, **179**

sauerkraut, 19, **183**
  with bratwurst and apples,
    135
sausages, 20, 21
  andouille, 90
  bratwurst, 135
  chicken-apple, 74
  kielbasa, 90
  linguiça, 78, 90
Schinus terebinthifolia, 32
Schmidt, Jimmy, 189
screwpine leaves, 119
seafood
  crab, black pepper, **110**
  crab boil, 166
  iodine in, 5
  shrimp
  dip for, 171
  roasted on rock salt, **63**
  salt and pepper, **104**
Sea Stars Co., 11, 213
seaweed
  stock(*dashi*), **71**
  for wrapping food, 106
sel gris, 10, 68
  see also Celtic gray sea salt
seppuku, 27
sesame oil, 97
sesame seeds, 165
shakers, salt and pepper, 49, 50
shallots, 118, 168, 171, 173, 179,
  180
  artichokes, and potatoes, salt-
    roasted, **100**
  fried, with rice, 119
sherry, 104
shrimp, dried, with crab, 110
shrimp paste, 179
Sicily, 20
  salt from, 12, 212
sikarni, 185
sin eaters, 23
Slater, Rabbi Jonathan, 21
smoke, liquid, 122
sōmen, in red miso soup, 72
soppressata, and mâche salad,
  157
sorrel
  butter, 113, **173**
  for wrapping food, 113

soup
    black pepper, **73**
    ginger beef noodle, **80**
    mulligatawny, **74**
    pear, chilled, **188**
    red miso, **72**
    to season, 70
    spicy sweet potato, **82**
    see also chowder
South Africa, salt from, 162
soybeans, fresh, and sea salt
        (*edamame*), 56
spaghetti
    carbonara, **85**
    with pepato, black pepper,
        and nutmeg, **86**
spices, 34, 51, 138, 159
    mixtures of, 166
spinach, on bruschetta, 60
squash
    summer, black pepper, **146**
    Tahitian Melon, 145
    winter, with black pepper
        and cilantro, **145**
Sri Lanka, pepper in, 33, 34
star anise, 80
stock
    beef, **80**, 131, 134
    chicken, 73, 74, 76, 78, 91,
        92, 93, 141
    fish, 76
    seaweed (*dashi*), 71
    veal, 134
    vegetable, 78, 91, 92
storage, in salt mines, 15
strawberries, roasted, with black
        pepper, **187**
sugar, red hot, **193**
sweet potatoes
    with apple cider and black
        pepper, **144**
    spicy soup of, **82**
syrup, simple, with pepper, **190**,
        197

t

Tamil Nadu (India), 74
Tancer, Forrest, 195

Tanner, Lesa, 205
tapenade, olive and artichoke,
        59, **174**
taramosalata, **64**
tarragon, 98, 154
taxes, 6, 8, 45
tea, 195, 199
    see also chai
Tellicherry (India) pepper, 32,
        52, 199, 214
tequila, chipotle, 202, **204**
Thailand
    pepper production in, 33
    recipes from, 76, 179
thyme, 93, 153, 166, 175
Tibet, 17, 195
ti leaves, 122
Time, 9
TimeOut, 18
Tisdale, Sallie, 3
toast, Spanish, **58**
tomatoes, 90, 149
    on bruschetta, **60**
    canned, in soup, 78
    with mustard greens and
        rice, **97**
    salad of summer, **149**
    for Spanish toast, 58
Touch of Pepper pepper mill,
        52
Trager, James, 45
Trapani (Sicily), 12, 212
turmeric, 74, 166, 176

u

Underground Vaults and Stor-
        age Co., 15
Unicorn Magnum Plus pepper
        mill, 51
United States
    feta cheese in, 19
    pepper consumption in, 33,
        37
    salt production in, 8-10, 14,
        22
    and the spice trade, 45

v

veal stock, 134
vegetable/s
    sea. *See* seaweed
    to season, 47, 136
    stock (broth), 78, 91, 92
Vietnam, pepper production in,
        33
Vinaigre de Banyuls, 98, 123,
        157, 168, 171
vinaigrette
    green peppercorn, **171**
    salt cod (salad), **153**
    see also dressing, salad
vinegar, black peppercorn and
        red onion, 167, **171**
vodka, 66
    black pepper, **200**, 201, 203

w

walnuts, 174, 194
Walsh, Ed, 16, 26
Washingtonian, The, 6
watercress, 156
Weir, Gordon and Doris, 185
William Bounds Ltd., 44
Willinger, Faith, 22
wine
    red, 130, 131
    white, 74, 112, 135, 188
Wine Spectator, 48
Wolfert, Paula, 100, 163
Wong Hoon Sing, 38, 40

y

Yale, Elihu, 45
yams, 144
yogurt, 1, 151, 152, 198
    cheese, 59, **185**

z

Zassenhause mills, 51, 86
zucchini, 73, 92
    black pepper, **146**

index